D187987

The Living Religions of the Indian People

The Living Religions of the Indian People

(Wilde Lectures, Oxford, 1932-34)

BY

NICOL MACNICOL, M. A. D. LITT., D.D.

GYAN

Published by

GYAN

Gyan Publishing House
5, Ansari Road
Daryaganj, New Delhi-110002
Phone: 011-47034999, 9811692060
E-mail: books@gyanbooks.com

Distribution Network
gyanbooks.com
India, USA, Canada, UK, Australia, France

ISBN : 978-81-212-2995-1 (PB)
First Published, 1934

2nd Impression 2021

Printed at: Gyan Press, Delhi.

The Living Religions of the Indian People
Author: Nicol Macnicol

The Living Religions of the Indian People

(WILDE LECTURES, OXFORD, 1932-34)

BY

NICOL MACNICOL, M.A., D.LITT., D.D.

AUTHOR OF "INDIAN THEISM," "PSALMS OF MARATHA SAINTS," "PANDITA RAMABAI," "THE MAKING OF MODERN INDIA," "WHAT JESUS MEANS FOR MEN," "INDIA IN THE DARK WOOD"

STUDENT CHRISTIAN MOVEMENT PRESS

58 BLOOMSBURY STREET, LONDON, W.C.1

PREFACE

This book contains—in somewhat enlarged form—the lectures delivered in 1932–34 in connection with the Wilde Lectureship in Natural and Comparative Religion at the University of Oxford. A considerable portion of the material was also made use of in a series of " Overseas Lectures " delivered in the Theological Colleges of the Church of Scotland and the Theological Faculties of the Scottish Universities in the winter of 1931–32.

While I owe my personal acquaintance with the religions dealt with to many years spent in India as a Christian missionary, the aim of the book is not to institute comparisons between the religions or to criticize them. In order that we may be able to help any people wisely in what affects them as profoundly as religion does, it is of much importance that we should understand, as far as possible, what religion has meant to them in their own lives. This book is intended to be a guide towards such a sympathetic understanding. It does not deal with the details of religious observance or of the theological or philosophical conceptions on which the religions are built or by which it is sought to explain them. Its purpose is to present, as far as a stranger may, the central elements in the various religions that give them their spiritual significance. The book may thus serve as an introduction to the further study of these faiths, whether it be continued by the help of their own scriptures or through contact with the lives of those who profess them and live by them.

I am deeply indebted to many followers of the religions of which I have sought to give an account for the glimpses that friendship with them has given me into the meaning and value to them of their ancestral faiths. To some reference is made by name in the book, and to them, as well as to many others whom I do not name, I desire to acknowledge my deep indebtedness. No greater gift can be given by one to another than to share such possessions as these. What I owe to others from among my own fellow-countrymen I shall not attempt to assess. One of them, however, I desire to name here, though he is no longer among us to receive the tribute of gratitude and affection that warms the heart at the remembrance of him. J. N. Farquhar more than any other in his time opened a road of exploration along which he himself travelled with a loyalty to truth and a faith in the divine purpose that still inspire and humble those who seek, however haltingly, to follow him along that same path.

N. M.

EDINBURGH,
December 1933.

ABBREVIATIONS

C.H.I.	Cambridge History of India.
C.I.R.	Census of India Report.
E.R.E.	Encyclopædia of Religion and Ethics.
S.B.E.	Sacred Books of the East.
Farquhar, O.R.L.I.	An Outline of the Religious Literature of India.
Rolland, P.N.I.	Prophets of the New India.
Dhalla, Z. T.	Zoroastrian Theology.
Moulton, E. Z.	Early Zoroastrianism.

CONTENTS

CONTENTS

Part IV

THE RELIGION OF THE SIKHS

Part V

THE RELIGION OF THE PARSIS (ZOROASTRIANISM)

Part VI

INDIAN CHRISTIANITY

INTRODUCTORY

THE SUBJECT, ITS TREATMENT AND ITS INDIAN SETTING

MUCH has been done by students of the various religions of mankind to trace their history, to study their inheritance of myth and legend and culture, to set forth the ideas that lie behind the tales or ritual, the theology or philosophy, implicit or explicit in their tradition and their practice. These investigations deal with the past and study the religions as so much dead and often desiccated matter, quite apart from their expression in the minds and hearts, and their government of the wills, of living men and women. All religions in their history accumulate masses of debris which to the investigator who approaches them from outside may appear imposing and important. It may even be the case that by the members themselves of the particular religion this deposit of the ancient past is considered to be very venerable, and around it much sentiment, that may be passionately felt, may gather. With such things as these the students of what is called comparative religion or of the history of religions are mainly concerned. They view the beliefs which they are investigating and cataloguing as if they were so many specimens of plant life arranged in a museum, not as if they were flowers actually growing in their beauty and colour in a garden. A real change must come about in the attitude of the student and in his selection of the materials of his study, if he directs his attention rather to the actual effects on the lives of men today produced by the religion he is considering. Just because religion is so vital an element in human life, awakening always personal interest on the part of those who sincerely accept it, it must be extraordinarily subject to change with the changing circumstances and attitudes of men. That is why there are so many definitions of religion and why no single one among them all seems adequate. If, indeed, that which is beyond time and change comes into the life of man, if his experience partakes not only of the temporal but also of the eternal, then there should be that in his religion which is unchanging; but it will have inevitably at the same time large elements that vary and take on new shapes, with his varying moods and needs. We have to recognise the inevitable variety of forms that even a religion that is believed to be something more than the product of human dreams and of the varying gusts of human desire is bound to take. For even a religion that has a core of what is called revelation within it, and that rests upon a basis of history, is bound to assume varying shapes according to the needs of men, just because it is something that satisfies the whole personality, answering the questions of man's reason, responding to the demands of his conscience and his heart, able to govern his will. Round about the core of that which we esteem eternal truth there will be a wide penumbra that is largely human in its source and in the shape it assumes. All religions have this shifting aspect, and, indeed, the existence of this atmosphere around them is just what shows them to be alive. Accordingly it is with the religions of India in their relation to these human needs and as satisfying, or as made use of with a view to satisfying, the human longings of men and women who are our contemporaries, that this study is specially concerned. The past history of a religion cannot, indeed, be ignored. We all are made what we are in large measure by our inheritance. But our aim is to find out how in the India of today the people seek and find satisfaction for their spiritual necessities through the medium of religion and what fashion these religions take under the stress of the actual demands and aspirations of living people.

When there are such things in any religion, there are living elements in it, and in the measure in which the religion possesses these elements it is alive. It may be the case in regard to any of the religious systems that there are in its sacred books or its sacred traditions and practices, truths and experiences and ritual performances that have satisfied, and that may again satisfy the needs of men, but if no one any longer makes use of them for these ends, because there are no questions in men's minds that they answer, and no thirst in their hearts that they quench, then the religion that enshrines these truths and traditions is a dead religion. It is dead until men bring their pitchers again to it to draw the water of life from it. It would seem, for example, as if that were the case in regard to Buddhism in large areas in China at the present time. Professor J. B. Pratt tells us that he found it there for the most part moribund. Even to those who knew most about the subject Buddhism was "rather an interesting philosophy than a living faith."[1] It seems—though the conclusion may be unjust and due to very imperfect knowledge—as if the great springs of truth and consolation that undoubtedly exist within Buddhism were becoming choked. In Shansi there are many great tombs that mark the graves of dead abbots. "Do they also mark the grave," asks Professor Pratt, "of a dead religion?"[2] Perhaps something not dissimilar is true of the Jewish people of today in their relation with a faith that was once, in the age of the great prophets, so full of life and power. Certainly this can be said with a large measure of truth in regard to Christianity in some periods of its history and even in regard to Christianity today in some regions where it is

[1] *The Pilgrimage of Buddhism*, p. 682.
[2] *Ibid.*, p. 688.

professed. A living religion requires not only that answers shall be given to men's questions that shall bring some kind of satisfaction and comfort, but that these questions shall be asked with urgency and a genuine desire to obtain an answer. It takes two to tell the truth or to establish any moral relationship among men: and, so also, it takes two to create any living religious situation, some Other than the worshipper or the seeker, on the one hand, and on the other hand one who sincerely worships or who, desiring, seeks.

That does not mean, of course, that the living elements in a religion are, because they are living, true; that is, that they are parts of a true interpretation of the whole of things. A religion of pure terror may be a religion that is in large measure false and evil, but it may be very much alive indeed, stirring the very depths of the worshipper's soul and may even accomplish in him a partial good. The comfort, again, that a religious belief or practice brings may be based on hallucination or ignorance or even on deception, and yet it may bring real comfort to troubled spirits and as such be sincerely used and have a certain limited value. In India there is a popular proverb in which there is, surely, a certain modicum of truth—"Where faith is, there God is." In much that we call superstition there may be, and often are, real movements of the troubled soul, flickers and gleams of vital religious longing, and responses also that issue from the divine side of reality. Alongside of fear and cruelty and grossness there may be, revealing itself through these, a real upsurgence of that which is deepest within the human spirit, that which always dwells there, though it may be seven times enfolded within it, like fire in a flint. The turbidity of the waters—to use an illustration that was a favourite with Dr. Edward Caird—really shows that an angel has been troubling them. Magic or fetishism or any of the primitive turnings of the soul towards the mystery that surrounds it may have the seed of religious life quick within it and may be rightly viewed as possessing the promise and potency of the ultimate faith of humanity. It has been said that the source of religion is the sense of creatureliness, and that sense—which implies an Other and Stronger—may drive men today, as it has driven men in the past, to do "damned deeds" as well as to do deeds that save and redeem: but both kinds alike, the lowest as well as the highest, are tokens of life because, however misdirected, they issue forth from living and awakened spirits. Dead souls are souls, if there are ever any such, that no breath from the unseen moves to aspire or to act: and a dead religion is one to which no one resorts at the impulse of the hope or fear stirred by the unseen Reality, whether it comes as an air from heaven or as a blast from hell.[1]

No one indeed can ever say of any religion that it is quite dead, unless he is able to search all the hearts that profess it, and certainly one who comes from outside to study the currents of religious life in India has no right to differentiate the living elements from the dead in the faiths of a land so vast, a land that encloses within the hearts of its millions so immense a variety of needs. We can see quite plainly that certain religions are living religions in that land, that they control the spiritual movements, and are bound up with the spiritual cravings, of multitudes. How far that control guides towards the noblest living or these relationships accord with ultimate reality is quite another matter. Whatever our view of these things may be, we can certainly affirm that there are religions in India that are alive because they are active within living and desiring hearts. What it is our aim to do here is to examine these living religions, so as

[1] "Religion is a playing with fire. The religious man is engaged in trying out the properties of an element which warms but also burns and scars. Thanks to the predominance of emotion over reason in it, religious experience is always hot. Gone cold it has gone out." Marett, *Faith, Hope and Charity in Primitive Religion*, p. 15.

to see—in so far as we can form a judgment on a matter necessarily, to one who studies the subject from without, so obscure and uncertain—what it is in these religions that at the present time appears to bring comfort and to yield satisfying answers to the questions of those who bring to them their problems and their needs. That is the guiding purpose with which we come to our study of the living religions of the Indian people. At the same time, however, the past history of these religions must by no means be ignored, for every adherent of them is a child of that past and his religion has come to him from it, coloured by the experience of many generations. He knows it, in some measure at least, in its setting in history and sees and feels it with that character. It is part of his heritage, and what it brings with it down the years flows in his veins.

This, then, is the method of our approach to the religions which we propose here to study. Our consideration of them will be to a considerable extent eclectic. We shall feel at liberty to neglect much in them that, while it may be of antiquarian interest, is not vitally related to the lives of the men and women of today who profess them. The primary occupation of our investigation is to be with that which, by the help it brings, or is believed to bring, to the adherents of these religions, preserves these religions alive today and is believed to give them a right to live.

We can claim that India affords a peculiarly favourable scene for such a study as we propose and that even today there are to be found within the bounds of that land in living operation, a greater diversity of religions than in any other country in the world. This is so because no other country provides within its borders so wide a variety of races and nowhere else are so many stages of cultural development represented. These are there exhibited for our study not merely as dead specimens in a museum but for our observation and our study, living and active in their control of the lives of men. Among the people of India are to be found racial representatives—to quote the words of Professor E. J. Rapson—of "the three primary ethnographical divisions of mankind" (Caucasian, Mongolian and Ethiopian); while its languages belong to "four of the great families of human speech" (Austric, Tibeto-Chinese, Dravidian and Indo-European) and have been greatly influenced by a fifth. Turning to the cultural variations that India exhibits to us, the same scholar proceeds, "We find at one extreme of the social scale, communities whose members are contributing to the advancement of the literature, science, and art of the twentieth century, and at the other extreme tribes still governed by their primitive constitutions, still using the implements and weapons, and still retaining the religious ideas and customs, of their remote ancestors in the Stone Age."[1]

These statements summarise the facts as to India's racial inheritance as these have hitherto been presented by scholars. It is supposed that one invasion after another from a period reaching far back beyond historical times swept down upon the land, bearing with them each its own culture. First of all, it has generally been conjectured, there came, at some prehistoric period which we cannot now determine, a Dravidian people who may be held to be "the earliest inhabitants of India of whom we have any knowledge."[2] This name is given to those in the south of India who speak Dravidian languages. Other students of the subject would reach still further back to a broad-nosed race whom they suppose to be the "aborigines." But whatever judgment one may form in regard to these speculations, we can now speak with confidence of the presence in India of a culture that ranks far above any of the cultures that these races may have

[1] *C.H.I.*, Vol. I, pp. 37, 38.
[2] Risley, *C.I.R.*, 1901, Vol. I, Part I, p. 508.

contributed. This is what has been called "the Indus civilisation," recently revealed as a result of the excavations at Mohenjo-daro in Sind. Sir John Marshall dates the antiquities that have been unearthed under his direction about 3250 B.C. and believes them to represent a culture that "must have had a long antecedent history on the soil of India, taking us back to an age that can only be dimly surmised."[1] This civilisation would thus appear to have established itself on the plains of India at a much earlier period than the great Aryan invasion which has hitherto been supposed to mark the beginning of civilised life in India. "Hitherto," writes Sir John Marshall, "it has been commonly supposed that the pre-Aryan peoples of India were on an altogether lower plane of civilisation than their Aryan conquerors, that to the latter they were much what the Helots were to the Spartans or the Slavs to their Byzantine overlords—a race so servile and degraded that they were commonly known as Dāsas or slaves. The picture of them gleaned from the Hymns of the Rigveda was that of black-skinned, flat-nosed barbarians. . . . Mentally, physically, socially and religiously their inferiority to their conquerors was taken for granted, and little or no credit was given to them for the achievements of Indian civilisation. Never for a moment was it imagined that five thousand years ago, before ever the Aryans were heard of, the Punjab and Sind, if not other parts of India as well, were enjoying an advanced and singularly uniform civilisation of their own, closely akin, but in some respects even superior, to that of contemporary Mesopotamia and Egypt. Yet this is what the discoveries at Harappa and Mohenjo-daro have now placed beyond question. They exhibit the Indus people of the fourth and third millennia B.C. in possession of a highly developed culture in which no vestige of Indo-Aryan culture is to be found."

[1] *Mohenjo-daro and the Indus Civilisation*, Vol. I, p. 106.

This discovery of a new centre of cultural influence established within India at a period when no influence of so high an order had been imagined as existing there will, as its significance is studied and its extent more fully determined, make it necessary that views that have hitherto been held in regard to the origins of this civilisation shall be radically revised. To what racial type or types this Indus people belonged is still uncertain, but that they were altogether apart from the Vedic Aryans seems scarcely doubtful. The Aryan invaders, who have hitherto been always reckoned as the great progenitors of Indian religion and culture, entered India, it seems probable, in the second millennium before Christ. They were not, as the Indus people would appear to have been, wealthy traders, dwelling in cities built of brick, but a pastoral and agricultural people, living in villages. Both in their case and in that of the Indus people worship would seem to have centred in the family, and the temple would seem to have as yet obtained no place; but the deities that the Mohenjo-daro excavations reveal to us are of a wholly different order from the sky-gods of the Indo-Aryans. No images were used in the worship of the Vedic deities; in those old cities of the Indus, on the other hand, many images of deities that were worshipped have been discovered. We are apt to relegate types of religion that we describe as animistic to peoples in the rudest stages of their development and to suppose that cults of that order that survive in India today derive from the pre-Aryan aboriginal tribes whom the Aryans conquered and drove into the forests or reduced to slavery. We forget that ruder and more elementary worships and superstitions form a penumbra around more luminous beliefs at all stages of religious development and among all races. Thus it is that we find the advanced material civilisation of these Indus peoples accompanied by a religion which, Sir John Marshall tells us, is hardly distinguishable from "that aspect of Hinduism which is bound up with animism and the cults of Śiva and the Mother Goddess."[1] We find also that phallic worship, which the Rigveda condemns, has an established place among this people, from whom, it may be supposed, it has passed down the ages, along with the cults of Śiva and of Śakti or the Mother Goddess, to take its place in modern Hinduism.

It is not necessary to dwell longer upon this extraordinarily interesting revelation of the primal roots from which the vast and ancient tree of Hinduism has sprung. Some sentences, however, may be quoted in which Sir John Marshall presents his conception of the religion that five thousand years ago was a living organism controlling the lives of that far-off people. "There is enough," he writes, "in the fragments we have recovered to demonstrate that, so far as it was capable of expression in outward, concrete form, this religion of the Indus people was the lineal progenitor of Hinduism. But these fragments give us a glimpse only of the popular, devotional and superstitious side of this religion. Of its other and more rational side; of esoteric ideas and philosophical concepts that may have been fundamental to it, as to later Hinduism—they have nothing to tell us. That is the misfortune of our possessing no documentary material that can be deciphered. Yet that there must have been such another side to this religion can hardly be doubted, unless we are to believe that a people, capable of evolving this highly complex and advanced civilisation were yet incapable of progressing beyond the primitive, animistic beliefs with which the pre-Aryans have hitherto been credited; or that, while they were superior to the Vedic Aryans in all that concerned material culture, they were yet hopelessly behind them in the ordinary processes of abstract thought." These are speculations that hardly concern us, but Sir John Marshall's contention, that to this prehistoric civilisation which the Vedic Aryans when

[1] *Op. cit.*, p. vii.

they entered India would find only in ruins and fragments modern Hinduism owes a large debt, can hardly be disputed.

These various elements that we have indicated, however they are to be described or discriminated, elements that we may indicate as those supplied by the Indus civilisation, by the aboriginal races—if we may still use that designation—by the Dravidians and by the Indo-Aryans, are the main sources from which the indigenous Indian religions are derived. That does not mean that there were not other immigrations of great significance into India after the Vedic period. One of these we must specially note for with it there was, in the words of Mr E. R. Bevan, "a sudden rift in the mists which envelop the ancient history of India."[1] That took place when in the fourth century B.C. Alexander and his Greeks made their swift incursion into the land, phalanx and legion thundering along her western border and then vanishing to leave little more than the echo, that still reverberates, of a mighty name. Still later came Scythian invasions, some of them as late as the Christian era, followed later still—from about A.D. 1000 onwards—by successive descents of Muslim conquerors, who brought with them not only the vigour of new blood but also the fervour of a great and virile religion.

As each of these racial waves swept into the land it brought with it—save only in the case of the Greeks—new ways of thinking and of worshipping. Just as there were, to begin with, among those whom we vaguely describe as aborigines, such practices as gather around Animism, Shamanism and cults to promote fertility, and as these presently were overlaid and mingled with the Aryan worship of the sky-gods, and as, later still, there came and dwelt among them, but somewhat apart, the grave monotheism of Islam—so some centuries earlier

[1] *C.H.I.*, Vol. I, p. 345.

than the Muslim conquerors there had come in very different guise a Christian apostolate—that of St. Thomas, according to the legend—bringing the Christian faith from Syria to South India. For a thousand years this remained the one centre of Christian life—a very sluggish life—within the sub-continent. Then in the sixteenth century a second apostle, St. Francis Xavier, brought the message of Latin Christianity and created a second centre of Christian life and faith. A third contact with the Christianity of the West was effected when, rather more than a century ago, the modern missionary movement likewise undertook the task of conveying to India, alongside of western commerce and western civilisation, the message of Christianity. Still another religion rooted itself in the land when in the eighth century of our era Zoroastrianism was conveyed to it, not by conquerors as Islam had been, nor by missionaries of the faith as in the case of Christianity, but by Parsi fugitives who, expelled from Persia, found a refuge and a home in India.

This brief survey is, perhaps, sufficient to indicate the complex of races and religions that India presents to us. For that reason we have opportunities within its borders of studying such a variety of religious attitudes and of expressions of the human spirit, as can hardly be found so easily accessible in any other land. This is especially true of six distinct religions that are to be found in India today, still living and still ruling men's spirits. These six which we propose to make the special subjects of our study, vary widely in their nature and their history and yet all alike are resorted to by multitudes in seasons of spiritual exaltation or distress or need and provide them in some measure with what such seasons demand. Three of them may be said to be indigenous, creations of what we may call the Indian spirit, and are deeply dyed with its peculiar colours. These are Hinduism, Jainism and Sikhism. Hinduism is, indeed, rather a vast treasure-house of religious experience and experiment, emotional, intellectual, ethical, than what we ordinarily mean by a religious system. It has so much variety within it, corresponding to some of the main necessities and demands of the human spirit at various stages in its growth, that it seems best that we should select three of these main phases and view them, as far as may be, apart. Jainism again is a system closely akin to Hinduism, expressive as it is, of some of the primary beliefs that seem to be associated with the ancient life of the people of the land, but clearly differentiated at the same time from Hinduism by some of its main tenets and by its origin and history. Sikhism, the third of the religions with which we propose to deal, is one of the most influential of the many reforming movements that have sprung up within Hinduism, and is notable as having achieved an independent life and as retaining its distinctiveness and independence down to today.

These three religions are closely related to each other and reflect, as the others do not, the peculiar temper of India in its long spiritual travail and the actions and reactions of its mind and heart. The other three have been transplanted to India from other soils and have acclimatised themselves there and adjusted themselves, no doubt, in large measure, to fit moods and needs that are specifically Indian. They are Zoroastrianism, the religion of Islam, and Christianity. All three have had a long history within India and may claim to have proved themselves to have that right of remaining there which comes from their being truly naturalised in their surroundings. Because the adherents of these immigrant religions—Parsis, Muslims and Christians—are Indians "in their bones," we have a right to study the faiths they profess as Indian religions in the same sense in which that is true of the first three which differ from them in the fact that they have had their birth and their entire development within the Indian land. These six roads of the spirit, made use of by the people of India and still today trodden by them with desire and hope and longing are the subjects to which we are to devote our study and investigation.

PART I

HINDUISM

CHAPTER I

ITS GENERAL CHARACTERISTICS AND ITS LITERARY DEVELOPMENT

THERE are few subjects of study that one can undertake that are likely to prove more baffling than that of the complex of aspirations and superstitions and speculations which is comprised within the general name of Hinduism. "Canst thou draw out leviathan with a hook?" Is it possible within any reasonable limits to convey a just idea of this huge, amorphous system and of its confused and shadowy history through four thousand years? To begin with, the question, What is Hinduism? is one to which no one is likely ever to be able to give a simple or a quite intelligible answer. It has no creed summing up authoritatively its tenets. It has no historical personality at its centre whose life dates its beginning. It has, indeed, no beginning that can be discerned. It may be described rather as an encyclopædia of religions than as a religion, a vast conglomerate, comprehensive in the widest sense, an amalgam of often contradictory beliefs and practices, held together in one by certain powerful ideas and by a system of social regulations. It is continually forming about new nuclei; it is agglutinative in its growth, made up of many accretions, imperfectly adjusted to each other and to the whole of which they are parts. Over the bizarre multiplicity of its beliefs and practices, what we may call the Hindu spirit, casts a fine-spun and subtle veil of its own which unifies them and gives them all alike a character which we recognise as specifically Hindu. Throughout the entire system or congeries there can be discovered a unity of characteristic and mood and attitude which makes the manifold a single whole.

To illustrate the complexity and strangeness of this religion, in contrast with the great world-systems that are reckoned its rivals, we shall quote descriptions of it by four friendly students of its doctrine and observers of its practice. Few foreigners have realised as fully as Sir Alfred Lyall the breadth and variety and mystery that make up Hinduism. He compares it in a well-known passage in his *Asiatic Studies*—thinking of it, no doubt, more especially at its lower levels—to " a troubled sea, without shore or visible horizon, driven to and fro by the winds of boundless credulity and grotesque invention." In that description Sir Alfred Lyall was not taking into account the Hinduism of ideas, its attempts, through the minds of its seers, to read the riddle of things. Of that side of the religion he was fully aware and he has shown himself able to enter with exceptional understanding and sympathy into its philosophisings. He is describing it in this place, however, in its aspect as a religion governing and guiding the lives of the multitudes of its ordinary adherents all over the land. We shall take as our second witness to the distinguishing features of this religion an able exponent of the mind of contemporary Hinduism, Sir S. Radhakrishnan. He has described Hinduism as " a subtly unified mass of spiritual thought and realisation." It accepts, he says, " all religious notions as facts and arranges them in the order of their more or less intrinsic significance."[1] It is essentially, in his opinion, a religion of experience, one of " the expressions of the spiritual experience of the race." The Hindu religion, he tells us, " is characterised by its adherence to fact. In its pure form, at any rate, it never leaned as heavily as other religions do on authority. It is not a 'founded' religion; nor does it centre round any historical events. Its distinctive

[1] S. Radhakrishnan, *The Hindu View of Life*, pp. 11, 31.

characteristic has been its insistence on the inward life of spirit."[1]

We may set beside these descriptions that of yet another able contemporary student of the subject, Babu Govinda Das, a Hindu scholar who passes judgment on his religion with much frankness. He goes so far as to affirm that "Hinduism is an anthropological process rather than a religion," and that much "degenerate tissue and toxic stuff" has been gathered into it during its long history.[2]

What these definitions actually imply as to the varied constituents that go to the making up of this religion is indicated in some detail in a reply given by an Indian friend to the writer of a recent book on India when he was asked to explain Hinduism to him. "It brings," he said, "under its sheltering wings all the religious, semi-religious and social practices and observances of the Hindu race. . . . Polytheism, monotheism, pantheism and atheism, have all flourished under the auspices, and in the name, of Hinduism—not necessarily at different times—and still form an integral part of recognised Hinduism. Demon worship, hero worship, ancestor worship, worship of animate and inanimate objects, worship of natural forces and worship of God, have all been woven into its web. It caters for every taste, every grade of life, every stage of development. This at once constitutes the bane and beauty of Hinduism, its weakness and strength. From the purest to the vilest form of worship, from the sublimest heights of philosophic thought to the meanest and crudest phases of intellectual and religious development, all the stages are provided for."[3] That account illustrates what Professor Radhakrishnan calls "the hospitality of the Hindu mind." "The Hindu tradition," he says, "by its very breadth

[1] S. Radhakrishnan, *An Idealist View of Life*, p. 89.
[2] Govinda Das, *Hinduism*.
[3] H. Harcourt, *Sidelights on the Crisis in India*.

seems to be capable of accommodating varied religious conceptions."[1]

It is obvious that it cannot be easy to present any succinct account of the history of a religion that gathers within its scope so wide a variety of human interests. We cannot sum up all the utterances of passion and desire, of love and hate and terror, all the conjectures, wise and foolish, as to the meaning of the life of man, that have issued from the minds and hearts of the Hindu race through these millennia—and yet that is what would seem to be demanded if this very human Hinduism is to be presented in its chequered history. The most that can here be done is to provide a summary record of the main changes and developments through which Hinduism has passed, as these are marked by the sacred literature which these successive stages in its development produced and which carry onward to today the tradition of their influence and their inspiration. It is true that a study of the literature of Hinduism and of its history as a literary development will convey a very one-sided and inadequate idea of the actual religion and its influence unless it is interpreted and corrected by an acquaintance with the facts of things as they are in the life and thought of living men and women. Especially in the case of a religion such as this is, so essentially human, so continually changing, " like the dust that riseth up and that falleth down again," it is necessary for its true comprehension that we keep as close as possible to the lives of those who have made it and have been made by it. At the same time our knowledge of the popular religion will inevitably be shallow and mistaken if we are not aware always during our study of it, of the great governing ideas that lie behind the ebb and flow of feeling and if we do not try to understand them as they can only be fully understood, namely by tracing the process of their growth. Hinduism has never lacked its seers, its thinkers,

[1] *Op. cit.*, p. 100.

its system-makers, and in the libraries of the religions its sacred literature occupies a notable and dignified position.

The head waters of Indian religious thought and aspiration, as far as they are disclosed to us in literary expression, are the Hymns of the Rigveda, perhaps the most remarkable collection in existence of the sacred songs and prayers of an ancient people. It is made up of ten books, containing 1017 hymns, lyrical utterances of worship and petition addressed to a pantheon of nature deities, such as the Sun, and the Sky and the Earth and the Storm and Fire. Few of these bright gods of the upper air survive under the same names as objects of worship in India today. They are the deities of a simpler, more unreflective and more objective people, such as the ancestors of the Hindus of a later time were during the period when they were descending from the high levels of Central Asia upon the plains of Hindustan. The prevailing view of Sanskrit scholars as to the date of this collection is that the oldest hymns may have been composed as early as 1200 B.C. The Rigveda is by no means the expression of the religious conceptions of a primitive people; it is the accompaniment of a highly advanced ritual worship, the work of the priesthood among those whose lives were largely spent in the activities of war and hunting. The gods are viewed for the most part as givers of gifts and the attitude of their worshippers to them is largely one of barter and of bargain. "Here is butter: give us cows." A deeper strain of devotion—one which has affinities with Hebrew religion—is found in connection with Varuna, the sky-god, who sits enthroned in the vault of heaven, watching men's sins with his thousand eyes, the guardian of the holy order (*rita*), the forgiver of sins. "With Varuna," says Professor A. B. Keith, "seems to have been bound up in the first instance the conception of *rita* as first cosmic and then moral order, and with his lessening glory these conceptions fade from Indian thought."[1] His "lessening glory" was probably due to the eclipse of the moral interpretation of life which he represented by another interpretation of which there are foreshadowings in the later hymns in this collection. The tenth book shows us the beginning of that pantheistic reflection which was to have such profound and far-reaching influence throughout the whole of the succeeding development.

When the Rigveda was composed the Aryan invaders would appear to have established themselves within India in the country round about the Saraswati river. The next stage in the literary development is marked by the production of the great ritual manuals called Brāhmanas. By this time the conquering race had advanced further westward as far as Kuru-kshetra, "the Field of the Kurus," the region of the Upper Jumna and Ganges. This is the famous centre from which through succeeding centuries Indo-Aryan culture radiated its influence throughout the whole land. The age of the Brāhmanas may be dated as extending from 800 to 600 B.C. These works are intended for the guidance of the priests and are occupied mainly with elaborate instructions for the proper performance of the great sacrifices. They are aristocratic works screening from view the popular worship which must have gone on alongside of these elaborate and costly sacrificial performances. The priests who perform them are mainly concerned with the profits they can obtain by means of them from the wealthy and the powerful. At the same time "the sacrifice is conceived as constantly recurring in order to maintain the existence of the universe."[2]

Such a formal and covetous priesthood and their official ritual observances can never sum up the whole of the religious life and aspiration of a people. Behind both

[1] A. B. Keith in *C.H.I.*, Vol. I, p. 103.
[2] A. B. Keith, *op. cit.*, p. 142.

the Vedic Hymns and the Brāhmanas there must have lain many things of which we can only catch now and then a glimpse—animism, fetishism, ancestor worship or tendance of the dead, the dread of evil powers, the belief in the efficacy of spells and of magical rites. The Atharvaveda is, no doubt, later as a literary composition than the Rigveda, but it contains a collection of magic spells and incantations which reveal what must have exercised a very ancient and potent religious influence. This lower order of religious belief and practice in all probability existed alongside of the higher Vedic worship which the Hymns reveal and it would certainly find abundant reinforcement from the fears and superstitions of the aborigines among whom the invaders, when they had conquered them had still to go on living.

We have already seen in addition how greatly the scope of the sources from which have issued the varied elements that go to the making of Hinduism has been enlarged by the discovery in recent years of the buried city of Mohenjo-daro and of the evidence that it has provided of the existence within India of an ancient and highly developed centre of culture. This " Indus civilisation " would appear to be quite independent of that of the Aryan invaders and also to be in some respects more highly advanced. Though its religious level, in the absence of literary evidence as to its character, cannot be certainly determined, it must have carried into Hinduism important types of worship. One of these, for example, was the cult of Śiva, which, reinforced, probably, by Vedic elements, has had an influential place in the later development.

There are thus, we may conjecture, at least three main sources from which the whole of the turbid stream of Hinduism flows forth. There is the clearly distinguishable contribution of the Vedic religion of ritual and sacrifice directed towards the higher gods, deities comparable to the Olympians of the Greeks. There are at the same time other large elements that, however they may be assigned to their sources, make their varied contributions to the religion—worships of trees and animals and rivers, cults that are usually associated with fertility ritual, including phallic rites and what is known as Śaktism, conceptions also that seem to be akin to the Yoga of a later age. There is also largely represented, and, no doubt, having many springs from which it flows, a religion of fear and gloom, concerned with the dark powers of the underworld, those chthonic deities that we now know to have been dreaded and propitiated by the Greeks alongside of Zeus and Pallas and Apollo, just as these gods and godlings were worshipped and are still worshipped in India alongside of the bright gods of another rank and kind.

But in India about this period certain powerful ideas of man's life and fate began to lay hold of the minds of men, ideas which from this time onward come more and more to govern all their speculation and belief. These are the doctrine of transmigration and following hard after it, that of *karma*. It is the view of some of the ablest students of this subject that the belief in transmigration was arrived at through a double influence, that of the Aryan teaching which in the scriptures called *Brāhmanas* speaks of repeated death, if not of repeated birth, and at the same time that of the lower fears and fantasies of the non-Aryan peoples whom the Aryans had subdued. "The extraordinary success of the doctrine," says Professor Keith, "shows that it was in harmony with the spirit of the Indian people, and suggests what is otherwise probable, that by the end of the period of the Brāhmanas the influence of the Aryan strain was waning, and that the true Indian character of the intellectual classes was definitely formed."[1]

These new conceptions of the meaning and destiny of the life of man teach that individual souls exist ever-

[1] A. B. Keith, *op. cit.*, p. 144.

lastingly from beginningless time, passing on from body to body in continuous rebirth, their condition and circumstances being throughout determined in every detail by the merit or demerit of the works (*karma*) that they have previously committed. Men thus found themselves in a prison-house of life and suffering from which they could not escape, bound to a wheel of rebirth that revolved unceasingly, the wheel of *samsāra*, as it was called. The absorbing concern accordingly of all who reflected upon life at all henceforward was to find a way of escape. Release (*moksha*) is the great object to which the philosophical constructions of their thinkers and the insight of their seers are directed. These doctrines of rebirth or transmigration and karma date from about the seventh century B.C., and alongside of them and deeply occupied with the problems they present appear the great works of Indian religious reflection and speculation, the Upanishads.

These remarkable documents have a unique place in the literature that records man's efforts to probe the mystery of the universe. They are unsystematic and do not formulate any consistent doctrine. We may accept as the view of the Upanishads which has always prevailed in India since the days of the Rishis or Sages, whose utterances they contain, the words of Professor Das Gupta in his *History of Indian Philosophy*. "The highest knowledge of ultimate truth and reality," he says, "was regarded as having been once for all declared in the Upanishads. Reason had only to unravel it in the light of experience."[1] We can also agree with him that the interpretation that has obtained by far the widest authority is that of Śankara, whose system we shall presently consider. At the same time there are other systems of importance that also claim to represent the teaching of the Upanishads. Nor need this claim be disputed for all students are agreed that various types of

[1] Vol. I, p. 41.

reflection find a place in these ancient scriptures. What they contain Max Müller long ago described as " guesses at truth." The key to their teaching is, however, recognised by all interpreters as contained in the sentence, " Thou art that," the recognition, that is, that the one ultimate reality is the Supreme Soul and the identification of the individual self with that Supreme Soul, the " One without a second." The sense in which this identity is to be understood forms one point of divergence among the interpretations. With the realisation of this final and controlling fact personality disappears and the way of release from the wheel of rebirth is disclosed. Around that doctrine and its meaning and implications centres the thought of India. To the philosophy that in its various forms derives mainly from this source is given the name " the Vedanta " that is, the end or crown of the Veda.

Along with the elaboration of the priestly ritual and the progress of speculation on the meaning and the end of life, there also grew up during this period that system of caste which for 2500 years has held in its grasp the social order of Hindu India, just as the doctrines of transmigration and karma have held dominion over its reflection. These are, each in its own region, the governing factors in the life and thought of India—caste on the one hand and the karma-rebirth conception on the other—and they are closely related to each other. The first outline of the social divisions that were to petrify into the rigid and elaborate framework of caste regulations can be discovered as early as the period of the Rig-veda. Slowly but continuously the system tightens its hold upon the life of the people. When Buddhism arose in the sixth century its tyranny was, in that particular region of India at least, not yet established, but not even Buddhism could overcome its steady progress towards complete control of all social relationships. Eventually this powerful order was able to expel the rival religion from the land.

It is impossible to give any clear indication here of a social system so complex and originating from so many varying causes. It must suffice to accept the description of one of the most experienced census officers of recent years in India, Mr. E. A. Gait. "The main characteristics of a caste," he writes, "are the belief in a common origin held by all the members and the possession of the same traditional occupation." It may perhaps be defined as "an endogamous group or collection of such groups, bearing a common name, having the same traditional occupation, claiming descent from the same source, and commonly regarded as forming a single homogeneous community."[1] It is, of course, an essentially religious system and cuts across, and usually ultimately controls, all the spiritual movements that have arisen within Hinduism. In the opinion of Professor Rapson the system "rests ultimately on two doctrines which are distinctively Brāhmanical—the doctrine of the religious unity of the family, which is symbolised by the offerings made to deceased ancestors, and the doctrine of *svakarma*, which lays on every man the obligation to do his duty in that state of life in which he has been born."[2]

It was soon to give evidence of its strength. Towards the end of the sixth century B.C. and early in the fifth two messengers of new doctrine appeared in India, Mahāvīra and Gautama Buddha, both of them apparently aroused to spiritual earnestness in large measure by reason of their hostility to the pretensions of the Brāhman priests. Gautama fled to the desert to think out a way of escape from the bondage in which, as it appeared to priest and philosopher alike, all men were held helplessly captive. To him as he sat in meditation under the Bô-tree at Buddh-Gaya in Behar came enlightenment, and he announced that life is suffering, that birth and rebirth are the consequences of desire and passion and that the way of escape is by the extinction of desire. This new

[1] *E.R.E.*, Vol. III, article "Caste," p. 234. [2] *C.H.I.*, Vol. I, p. 54.

religion and the kindred religion of Jainism, of which Mahāvīra is reckoned to be the founder and which arose almost contemporaneously, alike dispense with the necessity for any deity and represent a revolt against the Brāhman priestly domination, the blood-stained altars, the futile philosophising of the age. Buddhism is a practical and unspeculative religion of salvation. "Knowledge," says Dr. Hopkins, "is wisdom to the Brahmans; asceticism is wisdom to the Jain; purity and love is the first wisdom to the Buddhist."

Buddha is said to have died in 483 B.C. His religion gradually spread all over India and extended its influence to other lands as well beyond its borders until in the third century before Christ it attained its zenith under the great Buddhist king, Aśoka. Thereafter it seems to have steadily declined until by the eighth century of the Christian era it vanished from the land of its birth. The Brāhmanism of the priests and the philosophers had proved too much for it. "The most probable explanation," in the opinion of Professor Rapson, "of the very remarkable disappearance of Buddhism from the greater part of the sub-continent, where it was once so widely extended, is that Buddhism has been gradually absorbed into the Brāhman caste-system, which has also, though in a less degree, influenced the followers of other faiths—Jains, Muhammadans, Sikhs and even native Christians."[1] Jainism, indeed, lived on within its narrower sphere but the hierarchy of caste had proved its power as it was to prove it again and again in the succeeding centuries.

Apart from this development within the social order the greatest event thus far in the history of the Hindu religious idea may be reckoned to be the transformation of the ancient Aryan worship by the sombre reflection of the philosophers, centring all effort upon the necessity for escape from the bondage of life. We must conceive at the same time the routine of the worship of many

[1] *C.H.I.*, Vol. I, p. 55.

deities as proceeding with ever more and more elaboration among those classes whom the duty of living a secular life still controlled. The temples and the gods multiplied continuously. The influence of the older ideas of the indigenous people had helped to secure the acceptance of the doctrine of repeated births, and the same influence prevailed to secure the admission within the Hindu pantheon of the aboriginal deities. We can realise to some extent how complex and varied the religion of the land was becoming from the two great Epic poems which grew to completed form between the fourth century B.C. and the fourth century A.D., the Mahābhārata and the Rāmāyana, the longest epics in the world. The former, especially, is an encyclopædia of tradition, legend, ethics, and philosophy. "The religions and philosophical views of the Epics," writes Dr. E. Hopkins, "represent every shade of opinion from Vedic theism to philosophical pantheism with later forms of sun-worship (in both Epics) and sectarian cults of Durgā, Śiva and Krishna-Vishnu in the Mahābhārata, and Rāma-Vishnuism superimposed upon the cult of Rāma as a hero-demigod in the Rāmāyana."[1] The prominence of Krishna in the Mahābhārata and of Rāma in the Rāmāyana, both of them associated with Vishnu, point to the prevalence during this period of the cult of Vaishnavism. Vishnu and Śiva, both of them gods deriving from the Vedic age, divided the chief honours between them and were brought into close relationship with many other gods and demigods. The former of these dates from the Vedic period and bears with him into later Hinduism much of the elevation and benignity of a sky-god. If the lineage of Śiva, on the other hand, is really derived from the "Indus civilisation" his cultus may indeed be, as Sir John Marshall claims, "the most ancient living faith in the world."[2] The later development of the worship of this god was, no doubt, greatly affected by his absorption

[1] *C.H.I.*, Vol. I, p. 272 f. [2] *Mohenjo-daro*, Vol. I, p. vii.

of some of the characteristics of Rudra, the Vedic god of storms. His relation is for the most part with the darker shadows that brood over Hinduism, even as Vishnu, as is fitting in the case of a Vedic sun-god, is associated with its brighter aspect. Both these deities possessed qualities and, perhaps, traditions that made it possible for the philosophers to make use of them to represent the Supreme Soul of their speculations.

It is indeed a Scripture that is included within the Mahābhārata which, from this time onward until today, to a greater extent than any other since the Upanishads, has proved influential in guiding the life and thought of Hinduism. This is the Bhagavadgītā or " Song of the Blessed One," which was probably written about the beginning of the Christian era. The Blessed One is Krishna, an incarnation of Vishnu, who, in turn, is identified with the " brahman " or Supreme Soul of the Upanishads. The poem is thus, among other things, an attempt to interpret in a theistic sense the monistic teaching of the philosophers. It may not be the case, as has been maintained, that the Gītā " emanates from an un-Brāhmanical source," but it would seem to represent an attempt to bring together the doctrine of the identity of the individual and the Supreme Soul with the popular theism which centred in Vishnu and his incarnation Krishna. One of the main factors controlling the entire course of the Hindu development and producing within it from time to time agitation and conflict is the difficulty, and at the same time the desirability, of harmonising the claims of the theism of the worshipper of the gods and the pantheism of the philosopher. Buddhism represents one revolt which eludes both alternatives, but which, as far as India is concerned, had in the end to suffer defeat and extinction. The Bhagavadgītā represents, on the other hand, that way of compromise and mutual accommodation which was to prove much more congenial to the Hindu temper. The teaching of the Bhagavadgītā does not separate itself from the Hindu tradition, but is at the same time a protest raised in behalf of the claims of life and of reality in religion against what was either a dead rite or a barren and unprofitable speculation. It is an attempt to conserve on the one hand the activities of duty and on the other the devout life of worship, and to do so without abandoning either the gods or the "forest-sages."

By means of this Scripture, the Bhagavadgītā, the religion of the heart, which is called "*bhakti*," or loving devotion, obtains an acknowledged place in the theological development of the religion and from this time onward becomes a concern of the thinkers, even as it had long been a fact in the hearts of ordinary people where these hearts were alive with religious emotion. This type of worship which in the Gītā has attached itself to Vishnu and to Krishna, his *avatār* or incarnation, was also associated in South India with his great rival Śiva. These two gods divide the popular religion of the land into two main groups, the Vaishnavite and the Śaivite. The former is the more human and genial worship, often, indeed, fervent and passionate in its expression of devotion to its deity, and it is associated most frequently with one or other of the two chief incarnations of Vishnu, Krishna and Rāma.

The Bhakti development is marked by two significant stages in its history. In the first place, about the end of the eleventh century A.D. and the beginning of the following century, a South Indian thinker, named Rāmānuja, formulated for this worship associated with Vishnu and his avatārs a systematised doctrine, based upon his interpretation of the authoritative Scriptures of earlier centuries, the Upanishads, the Vedanta Sutras (manuals of instruction, expounding the Upanishads) and the Bhagavadgītā. He thus sought to establish the Vedantic orthodoxy of the Vaishnavas and "to get rid of the reproach of heterodoxy which had dogged the sect throughout its history."[1] By this important service

[1] Farquhar, *O.R.L.I.*, p. 244.

he gave to the popular theism a new standing and authority. On the other hand, at a somewhat earlier date—perhaps in the tenth century—a complementary service had been rendered to the religion of Bhakti by the appearance, probably also in South India, of the Bhāgavata Purāna. The Purānas are religious poems containing legendary and traditional lore of the gods, which are of great influence among the common people. The Bhāgavata is occupied mainly with the story of Krishna and presents it in a form which became widely popular and produced an intense revival of the Bhakti worships. How this was so may be understood from such a description of its contents as is given by Dr. J. N. Farquhar. Some of its utterances on Bhakti, he writes, " are worthy of a place in the best literature of mysticism and devotion "; they are, in his view, " expressions of a living religious experience." " We may with absolute certainty conclude," he goes on, " that the work arose in some centre where there was a group of Vaishnava ascetics who lived a life of fervent devotion and that the writer's religious experience was rooted there." This may explain the powerful and passionate outbursts of devotion to Krishna or Rāma or Vithobā (a form of Krishna) which occurred in succeeding centuries, through the influence of this book, all over the land and created a vernacular religious poetry. The Bhāgavata seems to have been the torch that kindled this flame of fervour.

Earlier than Rāmānuja, in the ninth century, another and still more influential thinker had arisen—also in the South which seems by this time to have replaced the ancient Kurukshetra as the centre from which religious thought and inspiration issued forth. He was Śankarāchārya, the greatest of India's system-builders. His system belongs to the main stream of Indian speculation and, as we have already noted, is very largely accepted as the orthodox and authoritative interpretation of Upanishad teaching. It is a spiritual monism, linked with the doctrine of māyā or illusion. Like Rāmānuja and all the Hindu schoolmen Śankara's construction is based on the *Prasthānatraya*, the triple Canon of the Vedanta, that is, the Upanishads, the Bhagavadgītā and the Vedanta Sūtras. The distinguishing feature of his system is its interpretation of these authoritative sources as teaching that the material world is illusion. It is accordingly frequently referred to as māyāvāda Vedanta —the Vedanta based on māyā or illusion. The sole reality is the "One without a second," and with this brahman the individual soul is to be realised as identical. By passing from the ignorance that illusion creates to this true knowledge, liberation is attained. The ultimate One, the sole reality, is impersonal and the ultimate goal is absorption into that brahman. This doctrine is also and more frequently called advaita, or non-duality. Rāmānuja's doctrine, being theistic, stops short of this goal and is called Viśishtādvaita or modified monism. The teaching of Śankara overshadows the whole land and reigns, scarcely challenged, in its authority over the thought of India.

Any doctrine based upon the Upanishads must be, one would expect, essentially pantheistic in its character. It can hardly be disputed that that is, in general, the point of view of the seers whose insights are contained in these documents. Their central teaching is that of an Absolute conceived as spirit, though there may be differences of view as to the relation of this Absolute to the world, differences which we find elaborated in the rival systems of Śankara and Rāmānuja. There is, however, among the Indian interpretations of the universe, another of which we must take note, which is not monistic, like these others, but definitely pluralist. That is the philosophy that is called the Sāmkhya. This system is opposed to both of the Vedanta systems which we have considered much more radically than either of them is opposed to the other.

It is well that we should remind ourselves of the links

that bind together all these philosophies while taking note of their differences. All of them are agreed in accepting as basal to their thinking the theories of karma and constantly repeated rebirth or samsāra, and all of them are agreed in taking as the aim of their labours of insight and reasoning the discovery of a way of deliverance from this depressing prospect, a means by which "the fetters of the heart may break asunder." Even Buddhism —though in this case the position is complicated by its denial of the soul—and Jainism are in agreement with these others in this respect and all are, therefore, in view of this central purpose of release which governs them, rather to be reckoned as religions than as philosophies. With the exception of the Chārvāka materialists, Professor Das Gupta tells us, all the systems agree on three things which we may take as he describes them. There is, first, the karma-rebirth theory, "that whatever action is done by an individual leaves behind it some sort of potency which has the power to ordain for him joy or sorrow in the future according as it is good or bad." And this passes on from birth to birth. There is, second, the doctrine of mukti, the doctrine, that is, that this beginningless chain of karma and its fruits "had somewhere its end" and that end "was not to be sought at some distant time or in some distant kingdom but was to be sought within us." There is, in the third place, the "doctrine of soul." "All the Indian systems except Buddhism admit the existence of a permanent entity variously called ātman, purūsha or jīva."[1] The Sāmkhya, therefore, widely apart as it is, in some respects, from the Vedantic idealisms, shares with them those presuppositions which give to all Indian speculation its distinctive character. "The religious craving"—in the peculiar form which we have just noted—"has been," Professor Das Gupta rightly maintains, "universal in India, and this uniformity of sādhana" (that is, means of

[1] Das Gupta, *op. cit.*, Vol. I, pp. 71, 74, 75.

attainment) " has therefore secured for India a unity in all her aspirations and strivings."

We do not propose to examine the Sāmkhya teaching except in its most general outlines and as a means by which the great end of release is sought. How far the principles it teaches reach back into the past and whether some indications of its presence may be found even in the Upanishads we shall not consider. Its classical exposition is found in the *Sāmkhya Kārika* of Īśvara Krishna who is said to have belonged to the fourth century A.D. It derives its main characteristics from the fact that for it there are two principles, prakriti or matter and purūsha or spirit. The latter, whose number is indefinitely great, erroneously identify themselves with matter. Like Buddhism—and, in a measure, the Upanishads—Sāmkhya holds that all life is sorrow, and it seeks deliverance from sorrow. The way to this end is that the soul should know the principles of Sāmkhya. " From repeated study of the truth," says the *Sāmkhya Kārika*, " there results that wisdom, ' I do not exist, naught is mine, I am not,' which leaves no residue (to be known), is pure, being free from ignorance, and is absolute."[1] As soon as its karma is exhausted the purūsha attains release (kaivalya) "which is both certain and final."[2] The condition so attained is not one that can be described as bliss, but is clearly nothingness.

Sāmkhya is atheistic but it is often found, as, for example, in the Bhagavadgītā, in association with another system, the Yoga. The Yoga is a scheme of disciplinary practice, and is theistic. Frequently the two systems are placed side by side as philosophy and religion or as theory and practice.[3] The followers of Yoga, " despite their acceptance of an Īśvara, devotion to whom, by meditation upon him, is a powerful assistance to final release, nevertheless in their desire for release aim " (like

[1] *Sāmkhya Kārika*, translated by S. S. Suryanarayan Sastri, Sloka 64.
[2] *Ibid.*, Sloka 68.
[3] Keith, *The Sāmkhya System*, p.60.

the followers of Sāmkhya) " at the isolation of the souls from nature, not at union with the Absolute."[1] This attempt to assimilate to each other doctrines that are radically alien is a frequent feature of Indian religion. The object of Yoga is to obtain complete control over the movements of the mind and by such means as ascetic practice and meditation to obtain release. Its method and practice belong to very early times, indications of it having apparently been discovered among the remains of the Indus civilisation. There Śiva, who is Mahāyogī (the great Yogī) in Indian religion, is represented in a posture of Yogic meditation. Whether used for the purpose of obtaining miraculous powers or of practising devotion to the Lord (Īśvara) Yoga has always had, and still has, a great place among Hindu methods of acquiring insight or power.

We must now turn to take note of the invasion of the Indian scene by a wholly new power which could not but exercise a profound influence upon Hindu religion. With the coming of Islam into India about A.D. 1000 and the establishment of Muslim rule in Delhi in 1206 the vague and comprehensive polytheism of the land was confronted by a faith at once clear and definite in its outlines and in direct contradiction to Hinduism in its central tenets. It could not fail to happen that, in north India at least, the stagnating waters of the old religion would be deeply stirred by this new influx and that from the contact and intercourse of the followers of the two faiths fresh energies would emerge. The most notable names, representative of this new influence and its effects are these of Kabīr and Nānak, the latter the founder of the Sikh religion. Kabīr is an even more interesting figure than his more notable successor, though we can only discern him dimly, but the two are alike in their attitude to the competing religions in the midst of which they lived. " I am both the child of Allah and of Rām," said Kabīr. " I am neither Hindu nor Muhammadan,"

[1] Keith, *The Sāmkhya System*, p. 45.

said Nānak, " but a worshipper of the Formless." In Sikhism we see the fierceness and fanaticism of Muhammadanism asserting its grim influence, reinforced, perhaps, by the darker elements in Hinduism, the worship of Durgā, the terrible one. Hence the transformation of the sect, under Guru Govind Sing, into a brotherhood of fierce Puritan warriors, organised rather for battle than for worship.

Kabīr, on the other hand, is an altogether winning figure. He was born, it is believed, in 1440, and whether he was originally a Hindu or a Muslim appears to be doubtful. A dispute is said to have arisen over his body after his death, the Muslims desiring to bury it and the Hindus to burn it, but when the cloth beneath which it lay was lifted, there was found, according to the legend, only a heap of flowers. These things are at least a parable, and the fragrance of his life remains for us all in his poems. He calls men away from priest and idol, from temple and scripture, to the living God within. He calls the God of his worship Rām, but he is really " the letterless One." " Your Lord is near," he says, " but you are climbing the palm-tree to meet him." " We can reach the goal without crossing the road." He is believed to have died in 1518. Nānak, who was somewhat later in date than Kabīr, died in 1528. Circumstances, and especially the warlike character of his followers, established his movement in greater strength than that of Kabīr. While the followers of the older saint remained within Hinduism, the Sikhs established themselves as an independent religion and remain so to this day.

Another, and yet mightier influence laid its awakening grasp upon Hinduism when towards the close of the eighteenth century Christian missionaries began in earnest to make known the Gospel of Christ and when the Christian and anti-Christian forces of Western civilisation were let loose upon the land. This meant that whether for good or for evil, there began from that time and has continued increasingly ever since until today a tremendous ferment of thought and feeling ever widening in its influence and its effects. It is what Indian mythology would call a stirring of the Sea of Milk, so that from it flows now poison and now nectar of the gods. Certainly the influence of Christ has been powerful for good and no one can deny that it is the influence of His teaching and His example that has created much that is best in the reforming Theistic Samajes of the nineteenth century. Ram Mohan Roy, first and greatest of the founders of these Societies, declared openly his debt to the teaching of Jesus. No Christian could have affirmed devotion to Christ more passionately than Keshab Chandra Sen. Debendranath Tagore and M. G. Ranade leaned more decidedly than these did upon the ancient scriptures of India, but they, too, certainly owed much—and would not have denied it—to Christ's teaching. These are all great and notable leaders in India's emancipation, worthy to have a place among the great *risis* of the land, and their names have a high place among those of the world's liberators. But in recent years these influences have been replaced by others which have created a still more violent agitation in the troubled sea of Hinduism. Increasing enlightenment contends with an ardent patriotism, jealous for its country's honour. Reaction thwarts the aims of progress, and more than ever those who desire their people's highest good feel themselves baffled. Hinduism seems to be approaching once more a crisis of her fate when the power will be tested anew of those ancient ideas and those stubborn traditions that have through so many centuries of her past maintained their grasp upon her.

In what has been said we have endeavoured to indicate the chief historical features in the progress of Hinduism mainly as a body of ideas from its historical beginnings as the religion of the Veda to the developed and systematised doctrine which in various forms controls the thinking of Hindu India and subtly and often unconsciously prescribes its attitude to life and its duties. It has not been possible even to suggest the varied developments of Hindu religious life that are indicated by the word *tapas* or austerity, the kinds of world-renouncement that have led men and women so often to abandon the ordered life of the home and become homeless wanderers. Nor has it been possible to give any account, alongside of this articulate development in the region of thought, of the manifold of devout aspirations, fears and superstitions that express themselves in a multitude of ways, in a multitude of hearts and before innumerable shrines. Round Śiva—Mahādeva, or the great god, as he is often called—and his wife, Pārvati or Durgā, are grouped many minor deities, often aboriginal gods and goddesses that have been adopted into the Hindu pantheon. Attempts have been made to bring some order into this immense confusion or to establish a hierarchy of divinities. Thus over a large part of India the orthodox worship is recognised as that of five gods who are the objects of worship in the temple and the home. These are Śiva, Vishnu, Pārvati, Sūrya (the Sun) and Ganpati. This eclecticism (which some attribute to Śankarāchārya) does not imply that those who follow this rule may not, and do not, worship as well many other deities. There is, indeed, wide freedom of choice permitted to the worshipper. Behind the particular deity, the *ishta devata* or god of the worshipper's special choice, there looms a Supreme Being who is dimly discerned and acknowledged. Even the villager will recognise his ultimate authority, but there are many minor powers that he feels to be near to help or harm him and whom he dare not omit to propitiate. Yet certain great thoughts and powerful traditions overarch them all, welding them into one whole, incoherent in some respects and often containing elements contradictory to one another, but, as in the case of other low forms of life, singularly tenacious of existence and stubbornly resistent to change.

CHAPTER II

HINDUISM AT ITS LOWER LEVELS

We have already, in our general account of the Hindu development, referred to the invasion, soon after the descent of the Aryans upon the Indian plains, of their higher Vedic faith by elements of the aboriginal religions. We have also taken note of the large inheritance—whatever its source—that has been revealed by recent researches as passing down to later India from the advanced civilisation of the Indus valley. In spite of the wealth and dignity of the life that these researches discover to us, the religion that accompanied it appears, as far as the objects worshipped indicate, to have been of a primitive character, largely what we call animistic. As the Aryans became Indo-Aryans their beliefs became assimilated to their new conditions and the influence of the environment that these humbler nature worships created had its inevitable effect. Of those whom the invaders found already in possession of the land and whom they conquered little can be affirmed with any confidence. The word Dravidian, which has been made use of to describe one large element among them, denotes speakers of languages akin to the Dravidian tongues spoken in South India. These are believed, like the Aryans, to have been invaders and to have entered India in prehistoric times through Baluchistan. Alongside of them the Aryans found still more primitive aboriginal peoples, remnants of whom are still to be found in some of the hill tribes. These are all classed together in the Vedic Hymns as Dasas or Dāsyus, dark-skinned enemies with whom in the earliest period the fair-skinned Aryans waged constant war. The name given to them is interpreted as originally meaning merely "foe,"[1] but presently it bears, significantly enough, its later meaning of "slave." These enemies are outside the Aryan pale, since they are not worshippers of the Aryan gods, and "they are constantly reproached for their disbelief, their failure to sacrifice and their impiety." Professor Berriedale Keith is of opinion also that they were phallus-worshippers, though as early as the time of the Mahābhārata this cult had obtained a place—like much else no doubt among the practices at first despised—in the orthodox worship of the Indo-Aryans.[2] The fact that they obtained this place may be attributed to this worship having belonged, as we have seen, to the ancient "Indus civilisation."

By the period when the latest stratum was added to the Rigveda the term Śudra had come into use to describe the lowest of the four great caste divisions, and in that class, as sprung from the feet of "Purūsha," the primæval giant, are included the aboriginal "slaves." By this time we may be sure that the conquered were taking their revenge upon their conquerors, imposing upon them many of their dark fears and the worship of their earthly deities. We need not, indeed, suppose that the Rigveda sums up the whole religion of the Aryans. Another type of religious practice is suggested by the incantations that are to be found in the tenth book of the Rigveda, and by the whole contents of the Atharvaveda.

We have further evidence, if such were needed, that a religion of fear, a religion such as is usually described as of a primitive type, may accompany quite an advanced mode of life, in the discoveries of Mohenjo-daro. But there seems now to have surged up from beneath a powerful reinforcement of these more primitive conceptions of man's relation to the unseen, radically transforming the character of the religious practices of the

[1] Berriedale Keith in *C.H.I.*, Vol. I, p. 84. [2] *Ibid.*, Vol I, p. 85.

people. We have already noted in the previous chapter the probability that the belief in transmigration which colours so deeply and so darkly the later Indian outlook was largely a product of the beliefs of the aboriginal peoples. We may class along with these beliefs such a cult as that of the phallus and the worship of Śiva, which is associated with it, cults which were destined to have so influential a place in later Hinduism. This type of worship, whatever its source or sources, was probably assisted in its development by the contribution that came to it from the wild, but much less sombre, conceptions that gather in the Veda around the name of Rudra, the god of storms. Among the elements that have gone to produce this whole cult must be included, in the opinion of Professor Berriedale Keith, "an aboriginal god of vegetation."

Just as the Dāsas or Dāsyus were sometimes to the Aryans aboriginal peoples and sometimes fiends, so the name Piśāchas seems to have both implications. No doubt those dwellers in the mountains and the forests who were dangerous enemies of the Aryans in ancient times became associated with the dark powers that they chiefly worshipped, with whose ways they were familiar and whom they could invoke. It is accordingly this side of Hinduism that is so powerfully reinforced by the contribution of the Dravidian and other aboriginal races. Shadowy and dangerous beings, bhūtas, piśāchas, vetalas, ghouls, disease devils, earth-mothers, came in like a flood ousting to a large extent the greater and worthier gods. So much is this the case that, in the opinion of such a student as Mr. William Crooke, popular Hinduism consists of "a veneer of the higher beliefs overlying demon-worship, the latter being so closely combined with the former that it is now impossible to discriminate the rival elements." As is natural this condition of things is most evident in South India where the influence of the higher religion was late of asserting itself and where the

Dravidian elements to this day retain a real ascendancy. Hence it is, no doubt, that Śiva holds so great a place in this part of India, gathering around him not only the monistic philosophy of Śankara but the warm devotion of a religion of the divine grace. Hinduism does not even now close its doors against new gods and godlings. Its doors are always open for the admission from beneath of new forms of mystery to be propitiated, new influences of evil to be averted.

It is immaterial for our purpose what name we use to describe these lower reaches of the Hindu system. It has its animistic features, its magic practices, its fetishism, its shamanism. What concerns us mainly here is not to enumerate and examine these various forms of primitive superstition but to consider those practices among them that continue even today to exercise widespread influence over the Hindu people, especially in so far as they have a real effect upon conduct and life and supply what we may describe as religious needs. These are vague phrases, capable of many interpretations but in dealing with so vast and so varied a body of material as Hinduism at this level supplies any detailed investigation is impossible. What we seek—difficult as it will be to obtain—is a general survey guided by the rule that we are seeking, in this immense lumber-room of the spirit, for that which is of religious value. All we can hope to do is to present some specimens of the media that are made use of by those who are as yet at what we may call the animistic level in religion in order to quiet their fears and stay their spirits, and by their means to endeavour to form some judgment of the extent to which these ends are being attained. To form a true judgment is, indeed, beyond our reach. No one can tell what measure of comfort their faith brings to these inarticulate multitudes. At the same time cultus by itself is not religion and it is with the personal element in a religious act that its value is bound up.

It is not easy indeed for the student to find his way through the vast jungle of the lower Hinduism and to form an idea of how it governs the mind of the peasant today and how it is related to the higher levels of the religion. Let us begin by taking to guide us in our survey the place that blood has in the lower Hindu worship. Whatever the actual causes may be which have given it the place it holds in the religion one can see its intimate relation to the wild passions that religion has to deal with. It is the flag of terror and of anger—perhaps we may say of the sense of life itself. It is the gift that the gods, when they are viewed mainly as demons, will most of all demand. The Karens of Burma give the stones they worship offerings of blood for, "If we do not give them blood to eat," they say, "they will eat us." Hence the blood sacrifices—a fowl or a goat or a sheep—offered at so many rude shrines, and not only at these but in the great temple of Kāli at Calcutta and in many another temple of the deities that are grouped about the ancient Śiva, "the Great God." It is impossible to describe the whole medley of worships that belong to this order except as varieties of demonolatry which have not yet wholly sloughed their primal character. New reasons for these offerings other than those that drove the primitive worshipper so to placate a blood-drinking fiend have arisen in later times to explain them. Thus the fact that Śiva was described as the Destroyer, the Lord of life and death, served to justify the cultus that surrounded him, but he remains still in large measure what he was to the citizens of Mohenjo-daro.[1]

[1] "If a thousand altars stream with blood
Of the victims slain by the chanting priest,
Is a great God lured by the savoury food? . . .
That millions perish, each hour that flies
Is the mystic sign of my sacrifice."

Lyall, *Verses Written in India*, p. 99.

Whatever may have been the influences that brought the change about—and in regard to this scholars hold varying opinions—the rule that forbade animal sacrifices in many temples must be recognised as marking a great advance. That is especially the rule in Vaishnavite worship. It is mainly the less enlightened multitude that still resort in their dread of evil powers to the old methods. The village idols are still painted blood red in colour even if only cocoa-nuts are offered before them. "A red-painted stone," says the Vaishnavite poet, Tukārām, "only brats and women bow down to," but others as well, in hours of "asthenic emotion" betake themselves to these methods of averting evil. Those who turn away from the red paint and the blood and allow fear to be sublimated into something nobler are climbing to a higher plane of Hinduism. In general it may be recognised that around Vishnu these higher conceptions gather more freely than around Śiva of the phallus and the burning ghat. With Vishnu and his avatārs are associated feelings of hope and love, and these point towards a world of a finer moral quality than fear and dread create. There is an old story of the thirteenth-century poet, Nāmdev, which illustrates this difference. This poet-saint was at first a robber and murderer, but, repenting of his crimes, he betook himself to a village shrine of Nāgnāth, a form of Śiva. But he found there in the grim god no gleam of hope. In his remorse he cut himself till his blood flowed before the idol. Then, in his extremity, the story tells us, a vision bade him go to Vithobā of Pandharpūr who would cleanse his sins and give him salvation. Thenceforward he gave up his whole life and his remarkable poetic gifts to the service of this Vaishnavite god of compassion and kindness. It was a rebirth into a higher moral and spiritual region and is typical of an influence that has been at work leavening with nobler hopes the grim nature worship that lies at the root of Hinduism and still exercises its dark control over many multitudes.

"Religious emotion," Mr. Marett reminds us, "is ambivalent, exciting the mind at once for better and for worse." That double direction is evident in the influences that blood represents and lets loose. A similar double development can be seen issuing from the sex emotions which also have their place among the cults of this lower order. Even within Vaishnavism and the religion of Bhakti, of which a fuller account will be given later, the dangers that await those who travel along this avenue of religion make themselves evident. The hysterical devotion to Krishna which took as its example the tales of Rādhā and her divine lover has had disastrous effects in the history of some of the Vaishnavite sects. Mirābāī, the old legend tells us, renounced her kingdom and her Rajput husband because Krishna was the Sole Male and his worshippers were all females. She could have only one Lord. At the same time in the worship of Krishna as the husband of Rukmini—such worship, for example, as is directed to him under the name of Vithobā—we see the nobler aspects of human love exercised towards him and some nobler aspects also of divine love attributed to him in a fashion that creates a truly spiritual devotion.

When we turn to other effects besides that of the offering of sacrifices of blood that fear produces we find that these are of many kinds. But whatever its form the effects of fear as an emotion bear the double character that we have already noted. It creates magic and sorcery and all the armoury of amulets and charms and incantations that are their accompaniments. But it may not only cause recourse to such dangerous aids; it may, as in the case of Nāmdev, toss the terrified one to the breast of a deity of a much higher order. But this upward development, where it occurs, is usually the consequence of some rare upsurgence of hope and courage, through the means of some prophetic personality. When such a seer arises there may be what we may call an evangelical revival. But more often a sombre pall broods over the life of the Indian peasant.

Indeed a generalisation that one is constrained to make in reference to this stratum of Hinduism is that its prevailing characteristic is fear. This fear is created by dread of the dark and of the spirits of the dark. This is so largely the case in regard to their religion that one is inclined at times to agree with the thesis of the old Latin poet that fear created the gods. Professor Jacobi in his article on "Demons and Spirits" in the *Encyclopædia of Religion and Ethics* illustrates what he calls the "demonophobia" of the lower castes and forest tribes of India by a quotation from an account of the terrors that beset one hill people, the Tharus of the Himalayan Tarai. "The *bhuts* or demons," we are told, "lurking in the forest trees, especially the weird cotton tree, and the *prets* or spirits of the dead, lead them a very miserable life. When the last ray of light leaves the forest, and the darkness settles down upon their villages, all the Tharus, men, women and children, huddle together inside their fast-closed huts, in mortal dread of these ghostly beings, more savage and cruel than the leopards, tigers and bears that now prowl around for their prey. Only the terrible cry of "Fire" will bring these poor, fear-stricken creatures to open the doors and remove the heavy barriers from their huts at night. And even in the daytime, amid the hum of human life, the song of birds and the lowing of the cattle, no Tharu, man, woman or child, would ever venture along a forest-line without casting a leaf, a branch or a piece of old rag upon the bansati (Sanskrit, *vanaspati*, "King of the woods") formed at the entrance of deep woods to save them from the many diseases and accidents, the goblins and malignant spirits of the forests can bring upon them."[1] These

[1] S. Knowles, quoted in E.R.E., Vol. IV, p. 60.

fears that haunt the lives of many by day and by night are inspired by the belief that every gloomy region, every spot where a tragic or violent death has happened, every aspect of nature that is strange and sinister, is the dwelling of some power that is dangerous. And just as there are such powers lurking in dark places against which one must be protected, so spirits of the dead are especially to be feared and precautions must be taken lest they return to the homes of the living with hostile purpose. There are also spirits that enter into and possess their victims; there are those that bring disease, and there are—to bring our list to a conclusion—the mother-goddesses who, in spite of their name, belong to this evil and dangerous category.

It can hardly be considered strange, if life is exposed continually to so many perils, that protection should be sought by means of charms and amulets and spells and incantations. We can understand how a mother surrounds her son, perhaps her only son and therefore in the Hindu system a peculiar treasure and even necessity, if there is to be any happiness or hope in life, with such defences. The preciousness of a son to his parents—since he alone can perform their funeral ceremonies—is one of the causes, in view of the uncertainty of life and of those unseen perils that surround it, from which issue innumerable anxieties and fears and the observance of endless ceremonies and the making of many vows.

Such anxieties as these have especially to be suffered by the women, and those who are intimate with their lives bear witness how burdened they are by daily anxieties and haunted by dread. This has been described vividly even in the case of those who follow the customs of the twice-born, by a sympathetic student of their lives.[1] This writer tells us that such a woman is often like "a frightened child shut up in a dark, deserted house" with horrible powers and evil shapes pressing

[1] Mrs. Sinclair Stevenson, *Rites of the Twice-born*, pp. 436 f.

against the window-panes. If that be so of these, how much more may it be true of those who belong to what are accounted the less enlightened classes. But after all such terrors are a part of human life and are found even among those who have inherited in other lands faiths that might well have brought them courage. Another writer,[1] who has had exceptionally close contact with the lives of village women, gives a most affecting picture of their anxieties and of the means by which they seek to guard against them. " Fear," she writes, " was everywhere. Mothers in every community lived in fear of the jealousy of the gods and goddesses towards their children." She goes on to tell of some of the pathetic tricks by which they sought to outwit those jealous and malignant powers, tricks to which mothers in every province of India resort no less than those in the Punjab of which she writes. They clothe them in dirty garments and dress the specially precious boy as though he were merely a girl; they dissemble their love with abusive and depreciatory speech; they give them names like " Blackamoor " or " Rubbish " or " Twopence halfpenny."

It may be thought that in what has been said generalisations have been too hastily reached from the lives of women and of people of aboriginal and low-caste origin. The testimony we have adduced could, however, be amply confirmed by the witness of members of the highest castes. A convert to Christianity from Brāhmanism, a man of high character and intelligence, tells how the terror of a demon, associated with the huge Jain image of Gumateśvara oppressed the village in South Kanara where he was born. The fear of the villagers was lest, if they neglected him, he would set fire to their thatched houses. In the same village the Mother goddess, Mariamma, was worshipped by members of all castes from Brāhmans to outcastes. Their fear was that she would afflict them with the epidemics that she controls.

[1] M. Young, *Seen and Heard in a Punjab Village.*

He gives other instances to show how fear of demons haunts even the educated and intelligent. One of these, a Brāhman, believed himself to be possessed by the spirit of his dead father. He goes on to comment on these memories and experiences that he has been recalling. "It is one thing," he says, "to read about animism in text-books on religion; it is altogether a different thing to live through the experiences of the animistic consciousness. . . . It was a life under the tyranny of the spirit-powers of darkness, a life of abject fear."[1]

The conduct of life is indeed difficult for those who are surrounded by so many evil influences against which measures have to be taken. Not only must spells and charms and amulets (or what those who are governed by similar ideas in the West call mascots) be used, but the omens must be carefully studied before any enterprise is undertaken. A writer on South Indian customs gives a selection of some of the omens that must be observed by a man starting on a journey. "It is a favourable omen if he should see, at starting, a married woman, two Brāhmans, an umbrella, a cow, two fishes, an elephant, a black monkey, a dog, a parrot, honey; but he must turn back if he should see a widow, a smoky fire, a hare, a blind man, a tiger, a dog barking on a housetop, a quarrel, an oilman, or a beggar."[2] These latter portents are centres of danger, not to be ignored or lightly reckoned with. If one should meet an outcaste man, even he may be a minatory and perilous object, and if this happens when one is starting on a journey, it is well to avert the danger by showing him the respect of circumambulating him, as one does when worshipping an idol.

Removal from one district to another involves transference of one's circumstances from a relation with known

[1] *Types of Religious Consciousness, Hindu and Christian*, by M. Sanjiva Rau.

[2] Stephen Neill, *Out of Bondage*, p. 31.

and friendly influences to those which are unknown and may be hostile. A Hindu Government official may have to refuse promotion because it involves transference to another district and his wife, if not he, is afraid of the spirits there. Perhaps this is what causes a journey across "the black water" to be forbidden by orthodox Hindu custom and makes it necessary for an orthodox Brāhman of the highest culture to arm himself when he goes to London to attend the Round Table Conference, with the milk of "Hindu" cows, as well as water from the holy Ganges, and even a supply of holy mud from the same friendly source, the beloved "Mother Ganga."

The sources from which the greatest menace to life and happiness comes to the Indian villager are those that send disease and those that issue from the world of the dead. Many of the disease deities belong to the group of earth-mothers, so numerous and so apt to be dangerous if not propitiated. They may be neglected at other times but when an epidemic is abroad they have all honour and recognition. The cholera Mother will be borne by the villagers with all respect and veneration in a little cart to the village boundary in the hope that she will pass on and leave them undisturbed. Or when a child has recovered from smallpox the mother will go to the shrine and roll in the dust before it seven times, saying, "I thank you, Baliya Kākā, that you have done my child no harm."[1] "It is God who gives everything," said a Jat woman, distinguishing the supreme God from the disease goddess, Kāli, whom she worshipped so that her children might survive, "but something of help one gets from her also."[2]

It is in such circumstances that the *bhagat* is called in who follows practices that anthropologists call Shamanism. The deity possesses him; he lashes himself sometimes into frenzy with a whip; and under the divine influence he utters his instructions for the patient's cure.

[1] Mrs. S. Stevenson, *Without the Pale*, p. 31. [2] M. Young, *op. cit.*, p 90.

But there is nothing that creates so many dark shadows for the life of the simple village people in India as does their fear of the spirits of the dead. Troubled spirits that are feared and that need to be placated are, for example, such as have met with a sudden or a violent death, or death by some epidemic disease, or the spirit of a woman dying in childbirth, or the unmarried or the widow. Anyone, indeed, who may be supposed to have died with unsatisfied desires or embittered against life, may be suspected of seeking in jealousy or anger to avenge himself or herself upon the living.

Reference has already been made to the account by Mr. M. Sanjiva Rau of a Brāhman of his acquaintance in Kanara who was believed to be possessed by the spirit of his deceased father and also by the demon worshipped by the family through many generations. He suffered endless miseries and was almost driven to commit suicide. He was delivered by the same power as brought back to sanity the Gadarene demoniac. "Jesus Christ has changed me," he said of himself, when he was, like his prototype, clothed and in his right mind. "I am like a copper vessel, scraped and tinned inside and outside."[1]

Miss Miriam Young, whose book on Punjab village life has already been quoted, tells of one unhappy Hindu woman, haunted, she herself believed, by a Muhammadan Pir or saint, to whom was attributed the illness by which she wasted away. "To be tormented by the gods, they said, was bad enough, but to be tormented by dead people was torment untold."[2] Many plans are

[1] *Op. cit.*, p. 12. Compare also what Mr. H. A. Rose says of another region of India, the United Provinces: "In the Kumaon division of the United Provinces the lowest class, the Doms, and even the lower classes of Brāhmans, the Khas Brāhmans and Rajputs—in fact the bulk of the population—believe in the powers of the malevolent or vindictive dead. Thus if a man has two wives and drives one to suicide any disease afflicting the other wife's children is ascribed to her ghost which must be propitiated and gradually comes to be treated as a god. If a man is killed in a quarrel every misfortune befalling his slayer or his children is ascribed to the ghost." *E.R.E.*, Vol. VIII, p. 36.

[2] M. Young, *op. cit.*, p. 164.

resorted to so that the ghost of the dead, when the burning or the burial is over, may not find its way back to its old home to haunt it. Some of these are similar to the old custom in western countries of burying the suicide at crossroads with a stake through the body.

It is not difficult to see how deeply the life of the village people must be affected, and how grievously they must be harassed, if they are beset by such fears as these. At every haunted place in the hills or valleys that they have to traverse day after day, measures for their protection have to be taken. A cocoa-nut must be broken at the foot of some rock that appears to the wayfarer sinister and threatening, every time the bullock-cart—or it may even nowadays be the motor-car—goes past; the blood of a domestic fowl has to be poured forth at a shrine which marks the spot where the dangerous spirit of a murdered man, or a man killed by a wild boar or panther may be met; or it may be that a brandy peg is offered at the tomb of a powerful foreign sahib who is believed to like such gifts. "Not every man has mana, nor every ghost; but the ghost of a man of power becomes as such a ghost of power, though in his capacity as ghost he has it in greater force than when he was alive."[1] The deity worshipped may have even been an outcaste man, as in the case of the man who in the Hyderabad State is worshipped as "Māng Ir," the Māng hero, in shrines in the walls that surround some villages. He was probably built into the wall as a sacrifice to the dark powers he represents, to make it strong, and now he ranks as a divine being.

These spirit influences that surround the village Hindu may not always be malevolent, but it does not do to count too much upon their kindly character. It is the course of wisdom in any case to be on the safe side. When Dr. J. M. Macphail, who lived and worked among the Santals asked if they thought that the objects

[1] Marett, *The Threshold of Religion*, p. 134.

of their worship could do them any good, an old man replied, " No, they can do us no good, but they can do us a great deal of harm."

At the beginning of his book, *Faith, Hope and Charity in Primitive Religion*, Mr Marett asks the question, " Is hope or fear the mother feeling in religion? " He gives his vote for hope. " The fear of the God-fearing man," he maintains, " is but the accessory feature of a mood founded on the bed-rock of hope "; for " religion is an epitome, a concentrated version, of life itself, that bold attempt to persist in being and to crown it with well-being."[1] It would not be untrue to maintain further that, while fear and hope are born from the same matrix, when hope prevails and being is crowned with well-being this achievement is most often reached through some man of insight or prophet, through, that is to say, some revelation. A new vision of God breaks upon someone, manifesting Him as higher than a demon, and in this way perhaps a whole countryside experiences what Mr. Marett calls a " spur to the life force."[2] Reference has been made already to the bitter sufferings of a Brāhman in Kanara, possessed, as it seemed to him, by his dead father's spirit and to the deliverance and the new birth of hope that came to him by such an experience of a higher God. But while this came in that instance through Christianity it may come, and not seldom has come, through a new discovery made within Hinduism. In the twelfth century in this same district of Kanara such a discovery was made by Basava, the founder of the sect of Lingayets or Vira Śaivas. He lived and grew up in the midst of such fears as have been described, but he himself tells the story of how a new life came to him through surrender to a nobler conception of God. " Those who have wealth," he said to God, " build temples for Thee. What shall I who am poor build for Thee? This body is Thy temple."

[1] P. 22. [2] *Faith, Hope and Charity in Primitive Religion*, p. 39.

His preaching is summed up in this passage: "To the faithful wife but one man is the husband. To the devotee who is truly devoted but one God is God. Cast away, cast away your thoughts that turn to other divinities. To think of any other God, that is evil indeed." He found a refuge from fear in this God's purpose for his life. "That which may befall us tomorrow, let it come even today. That which is to befall us today, let it come even now. Who will fear to face it? Who will shrink from it? The divine decree is that whosoever is born one day shall die another day." He still gave, as he had been accustomed, the name of Śiva to God and he retained the linga or phallus as the symbol of discipleship, but by what he taught of God he opened the way for those who followed him into a new life of joy.[1] He rejected, we are told, the fundamental Hindu principle of rebirth and with it the prospect of gloom and of uncertainty that it brought into man's life; he rejected also the widespread belief in ghosts[2] and was able to find an escape from the paralysing fears that belief creates. What this seer did for his followers in Kanara was done by many others in various provinces of India throughout the centuries, men and women who awakened the hearts of their fellows to hope in God. This was especially the contribution that was made to Hinduism, as we shall see in more detail later, by the saints and singers of the Bhakti faith.

The worship of the people of the villages and the hills is not all fear, otherwise it could hardly continue long to hold their allegiance. We can agree with Professor Robertson Smith when he says, writing of the religion of the Semites, "It is not with a vague fear of unknown powers, but with a loving reverence for known gods, who are knit to their worshippers by strong bonds of

[1] I am mainly indebted for this account of Basava to Mr. M. Sanjiva Rau's *Types of Ethical Consciousness (Hindu and Christian)*, pp 37 ff.

[2] See R. E. Enthoven in *E.R.E.*, Vol. VIII, p. 74.

kinship that religion in the only true sense of the word begins."[1]

Even the Earth-Mothers, though they belong to the dark underworld, have a benignant aspect, and can be classed among the village guardians. Many of these demons, too, have been partially civilised and humanised by being taken into the company of the higher Hindu gods. Hanuman, for example, or Maruti, the monkey-god, may have been originally, like not a few others, a theriomorphic deity of the aboriginal people, but he has become, in spite of his origin and his appearance, the tutelary god of the village, viewed, because of the help he gave to Rāma against the demon Rāvan, as a friendly and gracious god.[2] If Sīta, as Professor Jacobi suggests, was originally a chthonic deity, she certainly underwent, under whatever influences, a most gracious transformation.[3]

Similarly we see how the dread of ghosts and ghouls becomes transformed into an altogether higher order of religious observance. The ceremonies that are performed come to be viewed not mainly as rites of "riddance" but as means by which to bind the departed in friendship and affection to those left behind. When life becomes less of a struggle of wolves, and the security and mutual confidence of an ordered society is established, then even the dark places of the jungle may become less haunted, and the spirits of the departed may be recognised to be after death, as they were before, friends to their friends. Even when these spirits are viewed with dread, the precautions taken against them are not continued for long and after a while the fear passes away. Thus from those dark roots may grow, and has grown in the case

[1] *The Religion of the Semites*, p. 54.

[2] "The present writer is inclined to believe that Hanuman was a godling before Valmiki sang of his friendship with Rāma, whereby he came to be recognised as a popular deity throughout India." Jacobi in *E.R.E.*, Vol. VI, p. 661.

[3] Jacobi, *ibid.*

of Hinduism, a culture that has chiefly to do with the comfort of the departed spirits. Ancestor-worship, it has been suggested, has its origin "at once in the fear of ghosts, in filial affection and in the desire to preserve for the family the benefits of paternal protection."[1] The ceremonial performance of *Śrāddha*, as it is called, that is, ritual undertaken for the comfort of the dead, has a place in the most highly developed forms of Hinduism, but its roots stretch back to animistic practices and beliefs, and in the case of many among the less civilised classes and tribes rites that are obviously animistic, that is, that have as their aim the laying of a troubled spirit or the nourishing of an uneasy ghost with food, are still performed in all simplicity.

The religious worship and the religious conceptions of the peasant have thus climbed gradually out of their penumbra (as Sir Alfred Lyall calls it) of half-lights and dreads into an atmosphere of greater clearness and comfort. Even to have Śiva or Mahādeva in chief charge, as it were, of the chthonic powers, by establishing order established also confidence. With him and with his wife Kāli or Durgā became associated many of the deities of lower and less reputable rank. We have seen how ancient is the association of this whole group of deities with phallic worship, but many other evil traditions such as temple prostitution and the gross practices connected with such a festival as the Holi have similar affiliations. It is only very slowly that Hindu opinion is turning away from these customs, which, no doubt, have their deep roots in the fertility cults of a very early age. A god that presides over the process of life's natural changes, of life and death, the joys and the sorrows of our physical existence, has inevitably a powerful hold of those who live so close to the earth and are so immediately related to its rewards and to its tragedies as are the peasantry of India. It was not found to be impossible at the same time to

[1] Goblet d'Alviella in *E.R.E.*, Vol. I, p. 536.

associate this god with the final solutions that the philosophers sought after of the mystery of the universe. As Sir John Marshall suggests, this association may date from the ancient days when Śiva and Śakti were worshipped in the Indus valleys. We are told that in South India when a struggle was in process in the early centuries of the Christian era between Hinduism and the more ethical Jain and Buddhist doctrines the adherents of these latter faiths would say of such a Hindu deity as Śiva, "How can this demon be the life of the soul of all?" But perhaps that need not be thought impossible if this demon is one who

> "Governs the tides of the sentient sea
> That ebbs and flows to eternity."[1]

It is not, however, in his philosophic aspect that this god with his attendant godlings attracts the humble peasants; when the rains fail or cholera is abroad, then he has his opportunity.

There are two other types of worship that neither the peasant nor indeed any orthodox Hindu will ever neglect. In an attempt to define the Hindu, an experienced student of the people and their customs once suggested that he was one who reverenced Brāhmans and worshipped the cow. Neither that nor any other definition would include the endless variety of kinds of Hindus,[2] but it includes most of the common people in the villages of the land. What the place of the Brāhman in past days was we can learn from what Tulsī Dās writes in the sixteenth century in his *Rāma-charit-mānas*, a book of which Dr. Farquhar writes that "it has probably influenced a far larger number of Hindus in these last three centuries than any other work." For him the Brāhman is "the very root of the

[1] Sir Alfred Lyall, *Verses Written in India*, p. 100.

[2] A modern Hindu of authority, Babu Govinda Das, despairing of any narrower definition, has suggested that "everyone is a Hindu who does not repudiate that designation." *Essentials of Hinduism*, p. 60 (Madras, Natesan & Co.).

tree of piety, the destroyer of sin." "A Brāhman," he says, "must be honoured though devoid of every virtue and merit, but a Śudra never, though distinguished for every virtue and learning." "My soul is disturbed by one fear," he adds, "the curse of the Brāhman is something most terrible." Still today in great measure their power and prestige remains. "The right of Brāhmans to dictate may be challenged in the cities," writes an authoritative observer in North India, "but in villages like ours their control is absolute."[1] At a wedding, a festival, or on any other religious occasion gifts must be given to Brāhmans and no act of merit is more likely to bring a rich reward than the feeding of Brāhmans. But perhaps everywhere it is on the whole true, as an observer in the Punjab affirms, that the peasant, though he feeds and venerates, does not respect, the Brāhmans.[2] The authors of *Behind Mud Walls*, who write with the authority of an intimate knowledge of a village in the United Provinces, put into the mouth of a villager this account of the Brāhmans he knows: "The men who devote their lives to priestly duties visit us, to be sure. But they come with a conch or a bell, the sound of which sends our women folk scuttling to the grain jars. At our doors they stop just long enough to have the donations poured into their bags."[3] What Tukārām, the Śudra poet of the Deccan, wrote of the Brāhman mendicant in the seventeenth century is, no doubt, what many feel in regard to him still:

> "A greedy cat he steals
> From door to door, begging from men his meals.
> What Tukā says is true,
> The sack is empty and the measure too."

The villager feels often enough, we may be sure, that the Brāhman sack has nothing in it for his religious needs.

The worship that is rendered to the cow belongs to a

[1] Wiser, *Behind Mud Walls*, p. 19.

[2] See *E.R.E.*, Vol. V, p. 20.

[3] Wiser, *op. cit.*, p. 164 f.

very ancient tradition coming down through the centuries from very early times. We find also that in the " Indus civilisation " the bull, though not the cow, had an important place among the objects of veneration. Nor does the reverence and affection that the Hindu feels towards this favoured animal, whatever its source may have been, appear to have grown less with time.[1] It is indeed said that economic need nowadays causes the peasant in the Punjab to sell his cattle to the Muslim butcher knowing well their destined fate. But economic necessity is a tyrant which drives Hindus, as it drives other peoples, to courses that they are very loth to take. Further, cow protection, it has to be recognised, has become a symbol of Hindu patriotism, and so may often be used for political purposes to arouse hostility to the Muslim. But it is true all the same that the cow still stirs in the hearts of many an emotion of almost religious devotion.

While cattle are, naturally enough, held in honour and affection among peoples whose past reaches back to a pastoral age, this place of reverence accorded to the cow is something altogether exceptional. It is not in the heart of the Hindu peasant alone that warm emotion is felt towards this animal. We see in the case of Mr. M. K. Gandhi this primitive reverence sublimated into something that may claim to be of a higher order and to be based upon grounds of reason. In his exposition of the Hinduism which he professes " cow protection " has an important place. This is, he says, " the central fact of Hinduism." " To me," he goes on, " it is one of the most wonderful phenomena in all human evolution; for it takes the human being beyond his species. The cow to me means the entire sub-human world. Man through the cow is enjoined to realise his identity with all that lives." [2] Thus Mr. Gandhi gives to this deep-rooted

[1] Nothing has ever aroused more violent resentment against Mr. M. K. Gandhi among the orthodox than his merciful action in putting to death a calf whose life was a burden to it.

[2] *Mahatma Gandhi's Ideas*, by C. F. Andrews, p. 38.

tradition an interpretation which links it with another equally ancient belief, that of ahimsā or "non-killing." By many thoughtful Hindus of today the Sanskrit saying, which is widely familiar among all classes, "Ahimsā paramo dharma," "Non-killing is the supreme religious duty," is re-interpreted, in a similar fashion to Mr. Gandhi's interpretation of cow protection, as a summons to love. Ahimsā, Mr Gandhi declares, forbids men to harbour even an uncharitable thought.[1] Within the scope of these two ancient laws is thus comprehended an ideal of love towards all living beings, human and sub-human. What was originally an animistic conception of the sanctity of all life, has become moralised and so can claim justification before the bar of an ethical faith.

The peasant has some roads of escape from the burdens and shadows of his life. Among these are, especially, the religious festivals. These often bring brightness and variety into dull, monotonous days. When the festival comes round, it may be that a vow has to be fulfilled in gratitude for such a gift as that of a longed-for son; or it may be that the whole family will journey together, children and all, to the distant village where the god holds holiday, for what is probably to them little more than a picnic, or, if a deeper feeling moves them, it will be to gain the *darshan*, the auspicious view, of the face of some god and so to be assured of his favour. In any case it is an occasion for cheerfulness. This is specially so if the festival is that of one of the gods who draw forth bhakti or loving devotion and if they travel to the place of festival, as in such cases is often the custom, in companies with the singing of songs. We shall review in the next section more fully this important department of Hindu worship, but here we would simply note the fact that there are many villages to which the comfort and inspiration of this message of a God that can be loved has come. One may hear even an outcaste singing, as he sits by his

[1] *Mahatma Gandhi's Ideas*, by C. F. Andrews, p. 103.

hut door, as the writer has heard one sing, such words as these:

> " Sinners are we, I and you ;
> Vithobā alone is true ;
> He receives the fallen, too."

One of the poet-teachers of this school, who has followers all over North India—many of them outcastes—is Kabīr, the weaver-saint of the fifteenth century. Of a Dhed (an outcaste) who belonged to this sect we are told that he was fond of quoting this verse attributed to Kabīr as summing up the substance of his mystical creed:

> " The Word is the Key, the Word is the Lock,
> The Word by the Word created the Light ;
> He who knows the mystery of the Word—
> He can know the Creator and the God." [1]

The doctrine of the *śabda* or word which is referred to here and which has a considerable place in the teaching of the Kabīr Panth shows us how what originates as magic may grow into something of really deep spiritual significance. The mystery of speech as that which expresses thought creates the conception of the mantra or spell with its magic power. This next grows to become the inspired message of the spiritual teacher and through him furnishes the key to the meaning of the universe. " Everything connected with the three worlds is contained in the fifty-two letters." [2] With Kabīr the lower Hinduism is passing from the stage of ritual and spell to become a prophetic religion.

The meetings of congregations of these worshippers of " the formless One," when they spend the whole night in singing, and similarly the *Kīrtans*, or song services of other similar sects, are occasions when the soul of the peasant is often deeply stirred with religious devotion. And when they go, on some great day of festival, to such a place of pilgrimage as Pandharpūr, where stands the

[1] Mrs. S. Stevenson, *Without the Pale*, p. 76.
[2] *Adi Granth*, Gauri 1, 2.

chief temple of Vithobā, the occasion is one of much rapture. One of the Bhakti saints of the Marāthā country, Chokā Melā, was himself an outcaste. His shrine stands opposite to, and, of course, outside of, the main door of Vithobā's temple at Pandharpūr. He was not permitted to worship within the temple along with the members of the divine social order of Hinduism, but he shared their faith in a God of love whose name to them is Vithobā and of whom his fellow Marāthā Tukārām sang, "We have embraced his feet and thus we have set ourselves free."[1] He meant, no doubt, free from repeated birth, but the liberation was from other fears as well.

Those things that arouse their fears, and those things that move and win their hearts are in the case of the Indian village people, as of most people everywhere—the things that mean most in their religious life. And in the Indian village the former much predominate. Even for those who are not greatly troubled by the terrors of the dark, there is little that is cheerful that can be said of the life after death. Of what happens then, Miss Young writes, "Almost without exception they professed entire ignorance, but entire scepticism as to the possibility of future recognition."[2] With doctrines of rebirth they have a shadowy acquaintance, but in the case of most of them such speculations have little reality. All that can be said of the dead is, "He is gone." So with all the higher ideas of Hinduism; they have no hold on their hearts. There is a Marāthi proverb that says that "when the cord of the higher gods breaks, the lower gods howl." But the restraining cord of the higher gods leaves the lower ones much latitude. "Parmeśwar (the sole God) on the whole didn't interfere with anything these others (the lower gods) might do." Still there is that final court of appeal, however shadowy it may be. "'Do you ever go to any temple to worship?' we asked an outcaste man," writes a South Indian observer. "'No, we should not be

[1] *Temple Bells*, p. 69. [2] M. Young, *op. cit.*, p. 199.

admitted; we have nobody but God,' and he pointed upwards. 'Do you pray to Him?' 'Yes, we know nothing, but we cry out, O God, O God!'"[1]

Such are some examples of the variety and confusion which we find in Hinduism as it is continually climbing up from the lower level of fear and falling back again. It is not possible to give any just conception of a religion that, at this level especially, is so mingled in its constituents. It springs up at times and in one region or another into faith or even fanaticism; then it dies down again to torpor. Bishop V. S. Azariah gives a survey of Hindu religious life among the Śudras or non-Brāhman middle classes of the Andhra country in South India which probably truly represents the normal religious situation in many other parts of India as well. "The religious beliefs and practices of these castes are rather disappointing. Vedic and philosophic Hinduism are generally unknown. The Gītā, even in the vernacular, is a sealed book to most people. Nominally they are Śaivites or Vaishnavites—largely the latter. But beyond a trace of this in some of their personal names, their allegiance to these cults is indeed little. Village deities play a large part in ordinary life. Religious practices are not many; some fast on Saturdays and at ekadasi (the eleventh day after new moon); often they have an annual village sacrifice, more often only when blessed with a good crop or visited by an epidemic. Sometimes they attend the annual Hindu festival in the neighbourhood. Even when there is a temple in the village itself they visit it rarely, probably only on occasion of family events. Marriages are under the presidency of the Brāhman priest, who is also required at cremations. They are mostly meat-eaters, though they never touch beef. A few groups keep their women *gosha* (secluded)."[2]

That is not a picture of a religion in very living or

[1] S. Neill, *op. cit.*, p. 33.
[2] *International Review of Missions*, Vol. XXI, p. 460.

active control of its adherents. The Bishop shows us at the same time that the desire for religion is only slumbering within them and frequently finds expression. "They understand sacraments and their significance. They are moved by devotion and prayer; worship and adoration are instinctively theirs." Hinduism is not by any means dead though in many parts of India it may be failing to find fit means of expression.

There is much movement and disquiet within Hinduism at the present time due to influences some of them new but some as old as Hinduism itself. Such are the economic difficulties that press upon them as they have always pressed, and the new, disturbing movements that political and national ambitions have brought in many areas even among the village people. The outcastes have begun to knock at the long-closed doors of Hindu temples and some are being opened to them. But for the most part only a faint ripple caused by these storms and agitations disturbs as yet the stagnant waters of village religion. Undoubtedly, however, the influence of Mr. M. K. Gandhi in recent years has deeply stirred these waters. But on the whole the peasants still go on living as they have always lived, walking in the roads of ancient tradition and worshipping as their fathers from all time have worshipped. What a cultivator of Bundelkhand is reported to have said during the Census of 1901 is true in large measure still of most villagers: "All I know about religion is that every day I call Rām morning and night. All my time is taken up in work. I do not do things which would outcaste me, associate with the low, or eat forbidden things. This is all my religion."[1]

[1] Quoted in *E.R.E.*, Vol. V, p. 20.

CHAPTER III

HINDUISM AS THE RELIGION OF BHAKTI

(a) *The History*

MENTION has already been made in the general account of Hinduism, of Bhakti which may be interpreted as meaning "loving devotion" and which forms one of the principal phases of the Hindu religion. The word appears first in the literature of Hinduism in the Śvetāśvatara Upanishad. In any theistic religion such an attitude to God as the word "Bhakti" implies would naturally be assumed by worshippers when their emotions were stirred. And indeed such an attitude can be found expressing itself even in the Vedic Hymns. But as the religion became more and more pantheistic little room would seem to be left for the expression of such a personal devotion. In the Śvetāśvatara, accordingly, Bhakti is recognised as something that can only with difficulty be reconciled with the prevailing monism of the Upanishads. With the appearance of the Bhagavadgītā some centuries later we have, as we have already seen, a more powerful assertion of the claims of a theistic worship and from that time onward Bhakti takes a high place among the religious moods of Hinduism. We may, indeed, be certain that it was there always, but ere it could take its true place in a land like India, it had to obtain philosophical recognition and the prestige that philosophy alone could give to it. In the whole of the Hindu religious development theism is fighting for its existence against the dominant monism. The fortunes of this warfare give much of its interest to the history through the centuries of the Bhakti movement.

The authority of the monistic interpretation was, however, too well established for this devotion to a personal god to prevail. Only by means of compromise was it able to obtain recognition alongside of knowledge as a road to that final release towards which all the efforts of the devout worshipper and of the " forest-sage " were alike directed. Such a way of compromise was suggested first in the Śvetāśvatara and it is reaffirmed with more confidence in the Bhagavadgītā which is the Scripture which more than any other, vindicates the right, as against the philosophers, of a theism that could arouse the ardour of a devout heart. At the same time the relationships of the rival doctrines are not defined and the uneasy balance continues between bhakti and jñāna, that is, between the theism that worships and the pantheism that does not.

This contradiction could not be indefinitely ignored. It could not be ignored, especially, when through the emergence of Śankara and the formulation by him in systematic form in the ninth century of monism in alliance with a doctrine of māya or illusion, the way of knowledge was established in unassailable authority. And yet it was about this very time, apparently, that the Bhāgavata Purāna appeared and that a great outburst of Bhakti ardour was making its influence felt throughout the Tamil country in the region over which Śankara had established his philosophic sway. Thus it came about that the warmth of Bhakti devotion had to reconcile itself with the chill system of Advaita, and it did so by accepting a place not in the region of ultimate truth, but in the lower sphere of ignorance and illusion. Ultimate truth belongs to the monistic doctrine where nothing is but "brahman." Release comes with the discovery of that truth. Thus Bhakti has to be content to take the second place and indeed to forgo, in order that it may exist at all, that release which is the supreme goal of Indian longing.

While this road of compromise has been for the most part accepted by travellers along the road of Bhakti, that has not always been the case. In Rāmānuja, as we have already noted, there arose at the end of the eleventh century a teacher, less influential, indeed, than Śankara, but who obtained and retains a wide influence in South India, and who promulgated a philosophic doctrine that gave to Bhakti the right to live in a world of reality and not merely of illusion. His doctrine of Viśishtādvaita or "modified monism" provided room for a personal God and for the worship of the devout heart. Such Bhakti is accordingly in his teaching a means, and the chief means, by which one may obtain release.

Rāmānuja thus achieved his aim of vindicating the Vedantic orthodoxy of the doctrine of Bhakti as followed by the Vaishnava sect to which he belonged. They, too, he showed, derive their faith from the ancient sources of wisdom and can worship without reproach. But simultaneously with these philosophers, and even before their time, a powerful religious quickening was in process in the Tamil country which transformed the character and influence of the Bhakti movement. The heralds of this new dawn in the religious life of the land were the Ālvārs, the authors of a body of hymns "which forms one of the devotional classics of the Tamil country and is sometimes called the Tamil Veda."[1] They date from the seventh century. The feature of this new birth of Bhakti that distinguishes it in all its forms throughout the country is the fervour of the emotion it expresses. From this time on through many successive centuries we find this ardent Bhakti surging upwards in the hearts of devout worshippers in every province of India and expressing itself in songs of rapture and praise. "Never," writes one of the historians of the "Dravida Saints," "from fear or shame that the bystanders might take him for a madman ought the exhibition of his Bhakti rapture that deluges his being to be suppressed. . . . The very madness is the bhakta's pride. 'In that very madness,' the saint exhorts,

[1] Hooper, *Hymns of the Ālvārs*, p. 19.

'run, jump, cry, laugh and sing, and let every man witness it.'"[1]

Not all the expressions of Bhakti are as uncontrolled as this description would suggest. In the north and in the west there is less of this "madness," but everywhere its note is intensity and passion. The apostle who carried the contagion from the lands of the south to the north was Rāmānanda, an adherent of the sect of Rāmānuja, who took up his residence in Benares about 1430 and gave the impulse to a movement which produced such notable personalities as Kabīr, who was almost his contemporary, and Tulsī Dās, who followed him a century later. Rāmānanda is little more than a shadowy name today, but the songs of Kabīr and Tulsī Dās's poem, *Rāmacharitmānas*, continue still to move the hearts and govern the lives of multitudes throughout the whole of upper India.

Earlier than the time of Rāmānanda—at the end of the thirteenth century—the impulse to this new glow of religious emotion was given in the Marāthā country by a poetical exposition of the Bhagavadgītā, the author of which was a Marāthā Brāhman called Jñāneśvar. The influence of this work was deep and continuous throughout the centuries that followed. The great name in Marāthī Bhakti is, however, that of Tukārām (1608–49), whose songs in praise of Vithobā echo still over all the Marāthā country and keep the flame of devotion alight among all classes of the people. These two names—"Jñānobā, Tukārām"—are linked together in the chants that the worshippers sing as they march in companies to the great festivals that are held in honour of Vithobā and his saints. Another of these upsurgences of emotion, but one that, while more uncontrolled in its expression, was less permanent in its influence, is that of which the leader was the Bengali who became known as Chaitanya (1486–1530), who seems to have spent the years of his sainthood in a

[1] Govindacharya, *Divine Wisdom of the Dravida Saints*, quoted by Hooper, *op. cit.*, p. 25.

continuous frenzy of devotion to Krishṇa. "His life," says one Bengali admirer, "was a course of thanksgiving, tears, hymns, and praises offered to God."[1]

The Chaitanya sect soon fell into disrepute and cannot be said to hold the place in the religious life of Bengal today that is held by other Bhakti cults. There are, however, the Baül singers to whom Professor Kshiti Mohan Sen[2] gives high praise for their religious simplicity and sincerity. They belong to all castes and observe no caste differences; they enter no temples but worship "the Man of the Heart."[3]

It is not possible here to give a fuller account of this Vaishnavite Bhakti—a movement which had effects so profound in the religious life of India, that one scholar—Sir George Grierson—who has studied it in all its phases, goes the length of claiming for it that it brought about "the greatest religious revolution that India has ever seen—greater even than that of Buddhism, for its effects have persisted to the present day."[4] He goes on to describe what this revolution achieved. "Religion is no longer a question of knowledge. It is one of emotion. We visit a land of mysticism and rapture, and meet spirits akin, not to the great schoolmen of Benares, but to the poets and mystics of Mediæval Europe, in sympathy with Bernard of Clairvaux, with Thomas à Kempis, with Eckhart, and with St. Theresa. In the early years of the reformation the converts lived and moved in an atmosphere of the highest spiritual exaltation, while over all there hovered, with healing in its wings, a divine gospel of love, smoothing down inevitable asperities, restoring breaches, and reconciling conflicting modes of thought. Northern India was filled with wandering devotees, vowed to poverty and purity. Visions, trances, raptures, and

[1] D. C. Sen, *Bengali Language and Literature*, p. 661.
[2] In Rabindranath Tagore's *Religion of Man*.
[3] Dr. J. N. Farquhar, however, says that "they are no better than the left-hand Śāktas," a severe enough condemnation. *O.R.L.I.*, p. 312.
[4] *E.R.E.*, Vol. II, p. 548.

even reputed miracles were of everyday occurrence. Rich noblemen abandoned all their possessions and gave them to the poor, and even the poorest would lay aside a bundle of sticks to light a fire for some chance wandering saint."

Sir George Grierson's description is based upon the *Bhakta-mālā*, the "Acta Sanctorum," as he calls it, of Bhakti, a record compiled in the sixteenth century. This stream of devotion has flowed continuously through the centuries in almost every region of India from Kashmir to Travancore, bringing quickening wherever it has gone. It bears within it what we may claim to be the real heart of Hinduism. To it the most religious minds in India still resort and find in the songs of its poet-saints kindling and consolation. Its power has proved sufficient, at least in its seasons of rapture, to overcome the rigidity and the cruelty of caste and to bring men and women of all classes together, moved by common devotion. Among its singers and its saints have been not only Brāhmans but outcastes, not only men but women, and these, some of them princesses and some of them beggars. Even Muslims appear in this company, so strong is this religious ardour to break down barriers.

For the most part the warmth of this devotion centres about the incarnations of Vishnu—Krishna and Rāma especially—but also in the case of the Bhakti of the Marāthi country about Vithobā, a village god, identified with Krishna. It is natural that this ardent worship should be rendered to gods that arouse emotions not of fear but love, incarnations of a Sun-god around whom the more gracious and luminous aspects of the earlier religion had been gathered. With such a god, the more elevating and what we may call the more evangelical, aspects of Hinduism can be associated. Vishnu in old legend has appeared as a deliverer, and he and Rāma and Krishna are gods of light and life and hope, who are capable of being cleansed from the grossness of the nature deity and of acquiring higher spiritual attributes. At the same time one cannot rule out any deity, however forbidding his aspect may appear to us, from among those about whom the human heart, in its longing for affection, may create a halo of imagined charm and to whom it may find it possible to direct its love. Thus even Śiva has been remoulded by the Indian spirit in the south into the form of a Saviour and upon him also has been bestowed this worship of loving devotion. The chief singer of this school of Śaivite Bhakti is Manikka-Vāchakar, a Tamil poet who flourished about A.D. 900 and whose influence achieved for Śaivism in the south a similar position to that which we have described as having been attained for Vaishṇavism in the north. "No cult in the world," writes Dr. L. D. Barnett, in reference to this Bhakti of Śiva, "has produced a richer devotional literature or one more instinct with brilliance of imagination, fervour of feeling and grace of expression." The doctrinal system with which this religion is associated is called the Śaiva Siddhanta which was formulated in the thirteenth century by a group of theologians of whom the most notable was an outcasted Brāhman, named Umāpati. Thus the influence of loving devotion triumphed over the tyranny of caste as well as over the associations of death and horror that belonged to Śiva and brought to South India a religious quickening which retains considerable power down to the present time.

It seems still more strange to find that there have been followers of the path of Bhakti among the Śāktas, whose worship traces its lineage from the cults of mother gods and devīs and which has not even in later times purged itself from the influence of an origin so gross. They, too, sought release by the way of loving devotion which they directed towards the goddess, and their chief scripture is the *Devī Bhāgavata* which Dr. J. N. Farquhar dates in the fourteenth century.[1]

Of the religious quality of the Bhakti singers more will be said in the following section. We shall conclude this rapid

[1] *O.R.L.I.*, p. 289.

survey of the history and literature of Bhakti with some notes on the literary character of the songs or psalms in which so many of its saints have uttered their hearts.

It is inevitable that such utterances of simple and sincere devotion should make use of the language of the common people, and it is an incidental result of this religious movement that it more than any other influence has created the vernacular literatures of India. The medium of expression in the case of most of these poets is usually a brief lyrical utterance, sometimes only two or three verses—little more than an ejaculatory prayer or aspiration. They are "swallow-flights of song," expressing the heart's needs and its longing for God and for His fellowship, or perhaps some other aspect of spiritual experience whether of dejection or of rapture. A single example may be given of one of the briefest of these songs, by a Kashmiri beggar woman of the fourteenth century, Lal Ded:

> "O heedless one, speedily lift up thy foot:
> Now it is dawn; seek thou for the Friend.
> Make to thyself wings: lift up the winged (feet).
> Now it is dawn; seek thou for the Friend." [1]

These poems are for the most part personal and individual utterances, and in indication of that fact, it is often the case that each one is, as it were, signed by the author in the closing couplet. This couplet, so signed, frequently sums up the poem or emphasises its leading motive. Thus one of the finest of the poems attributed to Kabīr and translated by Dr. Rabindranath Tagore, the subject of which is the love between God and His worshipper, concludes: "Kabīr says, 'Listen to me, brother; bring the vision of the Beloved into your heart.'" [2]

These poems are written to be sung, and it is when sung that they move the heart. What Dr. Appasamy says of Mānikka-Vāchakar is true of many others among

[1] *Poems by Indian Women*, p. 51.
[2] Tagore, *One Hundred Poems of Kabīr*, p. 105.

them as well: "From generation to generation devotees in the Tamil country have sung and wept over his hymns."[1] Their power to touch these chords is as great today as ever. Few of the authors of these lyrics have any secular learning but they are wise in the experience of life's sorrows and in their sense of the innate and inextinguishable thirst of the human heart for God. Their interest in the world and its concerns and in the beauty that it spreads around them is altogether secondary to their absorbing interest in their relation to God. The nature upon which their eyes are ever turned is their own human nature with its failures and its yearnings. The visible world is for them "a hieroglyphic of the spiritual world," and in that world their thoughts mainly dwell.

"Purity of heart, humility, self-surrender, forgiveness, and the love of God," says Sir Ramkrishna Bhandarkar in reference to one of them, "form the sum and substance of the teaching of Nāmdev." It need hardly be said that there is a wide gulf between a literature occupied solely with subjects such as these and expressing itself in regard to them in a hundred different tones of desire and submission and the literatures of the West. When these poets look up to the night sky it is not to see and rejoice in "the moon's beauty and the moon's soft pace," but to be reminded of the lotus longing for the moon's light even as their hearts long for God. The rain bird's shrill cry is the very voice of their spiritual craving; the lost and frightened fawn in the wide and desolate jungle is to them a picture of their soul's solitude and desolation. All nature is but a mirror in which they see their own sorrows, and its beauty is secondary to the pathos of their inward need. Through innumerable *abhangs* (legend attributes to Nāmdev alone many thousands) the one note sounds, the one absorbing subject is presented. Narrow as that outlook on the universe may appear to us today, monotonous as its expression must be with so

[1] *Temple Bells*, p. 10.

limited a range of music, these poets have in their possession the eternal theme of poetry. Seldom surely have the deeply implanted sense of exile and the longing to return been expressed with more simplicity and pathos than in the lyrical cries of such a singer as the tailor, Nāmdev. " It is the sorrow of separation," says Dr. Rabindranath Tagore, " that ever melts and flows in song through my poet's heart." That sorrow comes to us like the shrill cry of a lost child down the winds of the centuries from the days when Nāmdev clanged his cymbals and sang his heart out in Ghuman or in Pandharī.

(b) *The Religion*

This wide-spreading religious movement, whose history has been outlined, has always exercised and still exercises today, a living and active spiritual influence upon all classes of the Hindu population. It is not aristocratic or intellectual in its appeal; its power is conveyed through a literature that makes use of the vernaculars and speaks direct to the emotions of the plain man. And yet it is not only the outcaste, at one extreme of society, that acknowledges its sway, but, equally, the scholar and the thinker at the opposite extreme. Among the most powerful personalities in India in the last generation have been M. G. Ranade, the social reform leader, Sir Ramkrishna Bhandarkar, the distinguished Sanskrit scholar, and Mr. M. K. Gandhi. These three outstanding Hindus agree in acknowledging their deep debt to the Bhakti poet-saints and have been accustomed to make constant use of their songs in their worship. In the reforming theistic church of Bombay Presidency (the Prārthana Samāj), which has attracted to itself many of the sincerest religious men of the last two generations, it is mainly from the psalms of the Marāthā bhaktas, and especially from the abhangs[1] of Tukārām that the hymns

[1] The short poems that form the medium of Marāthi Bhakti are called abhangs.

are taken that are made use of in public worship and it is from them also that much of their religious inspiration is obtained. Two of the distinguished men named above, Mr. Ranade and Sir R. G. Bhandarkar, were all their lives leading members of this Samāj and they both made constant use of verses from these saints as the texts of sermons preached to the congregations of the Samāj, as well as for their own private devotions. Mr. G. K. Gokhale, the distinguished political leader, tells how when he was travelling by night on a railway journey with Mr. Ranade he was wakened at a very early hour by the sound of his friend and guru's not very tuneful singing of Tukārām's songs of aspiration and confession. "The fervour," Mr. Gokhale says, "with which he was singing was so great that I felt thrilled through and through." This is one of the abhangs Mr. Ranade was singing: "He who befriends the weary and the oppressed and the persecuted—he is the true saint and God Himself is to be found there." After singing one of these songs, "snapping his fingers and clapping his hands and swaying to and fro," his wife tells us how his face would be "suffused with a warm glow of love and his mind would be flooded with happiness."[1] Another example may be given out of many to illustrate how Tukārām and his fellow-bhaktas can still move with religious emotion some of the ablest and most cultured of the Marāthā people of today. An able young Indian had been absent from India for several years in England and Germany. Distance and disuse and the circumstances of his life in these foreign lands led him away from his former habits of worship and his experience of communion with God, but when he returned to India and heard once more the songs of Tukārām sung in the old fashion, his sense of God and his desire to worship Him swept over him once more like the returning tide. He rediscovered his early religion and has never ceased to own its sway over him.

[1] J. Kellock, *M. G. Ranade*, p. 147.

These illustrations of the still living influence of Bhakti have all been taken from one part of India and one type of Bhakti, that of the Marāthā saints of whom Tukārām is the most widely influential. In his case they bear witness to the sway of a village poet, who was a Śudra, over the hearts of men of the highest culture. The other name that is linked, as has been noted already, with that of Tukārām in the songs sung by the choirs at times of festival is Jñānobā, the Brāhman author in the thirteenth century of the Jñāneśvarī. This poem, which reproduces in Marāthī with much grace of poetic imagery the message of the Bhagavadgītā, still seems to find its way to the hearts even of the unlettered people. The writer has seen a company of plain men and women in Poona dispersing after their weekly meeting at which this poem was regularly expounded to them and noted how many were women whose shaven heads showed them to be widows, in much need, no doubt, of the comfort and help that they sought from this Bhakti teacher.

What is true of the influence of this type of religion in the Marāthā country, is equally true of its influence over high and low alike in other provinces. The hymns of the Śaiva saints of the South are memorised by Tamil children, we are told, just as Christian hymns are by children in the West.[1] North and South alike, a great company of plain and unlettered people carry these songs in their hearts and sing them as they journey by road to market or as they guide the plough in the field. The writer has often seen and heard a devout old man, employed as a messenger in a Government office, singing such religious songs as he carried letters to the post office, and keeping time with the cymbals that he always carried with him.

It would be possible to call many other witnesses to the vitality to this hour of the Bhakti message in the religious experience of all classes of the Hindu population. Rabindranath Tagore has told us how the Vaishnava

[1] Hooper, *op. cit.*, p. 1.

lyric poets helped at least to make him a poet and how the Baül singers of Bengal who, while neither Vaishnavite nor Śaivite, have much in their religion of the Bhakti spirit, attracted him, when he was seeking in his early years a spiritual resting place. Yet another name that can be added to this list is that of Mr. M. K. Gandhi. It is to the Gītā that he most frequently confesses his indebtedness, and that, no doubt, both on account of its call for " undivided devotion " and of its exaltation of service rendered without desire for reward. But, his friend, Mr. C. F. Andrews, tells us, " it is to the simple village hymns of the Bhakti saints that Mahatma Gandhi turns for his own comfort and support in his hours of difficulty and failure and penitence in regard to his own shortcomings." He has a " garland " of such hymns which he makes use of regularly in his daily services of prayer. Of these the one, we are told, that is his greatest favourite is by Mirābāī, a princess of Rajputana of the fifteenth century, whose songs express an intense devotion to Krishna. This particular song has for its refrain the words, " Now only He is mine." Part of it is translated by Sir George Grierson as follows:

> " Kanh have I bought; the price he asked I paid:
>   Some cry, 'Too great,' while others jeer, ''Twas small.'
> I paid in full, weighed to the utmost grain,
>   My love, my life, myself, my soul, my all."

We must now turn to consider what the elements in this religion are that enable it to exercise so widespread and so potent an influence over men's hearts. It is a religion, as we have seen already, of warm devotion to a personal God. That religion involves beliefs in regard to God, in regard to the future life and in regard to conduct and character in this life. Its teaching on these subjects must be understood if we are to realise the kind of influence it is creating and what place it has in the whole Hindu system to which it belongs. It has too little unity in its history and is subject to too many emotional impulses to permit of its characteristics being comprehended in a single formula or of its value being summarily estimated. Its teaching, however, in these three large departments of idea and action is fairly uniform and consistent throughout its various phases.

1. What then is the doctrine of God that this religion implies? It need hardly be said that, if Bhakti means "loving devotion," that is something which cannot be rendered to any object that is not personal and that does not draw forth affection. The result has been that this worship through all its history has found itself in conflict, consciously or unconsciously, with the pantheism which seems to be always accepted more or less explicitly as the bed-rock of Hinduism. One method that can be made use of in these circumstances to solve such a contradiction is to ignore or to deny the pantheistic doctrine, and that, no doubt, was often done and is done still. Before the monistic view had become powerfully established by Śankara's constructions this method, we may be sure, was often followed; and later, when, in the north, Muslim influences strengthened theism, Kabīr, at least, was able to pay little heed to pantheistic authority. But in a great part of India Śankara's doctrine holds an unchallenged place. Rāmānuja, indeed, was able to win for theism, by his *Śri-Bhāshya*,[1] to a certain extent the prestige that connection with a philosophical system, derived from the Vedanta, alone could give. In South India especially Rāmānuja's modified monism was accepted by both Vaishnavites and Śaivites who followed the road of devotional theism.

Those adherents of Bhakti who are under the domination of Śankara's "māyāvāda advaita" (that is, the thorough-going monism which denies the reality of anything except brahman) themselves recognise that there is no final salvation to be reached by the road by which they travel. They have to be content—and many of

[1] His commentary on the *Vedanta Sūtras*.

them are content—to accept the view that their road is a lower and more earthly one than the way of knowledge which alone can lead men to release. This division remains in the thinking of many of them and creates conflict within their minds.[1] Theirs is an interim theology and the way by which they travel with such a devout ardour brings them, they believe, to no final goal. They are drawn in the one direction or the other by contrary desires—the desire for fellowship with God on the one hand, and the desire for release from rebirth on the other. Often they seem to rebel against the compromise to which philosophical authority has compelled them. "In the contact of the embrace," says Jñāneśvar, describing his experience of the solution that love brings, "the two become one naturally"; and Tukārām, perceiving the unreality of the religion of "the proud Advaitist," says of him bitterly, "He fills his belly, saying, 'I am Brahm.'" They resent the monistic doctrine, but they do not dispute it.

Tulsī Dās had in Rāma an object of devotion that embodied a very noble conception of God but, nevertheless, while he himself cannot do without worship of "the Incarnate" he gives to "Brahma, the unbegotten, the indivisible, the immaterial, nameless, formless," the highest place. Even so, though Kabīr is no polytheist and can say, "O God, whether Allah or Rāma, I live by Thy name," and though he was no philosopher either, and for him māya is just the deceitful world, a witch, a temptress, like John Bunyan's Madam Bubble, yet at the same time his outlook also is deeply dyed with the colours of Vedantic monism. Few in India wholly escape that subtle, pervasive influence. Dādū, indeed, the founder of a sect that is closely akin to the followers of Kabīr, seems to have himself rejected Vedanta but we

[1] An attempt to find a solution is contained in the following passage from an account of Tukārām written by Mahipati in 1774 and full of the glow of this religion: "Men, devoted to God, are united with His essence in such a way as to make no difference between them. But that unity is again divided into two parts so that the one continually worships the other." I. E. Abbott, *Tukārām*, p. 92.

are told that "much of the Hinduism against which he protested has crept back into his sect."[1] Professor Kshiti Mohan Sen probably goes too far when, describing Kabīr and Dādū and others of their spiritual kin in north India, he writes: "When our metaphysicians, dividing themselves into rival schools . . . had joined together in dismissing the world as māyā, then up from the depths of their social obscurity rose these cobblers, weavers and sewers of bags, proclaiming such theorems of the intellect to be all nonsense. . . . It is they, not the scientists or philosophers who have taught us of reality."[2] As a matter of fact their teaching—in this particular at least—was half-hearted and the opposing view was too strongly entrenched for them to succeed in holding their own against it. They had to be content with a secondary rank in the hierarchy of truth and to put aside the hope of final deliverance.[3]

What we find, therefore, in the Bhakti cults is a conflict between an instinctive theism on the one hand which craves the satisfaction that comes from worship and from an intuition of the divine love, and an authoritative pantheism on the other which imposes itself upon the adherents of these cults and weakens the confidence and hope that theism tends to bring to them. There is apt, as a consequence, to be a confusion and a contradiction lurking within their spiritual life which weakens their whole religious attitude. Even in the case of those theisms which have behind them the doctrine not of "advaita" but of "viśishtādvaita," that is, "modified monism," the fact that the laws of rebirth and karma still govern their thinking prevents the theism from being fully effective. William James describes the effect of

[1] Keay's *Kabīr and his Followers*, p. 163.

[2] Professor Kshiti Mohan Sen in Dr. Rabindranath Tagore's *The Religion of Man*.

[3] "The Bengali poet Ramprasad cries out in protest against the Vedantist: 'What is the use of salvation to me if it means absorption into the deity? I like eating sugar. But I have no desire to become sugar.'"

Times Literary Supplement, February 11, 1932.

theism as being "the affirmation of an eternal moral order and the letting loose of hope." Professor Rudolf Otto in an examination of the "Religion of Grace" of South India, which is a very advanced doctrine of this type, says: "Deep beneath him (Īśvara) rushes the stream of the world and humanity in *samsāra*, in ever-repeated circles of woeful birth and rebirth. In this world the wandering soul strolls, separated from Īśvara by its fall, lost in the confusion of the world. Then he inclines to it in pure, undeserved grace. . . . (The world) remains a *Līlā*, a sport of the Deity, a concatenation without goal and end."[1] It is evident that such a world-view falls far short of the kind of theism that William James describes.

It has further to be remembered that all—or almost all—of these bhaktas are worshippers of idols. They are often, indeed, contemptuous of the idolatry of the superstitious multitude. They claim to look beyond the idol to something greater that is there signified or suggested. So Nāmdev says: "No guru can show me God: wherever I go there are stone gods painted red. How can a stone god speak? . . . Everywhere I go they say, 'Worship a stone.' He is God whom Nāma beholds in his heart." And yet Nāmdev's shrine is at the gate of the temple of the idol Vithobā whom he worshipped with much devotion.

2. The same hindrances to the full realisation of what Bhakti is seeking are found to be operating when one passes to consider the beliefs that its followers accept in regard to the future life. Here again the thought environment of India compels a view which the bhaktas themselves feel to be inadequate. A religion of loving devotion is deeply rooted in the desire for fellowship. The bhakta desires passionately to have communion with God and he desires also—secondarily only to the other—communion with his fellow-believers, with the saints, as he puts it. There is thus no commoner picture of the

[1] *India's Religion of Grace and Christianity*, p. 70.

Deity in his relation with his worshipper, as presented to us by such a poet as Tukārām, than that of a mother with her child. Similarly the human worshipper is described in many passages as like a lost child longing to be back on his mother's breast. "From the beginning to the end of time," says Kabīr or someone of his school who takes his name, "there is love between me and Thee; and how shall such love be extinguished?"[1]

But it follows from what has been said above of their conception of God that their fellowship with a personal deity who, as Kabīr says, "is obtained for the price of the heart,"[2] has by many of the Bhakti saints to be admitted to be only a temporary joy. The only enduring haven is that which is reached through absorption in the impersonal One. The goal is release from all rebirth and that comes only when the soul recognises its identity with brahman and is merged in the ultimate All. Even the hymn in praise of love just quoted from Tagore's translation of *One Hundred Poems of Kabīr* concludes with what seems like that very extinction of love that, he suggests, is an impossibility. "As the river enters the Ocean," he says, "so my heart touches Thee." Certainly the road of Bhakti is abandoned and that of jñāna, which passes beyond personal relationships, accepted in its stead by Muktā Bāī, a learned Marāthā lady of the thirteenth century, whose Bhakti is sicklied o'er with the pale cast of thought:

> "Nivritti, who has torn from out his soul
> All seed of passion, certainly declares
> That all are One; and Muktā Bāī
> With mind firm fixed upon the road
> To freedom—road that ne'er can weary one—
> Attains the knowledge of the Endless One
> Who fills finite and infinite alike."[3]

---

[1] Tagore, *One Hundred Poems of Kabir*, p. 41.
[2] *Adi Granth*, Gauri 19, quoted in Keay's *Kabīr and his Followers*, p. 85.
[3] *Poems by Indian Women* (Margaret Macnicol), p. 46.

But there are others who find it hard to make this sacrifice. Even Muktā Bāī's brother, the great saint, Jñāneśvar, recognises that there are saints to whom

> " So dear the path of Bhakti, they despise
> The great Release."

Bhakti is indeed essentially a social religion, as it must be if it has in it the element of love. Its poets all sing of the joy of the fellowship of the saints. " Saith Kabīr, To whom shall I tell this, that heaven is in the company of the saints? " Evidence of how real this sentiment still is can be obtained at any of the festivals of these cults. The companies of pilgrims sing as they travel together along the dusty roads, and, when they reach at last the place to which they are journeying, whole nights are spent by them in rapturous fellowship. These facts indicate the intensely social character of the religion. In this it is in marked contrast with the aristocratic and solitary discipline of jñāna, followed by those who seek the bleak reward of moksha.[1] It is because he cannot renounce the bliss of fellowship with the saints that Tukārām sometimes is even constrained to say, " O God, hear my prayer: Do not grant me Release." [2] And Jñāneśvar, describing the raptures of the bhaktas, says:

> " To heaven they seldom go, but earth they fill
> Brim full of heaven, chanting my name until
> The world is cleansed from ill." [3]

3. A third aspect of this religion which determines its nature and value relates to the effect it has upon the life and character of those who profess and practise it. The *Bhakta Mālā*, the " Acta Sanctorum," as it has been called, of Bhakti, compares Bhakti in one passage to a growing tree. " Mark well its growth. Once but a feeble thing; now, shackled to its trunk, contentedly sway the mighty elephants of the passions." [4] It is true

[1] That is, release through absorption into brahman.
[2] See *Psalms of Marāthā Saints*, p. 82.
[3] *Op. cit.*, p. 36. [4] *E.R.E.*, Vol. II, p. 548.

that the mighty elephants are there but whether Bhakti controls them is a matter needing examination. Of the strength of the emotions it sometimes arouses there can be no question. We have seen how "the madness" of the Dravida saints of the South moved them and how violent were Chaitanya's raptures. But we have to ask whither these storms of passion carried those in whom they were aroused. All Bhakti is not, indeed, of this tempestuous character. That of the Bhagavadgītā and of the school of Rāmānuja was of a more meditative sort, and the saints of the west and of the north have the warmth of their loving devotion more under control than was the case with many of the bhaktas of the south and of the east.

The social character of this religion, to which we have just referred, tended, no doubt, to inflame its ardour, and there is also the fact that its stress is mainly on the emotions, the exercise of reason being temporarily at least suspended. Hence some of the aberrations that have brought discredit upon some of the sects that cultivate this spirit. An able modern student of Hinduism, Babu Govinda Das, goes the length, indeed, of condemning Bhakti as inevitably disastrous in its consequences. The body, he says, "is suddenly deprived of its guiding star"; it "wanders into the jungle of passions." "Headlong, unguided Bhakti makes for horrible degeneracy."[1]

It is not necessary to emphasise this danger, due to the emotional character of this type of religion. It is obvious that when such warm feeling centres around the figures of Rādhā and Krishna, the danger, if it lacks "its guiding star," is great. In the case of the Marāṭhā bhaktas whose record is ethically noble, one reason why this is so is that Vithoba, who is the form of Krishna that they worship, is the husband of Rukminī, not the lover of Rādhā. Similarly Kabīr and Tulsī Dās and others belonging to the northern sects are worshippers

[1] *Hinduism*, pp. 171 f.

of Rāma, a god around whom noble ethical conceptions can easily assemble. Of Tulsī Dās's poem on Rāma's story, which still exercises so wide an influence, Dr. Farquhar writes: " His (Rāma's) tender love for the humblest as well as the greatest of his devotees, his condescension in becoming incarnate for their sakes, his sympathy and endurance of suffering for those who are devoted to him, and his readiness to forgive are expressed with great power."[1] The spirit which such a poem creates in those who revere it and study it is bound to be ethically noble.

A very simple example of the devotional spirit of these bhaktas may be given, quite literally translated, from an obscure Marāthā psalmist, Tryambak, who is said to belong to the sixteenth century:

> " So long as I did not have Thy refuge, my mind was in great distress.
> But now I have gained courage, for I have heard of Thy goodness,
> O Infinite One.
> Confidence in Thee has settled deeply and with great power in
> Tryambak's heart,
> So, putting my hands together, I make my prayer.
> O God, take not Thy compassion from me.
> On whose neck shall I fall if not on Thine ? "[2]

At the same time it is undoubtedly the case that this emotional religion, attractive as it often is, fails in ethical effectiveness as a movement for the reform of evils in the Hindu social system. None of the Bhakti religions have proved able to achieve such a reformation; the strength of the established order of caste has always prevailed in the end. Chaitanya was called " the god-man who does not believe in caste," but his followers have not been able to maintain his standard. So also on festival days at Pandharpūr, the headquarters of the worship of Vithobā, caste distinctions are forgotten, and all are brethren for a brief period of rapture. But as soon as the festal day has passed and they take the road back to their homes the

[1] *O.R.L.I.*, p. 330.
[2] See J. E. Abbott's *Stotra Mālā*, pp. 78, 237.

old, iron despotism of caste regains its sway and the fires of devotional ardour die down once more.

There are many tales among the legends that have come down to us that condemn the spirit of class exclusiveness—tales, for example, of how Krishna dined with the Śudra Nāmdev when the Brāhmans refused to do so, and even of how he helped his outcaste worshipper, Choka Mela, to drag to his house the dead body of a cow, which is the outcaste's perquisite, but which to the true Hindu is tabu and to be dreaded and avoided. But these stories have no power to break the tyranny of established custom.

One of the emphases which Bhakti shares with most types of mysticism is its conception of sin as selfishness. This is a conception that is usually found in any religion that makes fellowship with God its central aim. It is not indeed possible to be confident in the case of a Hindu whether a prayer for deliverance from the "ego"—as when Tukārām cries, "Break, break my 'me' and 'my'"—is a prayer for deliverance from the powers of moral evil or whether it is prompted by the Vedantic demand that personality itself shall be extinguished. Here as in so many other Indian contexts the saint's view of evil is inevitably affected by the doctrine of life as a condition in which every action good or evil binds the doer to the revolving wheel of birth so that the sole way of escape is by the submergence of selfhood.

Inevitably, also, such a conception of human life leads to asceticism. If temporal relationships are unreal, then to reach the real they must be trampled upon. "Through the desire of sensual things," says one of them,[1] "my mind has wandered very far from Thee. I have found my pleasures in my home, children, wife." By some of the simple people the word samsāra is used, significantly enough, as a synonym for wife. That relation binds them to repeated birth in the region of illusion.

Even Kabīr who might be expected, in view of his

[1] Keśava, a Marāthā Brāhman. See Abbott, *op. cit.*, p. 71.

Muslim affinities, to be less under the influence of Hindu conceptions, seems sometimes to succumb to them. When he says,

> " Saith Kabīr, All my sins have been blotted out
> And my soul is absorbed in the Life of the world," [1]

shall we call him a theist or a pantheist?

At the same time it is impossible to doubt that Kabīr and Tukārām and many others of the Bhakti saints experience a real sense of sin and come to God as penitents with a genuine prayer for forgiveness.

> " I am a mass of sin ;
> Thou art all purity,
> Yet thou dost take me as I am
> And bear my load for me."

That and other similar confessions of sin by Tukārām would seem to have the authentic note of contrition and of faith in a personal God.[2] It is not difficult to understand that many today for whom Vithobā or Krishna or Rāma is no idol but a traditional symbol of " Him whose name is unutterable " find in the Bhakti literature a solace for their hearts in hours of sorrow and a fit expression of their deepest longings. As a matter of fact, as has been already noted, the songs of the Marāthā saints are made use of in the worship of the theistic church of Western India, those names that suggest polytheism or idolatry being omitted or explained away. Thus " Hari " (Krishna) is explained etymologically as meaning the " remover " of sin.

The moral ideal which the bhakta holds before himself need not be considered here, as it does not seem to differ from the moral ideal that Hinduism by its philosophic teaching sets before its adherents. The *summum bonum* of the Hindu is the same in essentials whether he is an adherent of the emotional faith of Bhakti or of Vedantic

[1] Quoted by Keay in *Kabīr and his Followers*, p. 82.

[2] Dr. T. R. Glover says that some of the verse renderings of Tukārām's *abhangs* " if surreptitiously printed with Cowper's versions of Mme. Guyon, might pass without remark." *Progress in Religion*, p. 18.

monism. There is one prevailing ethos which is characteristic of the Hindu, whatever creed he professes. Individual exceptions there may be and perhaps one finds such an exception in the case of Kabīr who seems sometimes to put aside the flute of Hinduism and sound the trumpet-call of Islam. Such a note echoes, for example, in one well-known poem that is attributed to him:

> "In the field of this body a great war goes forward, against passion, anger, pride and greed:
> It is in the kingdom of truth, contentment and purity that this battle is raging; and the sword that rings forth most loudly is the sword of His Name."[1]

Before we leave this department of Hinduism two other methods of religious culture that are associated with, or akin to, Bhakti must be mentioned. The first of these is that reverence for the *guru* or spiritual teacher which has always had prominence in Hindu religious discipline. In the period of the Upanishads wise teachers in whose hermitages in the jungle the problems of existence were discussed, gathered round them pupils to whom they taught their spiritual mysteries. The tradition of profound respect for such a spiritual guide continues throughout the whole history of Hinduism. But in the later centuries and in connection with the Vaishnavite and Śaivite sects this reverence grew to exaggerated dimensions. The guru is not only honoured: he is worshipped and even recognised as greater than God. For many within Hinduism today the real deity is the guru. It is natural enough that the actual dispensers of spiritual gifts—in this case the illuminati who alone can guide to moksha or release—should receive from their credulous disciples the utmost reverence.

But it is not by any means only among the uninstructed classes that this relationship is recognised as one of the chief means of spiritual attainment. Many of the educated people of today have their spiritual preceptors to whom

[1] Tagore, *One Hundred Poems of Kabīr*, p. 44.

they resort for guidance and to whose discipline they submit themselves. Swami Vivekananda owed his inspiration to his guru, Rāmakrishna; Dayananda Saraswati, the founder of the Ārya Samāj, is said to have owed much of the impulse of his reform to a blind sage to whom he submitted himself; Arobindo Ghose is said similarly to be the spokesman of an obscure teacher belonging to another province who brought him enlightenment. Mr. Gandhi tells us that he is deeply indebted to the insight of a wise friend, but, he adds, "I could not enthrone him in my heart as my guru. The throne has remained vacant and my search still continues."

These words indicate how high is the spiritual rank of such a teacher. Mr. Gandhi goes on: "I believe in the Hindu theory of guru and his importance in spiritual realisation. I think there is a great deal of truth in the doctrine that true knowledge is impossible without a guru. Only a perfect *gñānī* deserves to be enthroned as guru."[1] A *gñānī* means literally one who has spiritual knowledge, that is to say, one who knows the path to Release. These gurus are of many kinds, from those deeply learned in scriptural lore and in the experience of life to those who appear to be ignorant charlatans. But it is claimed that even men who seem impostors or quite unintelligent sometimes have a good influence upon those who surrender themselves to them and who thus through their means obtain inward peace and satisfaction. We have already quoted an Indian saying which may explain how this may come about, namely, "Where faith is, there God is."[2]

[1] M. K. Gandhi, *The Story of my Experiments with Truth*, Vol. I, p. 211.

[2] "In a hovel across the city we visited a stark naked man, fat as a Śiva bull, who denied God so vehemently that, compared with his talk Ingersoll's and Huxley's words read like sermons. He had eyes like a parrot's, red with indignation, and a nose like a parrot's too. He said, 'God does not exist; men die, that is the end of them.' Turning suddenly on us, he roared, 'Begone from my presence. How can I have any use for you since I have no use for God?' Yet there were many men and women who said that this fat fellow helped them to live their lives better. There was no doubt in their minds that he was a holy man." Mukerji, *My Brother's Face*.

The other method of religious culture that deserves mention here is that of listening to the old legends and religious tales, as these are expounded in temples or in the home. The custom of reading such books aloud in the home is, we are told, disappearing amid the bustle of life today, but it seems to have been a refining influence a generation ago. Mr. Gandhi tells how as a boy he was enraptured as he listened to the Rāmāyana read in his father's house. The reading and expounding of Purānas (such as the Bhagavata) by skilled Brāhmans is a religious exercise that is carried on in many temples and for which large audiences gather. A charming description by the Bengali poetess, Toru Dutt, of a scene from her own childhood can be taken as true—though she was a Christian—of children in cultured and religious Hindu homes even today. She describes three happy children in a darkened room listening to the story of Sītā's faithfulness:

> " It is an old, old story, and the lay
> Which has evoked sad Sītā from the past
> Is by a mother sung. . . . 'Tis hushed at last
> And melts the picture from their sight away,
> Yet shall they dream of it until the day."

That is a picture of a Hindu home such as ought to have a place in any just account of the Hindu religion. The affection that binds parents and children, especially, perhaps, the devotion of the Hindu wife, *pativrati strī*, that is, the woman wholly devoted to her husband, are flowers of much beauty that have been nurtured by such influences as these in their religion. From the far-off times of Sītā or, in later times, of Mirābāī, until today the ideal of a wife's loyalty and her uncomplaining submission has deeply influenced the character of Indian womanhood and given to them a wistful charm. As new visions draw them and summon them to new tasks one may hope that the memory of these examples of devotion and of duty will not wholly fade.

CHAPTER IV

VEDANTIC HINDUISM AND ITS MODERN PHASES

It has been already indicated that in any presentation of Hinduism a strict delimitation of the frontiers of one phase of the religion from other phases of it is impossible. Hinduism is not by any means a highly centralised organism. While that is true, at the same time the various forms that it has assumed possess common characteristics that betray their affinity and prevent any rigid differentiation. This is seen especially in reference to those basal ideas of Hinduism which, as has been already noted, affect powerfully all the various phases of the religion. For the purpose of our study of a system so amorphous and so comprehensive it has been necessary to associate together characteristic modes of religious belief and worship under certain general classifications. Thus we have surveyed Hinduism at its lower, animistic levels, and again we have considered it as it approximates to a theistic religion of fervour and devotion in its *bhakti* forms. The phases of Hinduism that have now to be examined are those in which its intellectual constructions and its background of idea dominate the minds of its adherents and give to their religion its special characteristics. Professor A. N. Whitehead says of Buddhism —and, by implication, of Hinduism—that it is a metaphysic seeking a religion. We have already seen how at some periods in its history theistic instincts are to be found contending with metaphysical conceptions that it is impossible to reconcile with them. There have been other periods in its history and other phases in its development when its doctrines—especially the monistic doctrines that are so fundamental in its thinking—control unchallenged the Hindu religious outlook. In this section of our study we propose to survey the types of religion which emerge under these conditions and especially the forms to which Hinduism is being moulded as it is affected by "the acids of modernity."

(a) *The History*

We have already, in our general survey of the history of Hinduism in its literary development, noted the importance of the teachings found in the ancient Upanishads, providing as they do materials for the interpretation of man's life and his universe. These unsystematised "guesses at truth" make up what is called the Vedānta, the conclusion or crown of the Vedic development. We have also seen how, many centuries later, there appeared in South India first of all in the ninth century of our era, Śankarāchārya, and then, in the eleventh century, Rāmānuja, the two great schoolmen of Mediæval India. Like the schoolmen of the West they were philosopher-theologians, whose speculations were bounded by the authority of scripture, and were directed towards the attainment of salvation. These great teachers built upon the foundation of the authoritative teachings of earlier times two imposing structures, the one rigidly monistic, the other a system of "qualified" monism. To these two masters, and especially to the former, most of the later philosophising of Hindu India looks back and by the main lines of their thought it is still controlled. They were, and are still, the great interpreters of Vedānta. Śankara has always had the widest influence and his "māyāvāda Vedānta," that is, his interpretation of the Vedānta doctrine as involving a denial of the reality of the world, can be reckoned in India as philosophic orthodoxy. In regard to the well-known formula, "thou art that," a modern Indian exponent of Śankara's system writes: "The identity of the 'thou' and the 'that' is not possible, unless one alone is real and the other unreal."[1] Śankara, accordingly, is a teacher of "Kevalādvaita" or absolute monism. Rāmānuja, on the other hand, leaves room for a real world and for a relation between the Supreme Self and the individual self that is other than identity. In the thirteenth century a third and more definitely dualistic interpreter of Vedānta appeared—also in the South—in the person of Madhavāchārya, who taught a thorough-going dualism, in opposition to both Śankara and Rāmānuja.

While these interpretations differ, the authority of the Vedānta was left unquestioned, and of its various interpreters Śankara retained and still retains the chief authority. His influence passes on from century to century unimpaired in its hold of the mind of Hindu India. It would be easy to trace his footprints deeply impressed upon Hindu thought in all its various expressions. In the fourteenth century Jñāneśvar speaks with deep respect of this high advaita teaching, calling it "the *brahma vidyā* which rooteth out all idea of duality." Eknāth in the sixteenth century in a poem, the *Bhikshugītā*, which has always been popular in the Marāthā country, speaks of "the world, consisting of friends and neutrals and foes, which affects a man with pleasure and pain" as being "a phantasm of his mind due to ignorance and nothing else." It is obvious that the unreality of worldly existence is an axiom to this Hindu and there is little doubt that the attitude to life that is the inevitable consequence of such a view was very widely spread throughout the land. Similarly we are told by Tulsī Dās about the same time how rarefied a doctrine of brahman was held by the seer Lomas. Brahman is "the unwishful, nameless, formless, identical with yourself, you and he being as absolutely one as a wave and water." There must have been many seers who led men into this bare and trackless land.

[1] V. S. Ghate in *E.R.E.*, Vol. XI, p. 189.

It is not necessary to adduce further evidence of the dominance of these monistic conceptions. We shall pass on to the early nineteenth century and review in rapid sequence some of the movements that from then onwards betray the fact that new forces are beginning to agitate the placid surface of Vedāntic religion. Behind its façade of idea the life of Hinduism had by that time become rank and corrupt. Bengal, for example, the earliest of the modern Hindu reformers, Rājā Ram Mohan Roy, tells us, " was steeped in the most debasing form of idolatry; . . . the grossest superstitions had taken hold of the national mind." In regard to Vaishnāvism in that province Ram Mohan Roy's Bengali biographer testifies that " its immorality and corruption were simply revolting." The need of the time and the awakening influences that were abroad—among which Christianity was certainly the chief—called urgently for a leader in a movement of reform and the response came in the establishment by Ram Mohan Roy in Calcutta in 1828 of the Brāhmo Samāj. This is a theistic society or Church which from that year onward in Bengal and in other provinces of India has had an important part in cleansing and re-directing the religion of the thoughtful classes.

The fact that the leaders in this movement derived their inspiration in large measure from Christianity makes it not altogether appropriate to relate it to Vedānta, but at the same time though its religion is essentially theistic and hostile to the interpretations of the old scriptures that Śankarāchārya supplied, it is a movement which, as regards many of its outstanding leaders, looked back to the Upanishads and the Gītā and drank deeply from these springs. We shall do little more here than name the leading figures in this movement and the general course of its development.

The trust deed of the first place of worship established by the Samāj in Calcutta makes clear the main characteristics of this theistic reformation and its definite dissociation from similar efforts for reform in earlier times. It rejects in the strongest terms everything that savours of idolatry and directs " that no sermon, preaching discourse, prayer or hymn be delivered, made or used . . . but such as have a tendency to the promotion of the contemplation of the Author and Preserver of the Universe, to the promotion of charity, morality, piety, benevolence, virtue, and the strengthening the bonds of union between men of all religious persuasions and creeds."

Ram Mohan Roy died in England in 1833. In 1842 the second great figure in this movement, Debendra Nath Tagore, joined the Brāhmo Samāj. Presently divisions of opinion and especially the powerful personality of the third religious leader of this theistic movement, Keshab Chandra Sen, brought about the establishment of a second Samāj, but till his death in 1905 Debendra Nath remained faithful to the Church which Ram Mohan Roy founded and which came to be known as the Ādī (or original) Brāhmo Samāj. He was universally known as Maharshi, the great Sage, and his saintly and devout character, accompanied by a faith at once deeply Hindu and strongly theistic, indicates the type of religion that this Samāj has sought with diminishing success to preserve in Bengal.

The central place in this movement of religious reform was now occupied by Keshab Chandra Sen and his fervour and genius enabled the Samāj to exercise a powerful influence in the religious life of Bengal. He failed, however, to maintain its unity and further schisms occurred. It is not necessary to consider here the causes which produced so much strife and contention within the movement. Once Keshab said to his friends in reference to these disputes, " You are like the pins united in the pin-cushion."[1] (He himself was the pin-cushion.) This inability to maintain harmony has weakened the Samāj movement throughout its history and leaves it today

[1] Farquhar, *Modern Religious Movements*, p. 69.

divided into three sections, no one of them in a condition of robust health or exercising a great influence. Thus the Ādi Samāj appears to have little active life. The poet, Rabindranath Tagore, the son of Debendranath, was for a time associated with it as its secretary. It maintained, he tells us, "its standard of truth at its static minimum, jealous of any vital growth that exceeded its limits."[1] So he gave up connection with it. The New Dispensation Samāj which Keshab Chandra Sen founded in his later years when he had come under the influence of Rāmakrishna—about whom we shall hear later—has had a somewhat unhappy history. After Keshab's death in 1884 it declined into a position of comparative obscurity. The Sādhāran Brāhmo Samāj, which separated from the Ādi Samāj in 1878, is at the present time the most active and influential of all the products of this theistic reform movement. It is with it that the majority of the provincial Samājes are associated and it maintains a staff of missionaries and carries on theistic missions among members of the humbler and more backward classes.

In 1864 Keshab Chandra Sen visited Bombay and a few years later a theistic church called the Prārthana Samāj (or Prayer Society) was established there. The most distinguished figure in the history of this Samāj was Mahadev Govind Ranade, probably the most steadfast and the most widely influential leader in social and religious reform in India during the last twenty years of the nineteenth century. He along with Sir Ramkrishna Bhandarkar and Sir Narayan Chandavarkar gave the Prārthana Samāj a position of great moral authority during the period of their connection with it. But of recent years its influence has dwindled.

The movements of reform that belong to the type of the Brāhmo Samāj have in common a strongly theistic character which relates them even more to Christianity than to the Vedāntic tradition to which they all in greater

[1] Rabindranath Tagore, *The Religion of Man*, p. 109.

or less measure acknowledge indebtedness. The Ārya Samāj on the other hand, whose influence has been mainly exercised in the north of India, is characterised by zeal for the Hindu tradition, though not for orthodox Hinduism, and by marked hostility to Christianity. Its founder was a Gujerati Brāhman who came to be known as Dayananda Sarasvati and who combined in the aims of the movement which he inaugurated a summons to his countrymen to return to the religion of the Vedas with ardent patriotism. He set side by side political and religious objectives, thus reinforcing his efforts for reform by invoking the assistance of the nationalism which was just beginning to stir the Indian breast. The Vedic religion which he proclaims was a strict monotheism, fiercely antagonistic to idolatry. He retained in his creed, as part of the Vedic inheritance, the doctrines of transmigration and karma.

To understand the influence of the Samāj which Dayananda founded we must realise how forceful was the personality of the founder, but at the same time how far he was from being either a scholar or a thinker. His interpretations of the Vedas were often fantastic; much of his ethical teaching was crude; his methods of controversy were violent. Perhaps that is why the influence of his Samāj, while it has been considerable, seems now to be steadily declining. His message has this advantage over that of the leaders of the Brāhmo Samāj that it appeals to the rising tide of nationalism and the awakening pride in India's ancient heritage. But its roots are not deep enough. Since nationalism is now no longer its special prerogative but a common possession of every class of Indian, that wind has ceased to fill the sails of the Ārya Samāj as it did so effectively in earlier days. The Samāj appears at the present time to be dividing into two sections, one giving its strength to tasks of religion and education, the other mainly political in its occupations and interests. Among the institutions that engross the former group are the Dayananda Anglo-Vedic College at Lahore and the Gurukula at Hardwar where boys are trained in intellect and character from the age of eight under conditions that may be described as monastic. Of the political Āryas we may choose as a representative Lala Lajpat Rai, one of the outstanding nationalist leaders who was repeatedly imprisoned and died in the midst of political strife in 1928.

This movement, so full of that energy of action which its first leader inspired, had in 1921 468,000 adherents, all of them in North India and nearly half of them in the Punjab. With that may be contrasted the total of the membership in the same year of the three Brāhmo Samājes in Eastern India, namely, 6400. The latter figure, however, cannot be taken as a true indication of the influence that the Brāhmo movement has actually exerted during its long and honourable history.

We must conclude this historical record of some of the products in modern India of the new life that is stirring the thoughtful classes with a brief account of still another movement that is at once notable in itself and also in certain respects typical of what is happening to Hinduism under present-day conditions. This is the remarkable rejuvenation of Hinduism that, beginning in Bengal and deriving its inspiration from a Bengali sannyāsi[1] known as Ramakrishna Paramhamsa, is steadily extending its influence throughout India. We have already referred to the influence that this man, to whom the title of Paramhamsa has been given in token of his deep spiritual knowledge and sanctity, had upon Keshab Chandra Sen. In him we have a resurgence of the pure spirit of Hinduism expressing itself through a personality of singular quality. He was, like Spinoza, though in a very different sphere, a God-intoxicated man, and intoxicated, as he was, by a pantheistic deity. His spiritual struggles, his ecstasies, and the charm and simplicity of his character attracted

[1] Ascetic.

and bound to him a group of devoted and able disciples of whom the most notable, the apostle of this new Hinduism, was Swami Vivekananda.

Ramakrishna died in 1886. In 1893 Swami Vivekananda became known to the West by the great impression he produced at the Parliament of Religions at Chicago. In 1902 he died at the early age of forty, but by that time the Ramakrishna Mission had been established and two monasteries, where its workers could be trained, had been opened. In the years since then the operations of the Mission have gone on steadily expanding. It is now carrying on work not only in Bengal, but in Madras, in Bombay Presidency, in Behar and Orissa and in the United Provinces. Its expansion would appear to be due in large measure to the fact that it unites an exuberant Hinduism with an affirmation that all religions are equally true and that accordingly every man should remain in his own religion, as well as with a summons to Hindus to works of service for mankind. It would seem as if Hinduism, if it was to have any future, could have it only as it was able along these lines to accommodate itself to the modern situation. We have in this movement a deeply interesting attempt to adjust the old Vedānta orthodoxy to the needs and the demands of a new world.

The Ramakrishna Mission may be taken as representative of several attempts to acclimatise Hinduism to modern India. Another centres round Arobindo Ghose—also, like so many others among these new prophets, a Bengali—who from his refuge in Pondicherry, issues calls to his countrymen to rediscover their ancient faith. Similarly in Agra another sect, who call themselves Rādhā Soamis are seeking with some success to combine Vedānta orthodoxy with modern energy and industrial efficiency. Of a different kind and quality are the efforts of individuals to build bridges between the Hindu tradition, so much beloved in these days of awakened patriotism, and the Christian civilisation which has brought to India elements of good which thoughtful minds cannot reject. Such are Dr. Rabindranath Tagore and Professor Radhakrishnan. Both of these are making contributions, each in his own fashion as poet or as philosopher, to this difficult task of reconciliation.

These names may be taken as representative of the variety of the efforts at religious reconstruction that are proceeding within Hinduism at the present time. They reveal some of the directions in which the currents of religious life and thought are flowing and give unmistakable evidence of the fact that religion, within the borders of what may still be called Hinduism, remains a living thing. We have now to survey these various movements of the human spirit and to study their characteristics and their worth.

(b) *The Doctrine*

Our task here is somewhat different from that which we had before us in the two earlier sections dealing with other aspects of Hinduism. The animism that is still living in India is the same animism as troubled the souls of the Dāsyus in the days of the Aryan invasions. So also emotional religion is in the main an unchanging thing whether it stirs the heart of Tukārām, a village shopkeeper of the sixteenth century, or of Sir Ramkrishna Bhandarkar, a Sanskrit scholar of the nineteenth. But the situation is different when it is a philosophic faith with which we are dealing and when reason and not emotion is in the ascendant. Such a religion, if it is a living religion intelligently held by educated persons and not just a dead tradition, is bound at such a time as the present to be full of eddies and cross-currents, of receding and advancing tides. The condition of philosophic Hinduism is actually one of much confusion and disturbance and it is not easy to forecast whether its struggles indicate the renaissance of this ancient doctrine or its approaching dissolution. The system of Vedānta, however, which forms the steel-frame of this religion, possesses qualities of strength which have enabled it to preserve Hinduism with its essential characteristics little impaired through the vicissitudes of the centuries, and it remains to be seen whether it will be equally successful in resisting the solvent influences of the modern world.

There are, of course, those still, as there have always been since the age of the ṛishis, who accept the whole system of advaita Vedānta without question. To many the karma-rebirth doctrine has this attraction that it seems to supply an explanation of the sorrows and inequalities of life and so to make acquiescence in them easier. So also there is an attraction in a thoroughgoing pantheism as delivering one from the conflicts of conscience and the agonies of remorse. "The doer and the Causer to do are one," they say and, as they say it, both bereavement and moral shipwreck alike become less intolerable and less tragic. The universe which they look forth upon may appear to be "wide, grey, lampless" but their acceptance of it creates in not a few of them a serenity and dignity of deportment which is one of the attractive characteristics of the Hindu people. One to whom all but the qualityless brahman is unreal and who actually treats all else as such and so as contemptible, dwells above the battle, and for that reason often possesses a charm such as seems to be possessed in all times and among all races by the world-renouncers.

It may illustrate the problem which faces this type of Hinduism in the context in which it lives today with Western thought and Western systems of religion and ethics contending with it for the control of the mind of India, if we have before us an interpretation of the mind of a thoughtful Hindu by a sympathetic English student of Hindusim. Sir Alfred Lyall in his *Asiatic Studies*, writing more than a generation ago, represents Vamdeo

Sastri as expressing the thoughts of a typical Vedāntist. "We are incapable," the Sastri says, "of apprehending a personality, except in the sense of something that marks or represents an incomprehensible notion; and dogmatic systems are to us no more than the formal envelopes of spiritual truth. In short, for us Salvation comes, not by righteousness but by knowledge, not by the casting out of sin, though we long to be delivered from it, but by emerging out of ignorance. Of the two trees that stood in your Garden of Eden we Hindus should have chosen the tree of life, which has been mystically understood to symbolise the wisdom which apprehends reality; whereas by eating the food which gave discernment of good and evil, Adam fell down into the region of earthly pains and pleasures, of will and desire. Undoubtedly the multitude of his descendants in India are still in the lower state. . . .

"In all civilised countries the real basis of religion is no longer metaphysical but moral; the rules of faith have been codified; the lines of communication between earth and heaven have been laid down. But all this firm ground of belief and conduct becomes submerged in the vague, fluctuating intellectualism of the Hindus. Vainly you prove to us that the conception of an impersonal, unapproachable Being is ineffectual and ethically pernicious; we recognise the moral danger but it does not stop us, for we are like mariners whom some magnetic attraction draws ever further beyond all havens to the boundless sea."[1]

It must be recognised that the type of character that this "vague, fluctuating intellectualism" produces is not infrequently dignified and attractive. Nevertheless those who have become ethically awake in the midst of the conflicts and the questionings of the modern world find themselves unable to rest satisfied with the traditional attitude of Vedāntic indifference. They have become aware that while it is often beautiful it is also often

[1] *Asiatic Studies*, Vol. II, pp. 86 f.

ineffectual. It is this conviction that has caused some to turn away altogether from Vedānta teaching and has caused others to seek to reinterpret it in a sense that may prove more morally bracing. To attain this end two methods have been adopted by different religious leaders. The religious movements that we have just surveyed and that have arisen among the most thoughtful and awakened classes in recent times either are definitely theistic and hostile to monism, or seek to bring about a reconciliation between the old monism and the new spirit of ethical endeavour. To the former belong the various " Samājes "; to the latter those revivals of Hinduism of which the Ramakrishna Mission may be selected as typical.

The Samājes—that is, the various divisions of the Brāhmo Samāj and the Ārya Samāj, while all definitely theistic, differ in the extent to which they derive their inspiration from eastern or from western sources. Thus Debendranath Tagore in Bengal and the leaders of the Prārthana Samāj in Bombay owe perhaps their deepest spiritual debt to the Bhakti movement and the Upanishads. Debendranath, as is to be expected of a rishi, looked back to the inspired utterances of the forest sages and his " Brāhma Dharma " is based on a theistic interpretation of their intuitions. The Ādī Samāj with which he was so closely associated represents this tendency within the Brāhmo movement. While it is true of the greatest of the leaders of the Prārthana Samāj also that they trace the pedigree of their theism to the most ancient days, and Mahadeva Govind Ranade claimed for it the name Sanātana Dharma—the Eternal Religion—they would admit their indebtedness at the same time to Christianity. The same acknowledgement, indeed, would probably be made by most of those who associate themselves with the other Samāj movements. Christianity, one might say, provides them with the standard by which they measure their theistic faith. Thus Hem Chandra Sarkar, the leading theologian of Brāhmoism in Calcutta at the present time, expounding the Katha Upanishad, the most theistic of those old scriptures, and claiming that it is unique in Hindu literature, gives as its signal quality that "it is remarkably like the Christian doctrine."

This fact reveals both the strength and the weakness of the whole Brāhmo movement. Its strength lies in its kinship with Christianity; its weakness in its foreignness. Its theism is perhaps too cold and too Western to lay hold of the Indian heart. It is warmest when it is most Christian, as in the case of Keshab Chandra Sen, or when it binds to itself most closely the ardour of the Bhakti saints. And in the latter case these spiritual rewards can be obtained more fully, perhaps, elsewhere than within the Samāj. The great pioneering work of the Samāj has been accomplished and the leadership is passing to others. The very fact that it looked so much to the Christian West is today reckoned a disqualification for any movement that desires to obtain a popular response.

This is a movement which is entitled to profound respect for its magnificent achievement at a period when to lead in reform demanded heroism and self-sacrifice. Its leaders are among the greatest names in modern India, altogether worthy by their spiritual insight and their moral courage of the place they hold as heralds of a new dawn in the spiritual history of their people. The movement they inaugurated belongs, however, to the past. It no longer satisfies, it would appear, the temper and the ambitions that are now abroad in the land. One of the most thoughtful of the Samāj leaders, Mr. Sitanath Tatvabhusan, explains what he calls "the derailment of the Brāhmo Samāj" as due to the lack of that "spirit of free thought and direct communion with God" which, in his opinion, characterised the Samāj in earlier days. Another critic, Mr. M. C. Parekh, who also speaks from personal experience of the Samāj, gives an estimate of the present position which is perhaps too severe but which in the main direction of its criticism may be accepted. "The Brāhmo Samāj," he writes, "which started as an imitation of Unitarian Christianity, is today still merely a poor reflection of European rationalism. To this intellectual bias it has added another which may well be termed pharisaic and communal. It has become a kind of back-water of religious and communal life, separated by its own sense of self-satisfied superiority from the main currents of national life which flow past it with a power and rapidity which it can neither appreciate nor even understand."[1]

In one significant respect the Ārya Samāj has an advantage over the Bengal movement. It is intensely patriotic and so in tune with the time. Its patriotism, however, is of the surface and has no deep springs; it does not carry on the Hindu philosophical tradition. Dr. Griswold describes its God as "a great Cosmic Executive whose business is to preside over the inexorable processes of transmigration and karma." While it is able to champion the elder Hinduism, it does so in a fashion that does not satisfy the philosophic instincts of the Hindu. On the one hand it is strongly theistic, but, on the other hand, its God is reduced to impotence in His relation to men because of the retention of the karma and transmigration doctrines. By his return to the Vedas its founder, Dayananda, was able to cut the religious life of his followers free from a great mass of later accretions which stifled the religious life: he was able also to get rid of pantheism. But in retaining karma and rebirth he left men in a condition of perpetual bondage, without any hope of deliverance. Also his claim that the Vedas contain the "basic principles of all the sciences" is, of course, a claim that does not bear investigation. "This rough sannyāsin with the soul of a leader," as M. Romain Rolland describes him, had not the intellectual equipment necessary for the creation of an Indian theism out of the materials that the old Hinduism supplied—if indeed such

[1] *The Brāhmo Samāj*, pp. 279 f.

a reconstruction is within the capacity of any human being. His forceful personality gave the new movement an impetus that carried it forward a certain distance. There seems little doubt, however, that it is now nearing the limits of its effectiveness.

Its strength has lain in large measure in the patriotic ardour that inspired it as well as in the resolution with which it sought "to diffuse knowledge and dissipate ignorance." It linked patriotism with a courageous campaign against such evils as caste, child-marriage and intemperance. Its very name, Ārya Samāj, is, as Dr. Griswold has pointed out, "a social and political more than a religious name." In this it differs both by its name and by its character from the Brāhmo Samāj, which has always been primarily interested in the religious life and in worship.

When we turn to the Rāmakrishna Mission and the spiritual foundations upon which this movement rests we find ourselves in the midst of experiences and ideas that are much more characteristically Hindu than are those of the Brāhmo Samāj in any of its forms or even than those of the Ārya Samāj, despite its intensely patriotic sentiment. The patriotism of Rāmakrishna and Vivekananda is not political but spiritual. They are possessed by a passionate faith in the ancient religious tradition of their people and they would cure its failure, not by diluting it with Christianity, but by a rediscovery of what they believe to be its real source of power.

The conscious and deliberate reorientation of the message of Vedānta to new ends such as the modern world demands of it was the task of Vivekananda. Rāmakrishna was a seer, not an apostle. His personality, in which ancient Hinduism seems to flower and to disclose its beauty, found in his disciple and successor its interpreter; and thus Vivekananda became a prophet proclaiming a new message of salvation for India. The combination of these two complementary natures, the one the seer, the other the apostle, has supplied a remarkable impetus to their gospel and its influence continued to spread steadily from province to province even after the death of Vivekananda in 1902. Whether it has achieved the rejuvenation of Hinduism and will conquer the whole land remains yet to be seen. It has at least shown to Hinduism what would seem to be the one way by which it may travel to an assured future as a living religion. It has set itself to accommodate the ancient doctrine to the needs of a new world. What this movement seeks others besides its adherents see to be urgently demanded. It is thus representative of a widespread movement of thought and aspiration in the religious life of the India of today, and on that account may receive fuller consideration than perhaps its merits and its actual influence warrant.

There are two qualities of this new Hinduism in which we may discern some of the sources of its strength. On the one hand it finds a place for Hinduism alongside of the other faiths of the world; on the other hand it inscribes "service" upon its banners. Of these the former was a deduction from what is implicit in Hinduism in all its pantheistic forms; the latter seeks to transform into its direct contrary the Hindu tradition and ideal of dispassion and inaction. It will be worth while to examine more closely these two aspects of this movement.

1. That all religions are equally true, varying roads to the same goal, indeed varying illusive forms of the sole and formless Reality, is almost an axiom of the Vedāntic doctrine.[1] But this had hardly until the time of Rāmakrishna been recognised in all its implications. The tradition taught that he who had passed in this life beyond difference, beyond name and form, to the Undifferenced and the Nameless, and who abode in that bare land, could look down with equal unconcern upon all lower breeds and upon the deities of their crude

[1] Thus Pantheism is "the mainspring that moves the puppet-show of popular idolatry." Sir A. Lyall, *Asiatic Studies*, Vol. II, p. 11.

desires. That was the spirit and temper of the traditional Hindu sannyāsi. But Rāmakrishna was not just one more in the line of sannyāsis who taught that anæmic doctrine nor did he dwell in an atmosphere of languor and of death. ' " O Mother," he cried to the god of his worship, " let me remain in contact with men! Do not make me a dried-up ascetic." We have seen that there was a very similar longing in the hearts of many of the Bhakti sages and that they were often torn between conflicting aims. Rāmakrishna, however, seems to have solved to his own satisfaction this antinomy that distressed them. God was both brahman and Kāli, both personal and impersonal, but he himself remained, " for love of humanity," a worshipper of " the divine Mother."[1]

What is relatively new in his attitude is his application of this pantheism to the claims of the religions amongst which he and his fellow Hindus lived. " He who is called Krishna," he said, " is also called Śiva and bears the name of Primitive Energy, Jesus, and Allah as well—the same Rāma with a thousand names."[2] His fervour, which he owed to his Bhakti heritage, seems to dissolve the distinctions of personal and super-personal Vedānta, as well as of Hinduism, Islam and Christianity, and of the world and the self, merging them all in an ultimate One, which he calls his divine Mother and to which he can maintain an attitude of rapture and of ecstasy. " She is the parent of the world and the world carries Her in its heart. She is the spider and the world is the web She has spun. The spider draws the thread out of Herself and then winds it round Herself. My Mother is at the same time the container and the contained. She is the shell, but She is also the kernel."[3]

[1] " He sang the identity of the Divine Mother with the Absolute. He sang the joy of the flying kite of the soul, launched by the Mother while She kept it attached to her by the string of Illusion." Romain Rolland, *Prophets of the New India*, p. 126.

[2] *P.N.I.*, p. 56.

[3] *Ibid.*, p. 47.

As a consequence of the dissolvent powers of this triumphant monism Vivekananda took upon himself an apostolate of inter-religionism, or perhaps we might say, of super-religionism. To America he said, " Never forget the glory of human nature! We are the greatest God. . . . Christs and Buddhas are but waves on the boundless Ocean which *I am*." He founded the Rāmakrishna Order on Christmas Eve. Its members celebrate the birthdays of Buddha, Krishna, Christ. They even seek sometimes to join with Christians in the Sacrament of the Lord's Supper. One of the aims they set before themselves is to unite all religions, a task which is theoretically easy in the case of a pantheism so thorough-going as that of Hinduism. Rāmakrishna and Vivekananda only set open to a wider world the gates of a religion that has always been by its nature hospitable. Hinduism is given a new standing—no longer an outcaste among the world faiths, but rather their great-hearted Mother who takes them to her breast.

2. The other outstanding feature of this religious movement, its declaration of the service of humanity as its aim, is one that it is less easy to deduce from its basic principles. " Well-doing by works " did not hold any important place, we are told, in Rāmakrishna's teaching.[1] " ' Kind to all creatures,' he said, ' kind? . . . Are you not ashamed, insignificant insect? How can you show pity to God's creatures? Who are you to show mercy? . . . No, no. Mercy is impossible. Serve them as if they were Śiva.' " Then Vivekananda proceeds to interpret these words of the guru " in the light of the doctrine of service, which reconciled the high love of God with beneficent activity."[2] To this interpretation Vivekananda devoted much of his eloquence and energy during the last crowded years before his death in 1902.

What he realised was that " the faith of the rishis must become dynamic " and to this task of transformation

[1] *P.N.I.*, p. 156. [2] Quoted in *P.N.I.*, p. 165.

he gave himself, travelling all over India and the world proclaiming his message. We may say that for him the Kāli whom Rāmakrishna worshipped with such devotion was replaced by the cause of his fellow-countrymen and of India. " It is a man-making religion that we want," he said. And again, " For the next fifty years . . . let all other vain gods disappear from our minds. This is the only God that is awake, our own race, everywhere His hands, everywhere His feet, everywhere His ears; He covers everything. . . . What vain gods shall we go after and yet cannot worship the God that we see around us. . . . The first gods we have to worship are our own countrymen." " What our country now wants are muscles of iron and nerves of steel. . . . That is what we want and that can only be created, established and strengthened by understanding and realising the ideal of the Advaita, that ideal of the oneness of all. Faith, faith, faith in ourselves."[1]

Swami Vivekananda's " Practical Vedānta " is an effort to turn the channel of Vedāntic aspiration in a new direction. To say " Thou art that " had meant hitherto entry into a kingdom of darkness and stagnation and apathy. He would put blood into the veins of brahman. He who can say " thou art that " " becomes a world-mover for whom his little self is dead and God stands in his place." He finds also in this belief the root of all service of others. " It is not a selfish faith. . . . It means faith in all because you are all. Love for yourselves means love for all, for you are all one."

It is not necessary to multiply evidence of the transformation that Vivekananda sought to effect in the whole outlook of ancient Vedānta. As one of his admirers expresses it, he sets " Vedānta on horseback "—giving it a momentum without which it could hardly justify its existence in a world that calls men to duty and to service. The claim is indeed made that the doctrine that all is

[1] *P.N.I.*, pp. 319 ff.

one is the true foundation of all ethics. Whether that claim is justified or not, it is deeply interesting to find the growing strength of the demand—not only on the part of the Swami but of others as well since his time—to bring about a radical moralisation of Vedāntic monism, and so to escape from that apathy and indifference that seem its inevitable consequence. At least two obstacles stood in his way when he undertook this task of re-interpretation. First, there is the old and rigid karma doctrine. The Bhagavadgītā with its teaching of *nishkāma karma*, action that, because done with no desire for reward, imposes no bondage on the doer, opened the way to a life of service. Rāmakrishna went further when he represented his Divine Mother as saying, "It is I who make and unmake laws. I order all karma, good and bad. Come to Me! I will lead you through this world, the Ocean of action." His disciple advanced resolutely along that open road, calling men to vigorous endeavour. And similarly he re-interprets māyā. For him it is the veil that covers the real: it is indeed, if rightly understood, the real itself. His interpreter to the West, M. Romain Rolland, claims that Vivekananda's māyā can be defined by a word that has come into common use since his day, the word Relativity.

The new Vedānta of Swami Vivekananda was thus a powerful summons to manhood and to action. He based his gospel on the doctrine of the identity of the individual soul with brahman, that is, upon the divinity of man. The divine was not for him, however, a quality-less, undifferenced brahman. The ego is not to evaporate but to become powerfully energised. The peril, indeed, of his teaching is that it may create "a delirious superman." "Without my will the Sun and Moon could not move," M. Rolland quotes Vivekananda as saying. "At my will the Universe goes like a machine." As a matter of fact the history of the Rāmakrishna Mission shows that the direction of the activities of its members has been towards works of service and of help of those in distress. The remarkable growth of its influence seems largely due to this feature of its work.

The two aspects of the teaching of this religious movement, namely, its emphasis on the unity and the common truth of all religions, on the one hand, and its call to action and service on the other, correspond to, and were, indeed, called forth by, the spirit of the times. Hinduism obviously needed to be re-interpreted if it was to find a place in the new world that now surrounded it. Animistic and polytheistic worships have to prove their respectability if they are to obtain a place in the religion of those who call themselves civilised. That could be done if the pantheistic implications of Hinduism were followed to their logical conclusions. At the same time the various levels in religion that are apparent within the wide bounds of that religion are explained as due to "gradations in spiritual evolution" and to the need of "catering for the spiritual needs of each section."[1] Similarly Professor Radhakrishnan writes: "Hindu thought believes in the evolution of our knowledge of God. Hinduism does not distinguish ideas of God as true or false, adopting one particular idea as the standard for the whole human race. It accepts the fact that mankind seeks its goal of God at various levels and in various directions and feels sympathy with every stage of the search." Thus Swami Vivekananda's doctrine of relativity in religious truth is operating to explain and justify the varied religious phases within Hinduism, and in consequence reform becomes less urgent than it appeared to be to Rājā Ram Mohan Roy and Dayananda Saraswati. Brajendranath Seal, a highly cultured and very "modern" Bengali, tells us of his stupefaction at seeing Swami Vivekananda, "a creative and dominating intelligence," worshipping before Kāli and her priest, "caught in the meshes of an uncouth mysticism," but

[1] Sir Lalubhai Samaldas in a Lecture on "What is Hinduism?"

he goes on to explain how later he was able to read the riddle. The defence of Hinduism has found a rational basis and has been made respectable. Mr. Gandhi's attitude to Hinduism and to all religions seems to issue in part from this same root, that is, from what a Hindu would consider the axiom of pantheism, and in part from his deep-seated agnosticism. "To a colleague who asked him, 'Can I not hope to give my religious experience of God to my friend?' Gandhi replied—'Can an ant desire his own knowledge and experience to be given to an elephant?'" Mr. Gandhi is not a systematic thinker. He is guided by intuitions and so is able at the same time—in spite of both pantheism and agnosticism—to practise prayer with a conviction that would seem to be possible only for a theist.

We are told that Rāmakrishna on one occasion towards the close of his life, "realising in full the identity of all within the one Being," saw that "all three were the same substance—the victim, the block, and the executioner," and added, "My God, what a vision!" Again we are told that Vivekananda was affected for life by "a lesson in humility given him by a little dancer." When, displeased that she should have been brought in to entertain the company among whom he was, he rose to go out, she sang a poem by a Vaishnavite saint, Surdās: "O Lord, look not upon my evil qualities! Thy name, O Lord, is Same-sightedness. Make of us both the same brahman!" This recognition of the divine life as present in everyone, the sinner as well as the saint, is a marked characteristic of religious Hindus, and "service" on their part takes the form of an endeavour to evoke the buried divinity in men. Of another modern Hindu teacher who has had considerable influence, Swami Ramatirtha of Lahore, we are told that he taught those who followed him to reach down to the divine in men and, perceiving this beneath their evil-doing and their faults and limitations, to love them and rejoice in them.

This attitude is interpreted by M. Rolland, in the case of Vivekananda as involving "the relativity of virtue." The Swami, however, seems to have deduced from it a call to the service of men and especially of his own unhappy fellow-countrymen. "May I be born,' he cried, "and reborn again and suffer a thousand miseries if only I am able to worship the only God in whom I believe, the sum total of all souls, and above all my God, the wicked, my God, the afflicted, my God, the poor of all the races."[1] In this spirit at sixty-eight centres throughout India and beyond India the Ramakrishna Mission is carrying on its activities at the present time.[2] By its efforts "the lion of brahman," asleep in the heart of each man, is to be awakened.[3]

These are some of the means by which it is hoped that the religion of the modern Hindu will be rejuvenated. One could hardly have pictured the brahman of the Upanishads as a lion—that brahman which has been compared to the silent sea into which the ātman, like a dewdrop, melts; or which the sages tell us is like a dreamless sleep, or an unanswering stillness. But the demands of a new time call for qualities that ancient India felt little need of. Demands are being made on every hand by Hindus themselves that the old non-moral tradition must be amended, that, for example, the obscene images in the Jagganāth Temple at Puri must be effaced, that the dedication of girls to Hindu gods must be forbidden, that temples must be thrown open to the untouchables. Someone has said of Hinduism that it is a "religion condemned to die but determined to live." It has certain qualities that give it great survival power. There is, for example, as has been already indicated, its pantheism with the ability that accompanies pantheism to justify an old phase or to assume a new one, according as necessity requires. It may also be claimed, as M.

[1] *P.N.I.*, p. 250.
[2] Of these, six are in the United States of America.
[3] The phrase is Vivekananda's and is quoted in *P.N.I.*, p. 327.

Rolland claims, that the Vedānta doctrine is in agreement with a view of the universe that some modern scientific teachers in the West would accept. The "free man's religion," that of those who "without the bitterness of impotent rebellion" "resign themselves to the outward rule of Fate," is a goal towards which those who have inherited the teaching of Advaita may find it natural to direct their lives. A generation ago Sir Alfred Lyall saw that this accommodation between philosophic Hinduism and modern materialism would be easy. He went on to add that he could not see how pantheism could help India in seeking "not only an explanation of phenomena but a basis of morals."

This, however, is what many Hindus at the present time are anxious to make room for within the compass of their own religion. There is, it is true, a strong current bearing away from all religious belief those for whom the solvent forces that have come from the West have destroyed the traditions of their fathers. But others are more faithful to the deeply religious instinct of the Hindu and are seeking a way by which the old religion may obtain that ethical authority without which, they realise, it cannot claim to continue to govern men's lives. Thus Professor Radhakrishnan desires to make it able to "cure its followers of the swell of passion, the thrust of desire and the blindness of temper" and would persuade himself that the sannyāsi spirit is that of one "who dwells in love and walks in righteousness."[1] A more orthodox

[1] Professor Radhakrishnan seems, indeed, to fear that Hinduism is travelling too far in this direction. In his Hibbert Lectures he comments on the influence that teachers like Vivekananda, Gandhi and Tagore are having, so that "a social gospel is becoming popular." "The Bhagavadgītā," he says, "has become the most important Hindu Scripture. In religion accent is the vital thing, and it is now shifted to social reform." "But," he goes on, "we cannot forget that in essence religion is spiritual redemption and not social reform. Sanctity and holiness may imply service and fellowship but cannot be equated with them. Religion today has to fight not only unbelief and secularism, but also the subtler rival in the guise of social reform." The voice might almost be the voice of Karl Barth. *An Idealist View of Life*, pp. 72, 73.

but a more outspoken critic of Hinduism,[1] who was himself President of the Hindu Mahāsabhā, an organisation which exists to champion the traditional religion, states frankly what he conceives to be demanded of it if it would survive. "The one need of the times," he says, "is to expand the spirit of Hinduism, to liberalise it so that all those who profess it, however low and depressed, will find in it a living solace, a guide on all occasions when their minds are troubled. We must so reconstruct Hinduism that its meanest adherents, however degraded, will find in it solace, comfort and even enjoyment and respect." The awakened spirit of nationalism has brought many back to bow in the temples of the old, unreformed, impenitent Hinduism. In many cases this has no more of a religious motive behind it than is associated in other lands with the waving of the Union Jack or of the Stars and Stripes. And yet there may be and often is, much more that has religious value in the awakening that nationalism brings about. It stirs men from their mental lethargy and self-absorption and may so far advance them to be wise. That there is often a real quickening of religious interest none can doubt. Many more copies of the Bhagavadgītā are in circulation now, we are told, than a generation ago, "and most of the educated Hindus are able today to quote verses from that great Scripture." "Indian booksellers say," the Hindu observer from whom that statement is quoted goes on, "that, apart from the text-books prescribed in Schools and Colleges the only books which have a large sale are books on religion, especially those on the Gītā." "Above all," he concludes, "the typically Hindu character of Mahatma Gandhi has touched the heart of the masses throughout India and quickened the spirit of Hinduism more effectively than a thousand books could do. And it must be admitted that his experiments in Satyāgraha on a

[1] Mr. M. R. Jayakar.

nation-wide scale open a new chapter in Hindu ethics."[1]

Whether Mr. Gandhi's influence is bearing India away from the pantheistic tradition, drugged as it is "with all the drowsy syrups of the East," to a theism which will strengthen the moral fibre of the people one cannot as yet determine. Dr. Rabindranath Tagore's "religion of man" seems similarly to be somewhat apart from the main stream of the Hindu religious inheritance. In spite of the name which he has given to his religion it is hardly the same as what is known as Humanism in the West. He tells in his Hibbert Lectures how when he was eighteen "a sudden spring breeze of religious experience" came to his life. "That which was memorable in this experience," he says, "was its human message, the sudden expansion of my consciousness in the super-personal world of man." He thus combines as the object

[1] The writer from whom these sentences are quoted, Professor D. S. Sarma, M.A. (writing in *Young Men of India*, June 1931), sums up the evidence that seems to him to indicate the present condition of Hinduism as follows:

"No social worker who sees the conditions under which our depressed classes are forced to live can ever believe that Hinduism teaches the inherent divinity of every human being. No student of religion who witnesses the type of faith that satisfies too many even of our educated classes today can ever believe that Hinduism has at any time taught anything more than gross ritualism or achieved anything more than mere Pharisaism. In fact, when one sees the silent opposition to Mahatma Gandhi's campaigns against untouchability, or when one counts the number of child-marriages that took place last year to evade the operation of the Sarda Act, or when one considers the innumerable little sects and sub-sects into which the Hindu society is divided, each with its own walls of separation, for all of which a religious sanction is claimed, one may be tempted to say that Hinduism is nothing but a mass of dead wood cumbering the path of progress."

Nevertheless he concludes his survey on a more hopeful note:

"Young men have to be taught to face realities in religion, as well as politics, and not to waste their energies on empty formulas from which truth has departed. If this is done with courage and insight, there is no doubt that Hinduism, the most ancient of religions, with its great ideals of toleration and non-violence, its unique and elastic concept of Dharma, its doctrine of the non-violability of the moral law, its integral vision of an evolving universe and its rich and adequate conception of God as a Being both transcendental and immanent, both personal and impersonal, may still have a message to deliver to the world."

of his worship a super-personal Being to whom, as he says, the individual man is related as the molecules in a steel rod is to the rod itself, with a human element which enables him to call his religion the religion of man. The former would seem to be an inheritance from Vedāntic teaching and the latter from a Bhakti which, he tells us, he was taught by the wandering Baul singers whose religion he felt was alive with an emotional sincerity. "Their God is the man of the heart." To hold together these two theological conceptions is easier, no doubt, for a poet than for ordinary persons, and a conflation of pantheism and theism is what, as we have noted, the Hindu soul has often in its past history sought to accomplish. This attempt is still being made by many of the finest spirits in an India which is striving to reconcile the ancient heritage of Hindu religion with the moral demands that the modern world makes upon thoughtful men.

These instances of individual religious attitudes in the Hinduism of contemporary India have been cited as giving evidence of movements in various directions on the part of those who are seeking to reconcile the old doctrine with the needs of a new day. There are very many thoughtful and deeply religious minds within Hinduism who—like Mahatma Gandhi, Professor Radhakrishnan and Dr. Rabindranath Tagore—are seeking in many different ways to enable the Hindu without denying the past to inherit the future. There is specially the eager desire to enable its adherents to exchange ideals that have been "passive, static, ataraxic," for others by means of which they may become, in the words of one of their modern seers, Arobindo Ghose, "canals of action in this world."

In their desire to achieve this end many are turning away, not merely from traditional Hinduism but from all religion. It is natural that this should happen and that they should conclude, as they look back upon the long tale of Hindu oppression and Hindu superstition, and as they look around them at the religious enmities and conflicts that divide their people and hinder progress, that all religion is false and evil. They prefer to have no religion at all, rather than a religion which enfeebles and degrades them, which as Dr. Tagore puts it, creates in its followers "the Śudra spirit," that is the spirit that cringes. A Conference of non-Brāhmans in South India recently adopted a resolution which is a significant symptom of this rebellion. The Conference expressed its want of confidence in Mr. Gandhi for this among other reasons—"his undermining of the sense of self-confidence and self-reliance in the people by his deliberate invocations of God in all his acts and utterances." Thus both those who still cling at least to the name of Hinduism and those who would cast it and all religion from them in disgust are agreed in seeking new ideals for the remaking of man and the reinforcement of his moral energies whether these ideals are to be sought within the old religion or outside. In the midst of these questionings, and the distractions of conflicting views of the way of religious advance, the educated and awakened Hindu stands at the present time uncertain and perplexed. The travail of the Hindu spirit to create the new religious synthesis that India waits for is not yet accomplished. What course will ultimately be chosen and followed by the Hindu soul in its future journeyings cannot as yet be forecast. But when one reviews its long record of spiritual adventure and aspiration through the ages one cannot believe that it will fail in the end—however long delayed—to reach the true goal of all human seeking.

PART II

INDIAN ISLAM

CHAPTER V

ITS HISTORY

Of the six religions dealt with in this volume three may be said to be wholly indigenous to India, to have their home and practically the whole of their history within its borders. These are Hinduism, Jainism and Sikhism. Of the remaining three the religion of the Parsis had a great past elsewhere, but, having been transplanted to India, it has become so rooted there that that land may now be said to be its headquarters and its home. The two remaining religions are in a different position from any of the others. Both Islam and Christianity have had their main history outside of India and are, as none of the others are, world religions. They can both, at the same time, claim to be Indian religions because each has had a long history within India, though there is a wide difference between the kind and the significance in each case of that history. Both can also claim to be Indian religions because they have acquired through that history distinctive characteristics which make it possible to speak of Indian Islam and Indian Christianity. That at least is indisputably true in regard to the Islam of India and makes possible its treatment in detachment from the whole of which it is a distinctive portion.

Its importance in that whole to which it belongs is due to the great number of those within India who profess this faith, to the splendid record of their achievements in secular life, and to the strength and the characteristic quality of their religious belief. The number of Muslims in India, according to the census of 1931, is 77,743,928, a total which is reckoned to be nearly one-third of all the Muslims of the world[1] and a larger number than are to be found within the borders of any other single country. This total is also just under one-third of the number of the Hindus alongside of whom they have to live and with whom they have to share the guidance of their land. This fact and the influence that it has upon their lives and their religious ideas has helped to give Indian Islam its specific characteristics and to differentiate it from the Islam of Arabia or Turkey. The fact of its confrontation by so formidable and so different a rival and the problems thus raised have a central significance in determining what it has grown to be in the past and what it will become in the future. Various causes combine to give the Muslim the advantage over his rival of a more rapid increase in numbers. There is also the circumstance in India, as compared with the other chief Muslim lands, that Western influences are brought freely to bear upon the religion and are deeply affecting it. These are some of the features of the situation in which Islam finds itself in India which give a special interest and importance to the form and the direction that the religious development will take in days to come. It has already in the past exhibited characteristics of its own that are notable enough.

The secular achievements of Islam in India are not indeed to be summed up, as elsewhere they so largely are, in conquest and government, but include as well the dignity and splendour of the art and architecture by means of which mosques and palaces were created and adorned so that they have won the admiration of the world. It is the Islam that has had this distinguished past and that is facing somewhat anxiously an uncertain future, the Islam that has found for itself a colour and a shape that it owes to India and that belongs now to its

[1] According to Professor H. A. R. Gibb (*Whither Islam?*, p. 11) the most careful calculation gives a total of from 240 to 250 millions of professing Muslims in the world.

essence, that we have to deal with here. We shall accordingly begin by sketching as rapidly as possible the history of the growth of the religion and of some of its characteristic developments since Islam first descended in the guise of a conqueror upon the Indian plains.

It is not, of course, suggested that Islam is different in India in its essentials from what it is elsewhere. The Prophet Muhammad, according to tradition, when asked by the angel Gabriel, " What is Islam? ", replied, " Islam is to believe in God, to say the prescribed prayers, to give alms, to observe the feast of Ramadan, and to make the pilgrimage to Mecca." No doubt many Muslims in India, as elsewhere, can say, " All these things have I observed from my youth up." We shall take for granted that that is what Islam signifies for the pious Muslim everywhere. But within these boundaries there is room for a large measure of variation and of growth from the days when in A.D. 1001 Mahmud of Ghazni swept down upon India from Afghanistan to the day when Sir Syed Ahmad Khan opened a Muslim College at Aligarh in 1875.

India's relation with Islam is usually reckoned to begin in A.D. 1001, the year of the first of a series of successive invasions through the north-western passes. Three centuries earlier, it is true, Sind had come under Arab domination and has remained ever since predominantly Muslim in the religion that is professed, though here even more than elsewhere it is a Hinduised Islam that the people actually follow. The main stream of the Muslim invasion has, however, flowed, not from Arabia but from the Central Asian plains and the path of its entrance has been through the mountain barriers of the North-West. During successive centuries Upper India was spoiled and laid waste by invasion after invasion. In 1193 one of the Afghan conquerors, Muhammad Ghuri, established at Delhi the capital of his rule. That city continued till 1858 to be the capital of a Muslim empire that was seeking continually to extend its control over an increasing area of the land.

The motives of these invasions were compounded, no doubt, of brigandage and religious zeal. Mahmud of Ghazni is said to have destroyed a thousand temples, while of Muhammad Ghuri we are told that when he set up his capital at Delhi "the city and its vicinity were freed from idols and idol-worship and in the sanctuaries of the images of the gods mosques were raised by the worshippers of the one God." Mr. T. W. Arnold sums up the record of these invaders thus: "They at times during the early stages of the conquest exhibited a brutal intolerance towards the Hindus who opposed their armies, and ruthlessly massacred Brāhmans and razed the temples to the ground: but after the savageries of conquest were over a certain amount of toleration was allowed to their Hindu subjects."[1]

Not many of the Hindus were able, we may be sure, to accept this iconoclasm in the spirit of philosophic detachment of one of them, Nāmdev, a Deccan poet of the fourteenth century. "A god of stone," he says contemptuously, "and a worshipper who is deceived. . . . Such gods were broken in pieces by the Turks. They threw them into the water as all men know." It was not, of course, to be expected that toleration would be shown to idolatry by the fierce adherents of this monotheistic faith, Afghans, as they were, and Turks. A somewhat surprising instance of Muslim intolerance shows them persecuting, in the fifteenth century, the Parsis who, being like themselves "people of a book," were entitled to special consideration. These fugitives from Persia were settled in Sanjan in Gujarat under the protection of a tolerant Hindu ruler. After his overthrow by a Muslim invader the Parsis "suffered many wrongs at the hands of the Mahommedan troops,"[2] so that they had to flee for

[1] T. W. Arnold in *E.R.E.*, Vol. VIII, p. 895.
[2] *History of the Parsis*, by Dosabhai Framji Karaka, Vol. I, p. 47.

their lives, taking their sacred fire with them, and seek a refuge among the mountains. But the spread of Islam during these centuries was not wholly due to methods of force and fear. As early as the thirteenth century there were Muslim missionaries, such as Mu'in-ud-din Chishti of Ajmir, by whose efforts, we are told, whole tribes were converted.

A change came over the spirit of the Muslim rulers in India when, in 1556, Akbar, greatest of the Moguls, ascended the imperial throne. It is he — a direct descendant of Timur the Tartar, and, at the same time, it is said, of Chingiz Khan, the Mongol—who first among these Muslims revealed great qualities of statesmanship and proved himself capable of governing his alien subjects with understanding and insight. To this end, in order that he might fashion a united people, he sought to discover some means by which they might be made spiritually one. To combine within the bounds of a single faith attitudes and ideas so hostile to each other as those of Hinduism and Islam, might well appear an impossible dream, and so indeed it proved; and yet to have sought such an end, though the means he employed were superficial and ill-considered, in itself gives to Akbar a notable place among rulers. The Dīn-ilahi, the divine religion, which he projected and sought to establish, failed of its purpose, as any such attempt at the artificial creation of an eclectic faith was bound to fail, but it bears witness to his deep interest in religion and to a spirit of toleration that was exceptional at that period in anyone and especially in a Muslim. He seems to have abandoned Islam as his personal belief and to have been what one might call a devout sceptic, seeking truth but never able to find it. He died, according to Mr. Vincent Smith, "a baffled, disappointed man."[1]

Akbar illustrates in his person the subtle, invasive power that Hinduism exercises over so many minds.

[1] *Akbar, the Great Mogul*, p. 350.

His toleration of other religions and his expressions of reverence alike for Muhammad and for Christ seem to have been due to the influence upon him of pantheistic ideas. This was probably also the reason why he maintained that it was "a religious duty and divine praise to worship fire and light." "The deep-sighted," he held, "know better than to call this fire-worship."[1] So also sympathy with the Jain and the Hindu made him place limitations on the slaughter of cattle. He suspended the imposition of the *jizyah*, the poll-tax on non-Muslims, and took measures, in the cause of humanity, to restrain the Hindu practice of suttee. He thus showed himself both a far-sighted ruler and a social and religious reformer long before the days of reform. He declared himself no believer in the use of force to spread religion. "What constancy," he is said to have asked, "is to be expected from proselytes on compulsion."[2]

Akbar's statesmanlike efforts to unify his discordant empire found little support in the policy of his successors. During the long reign of his great grandson, Aurungzib, the traditional Muslim policy of oppression and persecution was fully resumed. When he died in 1707 the empire of the Moguls was well on the way to dissolution. The Sikhs and the Marāthās were engaged in conflicts with the Muslim power which were essentially religious, the products of bigotry and fanaticism on the one side or the other. The Muslim-Hindu hostility that flamed out then, in the rebellion of Sivaji, the Marāthā, is even today a cause of distrust and division and nowhere more than in the Marāthā country where the tradition of that old struggle still survives.

For the Muslim the state is a religious as well as a civil authority. It is the duty of the state to maintain Islam and to oppose all that hinders its extension. Thus it inevitably followed that the decline of the Mogul empire weakened and depressed the position of the

[1] *E.R.E.*, Vol. I, p. 273. [2] *Ibid.*, p. 27.

Muslim faith in India. As the power of the East India Company, and behind it of Great Britain, increased and that of the disintegrating Empire declined, the prestige of Islam declined simultaneously. This was all the more the case because the Muslim power had rested hitherto much more upon military force than upon any ascendancy of intelligence or statesmanship. The administration had long been in large measure in the hands of Hindus, and Akbar was making no radical innovation when he chose an able Hindu, Todar Mal, to be his minister of finance.

Thus it came about that by 1857 when the Muslims saw that the prestige and authority which had so long been theirs was rapidly vanishing, leaving them not only dethroned from their imperial power but in a subordinate place as compared even with the Hindus whom they had despised, a bitter sense of humiliation and anger overwhelmed them. The "Mutiny" of 1857 was, of course, only superficially a military rising. It has been called by a western historian "the first wave of anti-Western reaction," and by Indian nationalists the first war for India's independence. One element that largely entered into it was that of the outraged and embittered pride of a dethroned religion accustomed for long to a position of domination and authority. There is a parallel between what happened then and what happened sixty years later—when Turkey was defeated—in the anger in each case over what was accounted a religious humiliation and in the unreal alliance that resulted uniting Hindu and Muslim against a common foe. In both cases there was latent beneath all that united these two sections a hostility that remained and was only temporarily suspended. The consequence was that no substantial achievement could be realised through such an alliance and they were bound presently to fall apart again and experience the bitterness of disillusionment. In the earlier Mutiny struggle the memory of past Muslim power, in the later Khilafat struggle the hope of future Hindu power, were elements creating the situation in each case, and they were elements in each case preventing cordial co-operation. The future progress of India depends still upon a radical resolution of the antagonism that can so easily be rekindled between these two competing religious communities.

The Khilafat agitation which arose in India at the close of the Great War was due to resentment at the terms imposed upon Turkey and the Caliph as a result of that struggle. Mr. M. K. Gandhi set himself by the side of the leaders in this movement and sought to create a common front by uniting both sections in the demand for self-government. The real motive, however, behind the Muslim agitation was religious and its aim the restoration of the Sultan of Turkey to the headship of Islam. Co-operation in the demand for self-government was the price that the Indian Muslim was willing to pay in order that the dishonour done to Islam might be wiped out. When, accordingly, in 1924, the Angora Assembly deposed and banished the Caliph and abolished his office, the pretext that had united in an unreal alliance Hindus and Muslims was by that action destroyed and the fact revealed that the deep-seated differences between them had not yet been overcome. Tragic evidence of that was given again and again in fierce conflicts which broke out repeatedly during these years and which, whatever their primary causes might be, were inflamed by the fires of religious hate. In 1921 in the South of India the Mappilas or Moplahs, a fanatical Muslim community, rose in rebellion and set up a "Khilafat kingdom." Soon, however, what began as a result of political agitation turned into a religious jihad against the Hindus, very many of whom were massacred and over a thousand, it is estimated, forcibly "converted." Of these conflicts it is not necessary to give any full account. It is enough to say that it has been calculated that between 1923 and 1926 seventy-four such communal riots took place resulting in many deaths. In March 1931, at Cawnpore, perhaps the most hideous of them all occurred, leaving behind it a deep and dangerous resentment. On the occasion of this outbreak "murders, arson and lootings were widespread for three days; the number of verified deaths was three hundred but the death-roll was probably between four and five hundred. Many temples and mosques were desecrated or burned or destroyed and a very large number of houses were burned or pillaged."[1] The causes that are at work behind these tragic events are, no doubt, compounded of economic jealousies and political ambitions, as well as religious animosities, but religious hate has furnished the battle-cry and poisoned and embittered the conflict.

With this statement of the facts that stand forth most prominently in the position of Indian Islam today and cast so deep a shadow over its future, and indeed over the whole future of India, we shall conclude our review of the external aspects of the fortunes of the Muslim faith in India. Its position as over against Hinduism on the one hand and the British authority on the other, is that of a deposed state religion, looking back regretfully at its great past in this land and looking forward doubtfully to an uncertain future.

It has, however, another external relationship which affects its position as a religion and which must not be forgotten. Indian Islam is bound up through its cultural history with the other branches of the Islamic fraternity. This relationship, as recent history to which reference has been made has demonstrated, has a disturbing influence on Muslims in India such as is certain to affect their future as members of the emerging Indian nationality. Sir Theodore Morison, who was intimately associated with Indian Islam for many years, quotes a striking statement of the Muslim attitude in this matter that was made to him in the nineties of last century by the large-minded Muslim leader, Sir Syed Ahmad, the pioneer in

[1] Sir Theodore Morison in *Political India*, p. 99.

modern reform movements among Muslims in India. "When there were many Muslim kingdoms," Sir Syed said, "we did not feel much grief when one of them was destroyed; now that so few are left, we feel the loss of even a small one. If Turkey is conquered that will be a great grief, for she is the last of the great powers left to Islam. We are afraid that we shall become like the Jews, a people without a country of our own."[1] In India more than in any other country they have still the opportunity of playing a great part, but there, too, it is likely to be a part of less authority and eminence than it was in former days.

The position of Islam as a religion that seeks to exercise civil as well as ecclesiastical authority makes it no easy matter to define the boundaries between its political and its religious aspects, and renders difficult its adjustment to a condition of subordination. That is what it has had to reconcile itself to during the last century of its existence in India and what it will have to accept in the days to come. This readjustment is hard to accomplish in the case of a religion that creates in those who profess it a haughty spirit of dominance and exclusiveness and that teaches scorn of all idolators.

We must turn now from the outward fortunes of the Muslims of India to note some of the more inward and spiritual influences that were at work during these centuries giving to their religion its distinctive characteristics. The followers of Islam in India belong broadly to two main groups—those who claim descent from the Muslim immigrants into India from outside its borders and those who belong to communities that have exchanged Hinduism or animism for Islam. This distinction, it need hardly be said, is not a rigid one. There is a popular saying among Muslims to the effect that a Muslim who originally belonged to a Hindu weaving caste may progress with growing prosperity, after he has entered the

[1] *Op. cit.*, p. 95.

Muslim fold, until he is able to claim as a Sayyid, kinship with the Prophet's family. It is among converts, naturally, that the largest dilution of the pure doctrine of Islam is to be found. We have already noted that the converts in Sind follow practices that owe much to their Hindu origin. They are said to be "pre-eminent for abject devotion to Pirs and Sayyads, living or dead."[1] The large number of these saints in Muslim India is probably in great measure due to Hindu influences. Thus the *Panch Pir* or Five Saints worshipped by Muslims all over India may be a Muslim parallel to the Five Pāndavas who are equally popular among Hindus. In any case the five actually worshipped are in many instances Hindu godlings. "The enumeration," says W. Crooke, "varies from district to district according to the tastes of the worshippers or the local cults which have been absorbed." One may find a roadside grave of a Muslim saint owned, and ministered to, by a Hindu of low caste. In Bengal the interchange of worship between Hindus and Muslims is very marked, though a recent reforming movement of the Wahhābi type has checked the corruption of the faith. It has recently been revealed through the strong opposition of many Muslims to the Sarda Act, which raises the age of marriage, how widespread among them is the Hindu custom of child-marriage. In the days of the Emperor Jehangir even suttee was practised in some Muslim circles.

We must not, however, conclude from such facts as these that the Muslim faith, in the case of those influenced by Hindu contacts or of those converted from Hinduism, is necessarily a superficial thing. A generalisation must be made with much caution. Thus the Mappilas or Moplahs of Malabar are in large measure made up of descendants of converts from Hinduism but they are said to be extremely fanatical adherents of the faith they have adopted, and they gave grim proof of this in the

[1] *Gazetteer of Sind*, quoted in *E.R.E.*, Vol. XI, p. 572.

outbreak of 1921 already referred to. Kashmir, where 76 per cent of the inhabitants are Muslims, has recently been the scene of similar religious conflicts aroused by jealousy on the part of the Muslims of their Hindu fellow-citizens and their Hindu ruler. But this Muslim zeal is apparently no proof of depth of Muslim conviction if the evidence that Sir Walter Lawrence gives us is to be accepted. "When I was in Kashmir," he writes, "an Arab preacher visited me. His object was to put life into the languid observances of the Moslems of the Valley. I introduced him to the leading men of the country, but after a long tour through the villages he returned, baffled and dejected. He told me that he had found no true believers; in their hearts the Kashmiris of the Valley were as Hindu as were the Brāhmans of the capital."[1]

The recently accentuated rivalry of Hinduism and Islam has produced active efforts at what is called by the Muslims *Tabligh* or propaganda with a view to conversion, just as it has produced *Suddhi* on the part of the Hindus, that is, the reclamation to Hinduism of converts to Islam from that faith. Whereas it once was the case that those belonging to the two faiths who shared the life of the village together were often drawn together into accord and into kindly relationships there is much more of a tendency now to draw apart from each other and emphasise differences. Thus among the Muslim Malkanas of the United Provinces who claim to have brought about a conflation of the two rival religions so that they are said to worship both in temples and mosques, the Ārya Samāj is actively at work to prevent Hindus from thus falling away to the Muslim camp. How far these are genuinely religious movements and how far they are dictated by the desire to increase the number of members of the rival communities for political ends one cannot judge, nor yet to what extent success is being

[1] *The India we Served*, p. 161.

achieved by one religion or the other. There are some facts, certainly, that in any competition between the two faiths are in favour of the Muslims. One such, for example, is their comparative freedom from the caste exclusiveness of the Hindus. "It is the absence of class prejudice," writes Mr. Arnold, "which constitutes the real strength of Islam in India, and enables it to win so many converts from Hinduism."[1]

On the other hand, if we are to estimate aright the strength, at this lower level of the population, of the rival systems, we must take into account the deep roots of Hinduism and the superficial nature of a change from the worship of a Hindu idol to that of a Muslim saint. There is probably much to be said in many instances for the view of Sir Walter Lawrence, who has already been quoted in this connection. "I cannot express an opinion," he writes, "as to the prospects of the Tabligh movement, but I know intimately two large communities converted from Hinduism to Islam, and I am certain that most of these could be whistled back to the fold."[2]

But while at these lower levels Muslim belief and practice have undoubtedly been seriously corrupted by the animism and Hinduism upon which they have been superimposed, it is true, on the other hand, that at the higher levels of religious reflection a reciprocal influence has been exercised by the two religions upon each other. The most striking instances of this influence exercised by Islamic monotheism upon the thought and belief of Hinduism can be found in Kabīr and Nānak. Both of these religious leaders believed that they had discovered a higher way which included and transcended the rival doctrines. Kabīr (1440–1518) bears a name which indicates a Muslim origin, but he may have been a Hindu orphan child brought up by a Muslim. According to a legend he was accused before the Muslim ruler of his time, Sikander Lodi, of being no true Muslim, but

[1] Quoted by Titus, *Indian Islam*, p. 53. [2] *Op. cit.*, p. 293.

"hateful alike to Hindus and Muhammadans." He replied: "Hear, O Sikander; I am a pir (saint) of both religions." So Nānak also is said to have adopted as his slogan, "I am neither Hindu nor Muhammadan but a worshipper of the Formless One." Dr. Farquhar is convinced that both of these teachers, whose influence has been widespread throughout North India, were influenced by "the mystic Islam of the Sufis."[1] Kabīr much more than Nānak, though he calls the god of his worship Rāma, bears the impress of Muslim monotheism. He rejects all incarnations and, while he follows Bhakti in affirming the necessity of a guru, he does not elevate the human teacher, as Hinduism often does, to the rank of divinity. On the other hand by his acceptance of the doctrine of karma and transmigration he really aligns himself with Hinduism. Nabha Dās in his *Bhakta Māla*, which is dated about 1600, tells us that Kabīr "imparted religious instruction to Hindus and Muhammadans alike." "He had no preference," he goes on, "for either religion, but gave teaching that was appreciated by the followers of both. He spoke out his mind fearlessly, and never made it his object merely to please his hearers."[2]

Of Nānak's debt to Islam more is said elsewhere.[3] He was undoubtedly much influenced by Kabīr and the movement for the quickening and purifying of Hinduism to which Kabīr belonged, but Kabīr set himself free far more completely than Nānak from Hindu polytheism. Through these two personalities, and especially through Kabīr, a salutary infusion of Muslim teaching was conveyed to many within Hinduism. Dr. Farquhar gives a list of ten of the chief sects that sprang from the influence that Kabīr exercised by his life and by the songs that made his teaching widely known throughout the North. The record of their historical development is, however, significant. All of these sects, Dr. Farquhar says, were at first monotheistic and non-idolatrous in their worship,

[1] *O.R.L.I.*, p. 331. [2] Quoted by Keay, *Kabīr*, p. 49. [3] See chap. xii.

recognised no caste distinctions and admitted both Hindus and Muslims. The drift towards Hinduism, however, soon set in, incarnations were recognised and the worship of the guru, and presently idolatry was re-established. Thus here, also, in spite of the theistic and ethical character of the impulse that Kabīr had given, and in spite of the influence that a religion of the elevation and the prestige of Islam might be expected to exercise, the stubborn strength of Hinduism, allied with certain deep-seated instincts of ordinary human nature, ultimately—when that ordinary human nature was left unsupported—re-established its sway.

It is highly probable that Kabīr and Nānak were in contact with Sufi teaching. There is very much in the doctrines of these mystics that would find an echo in the hearts of Hindu ascetics and lead them to compare their kindred intuitions. Inevitably Sufism with its somewhat precarious combination of a monistic philosophy with a longing for fellowship with God would commend itself at once to those who by means of Bhakti were seeking to establish a similar alliance with Vedāntic Hinduism. The bias of the Hindu bhakta was usually, as we have seen, too far towards a monism that seemed to strangle all hope of real communion; the predominant partner in the alliance in this case was Advaita. Sufism, on the other hand, issuing as it did from a powerfully established faith in one personal God, could bring to the devout heart of Kabīr an assurance that delivered him from the perils of Hindu monism. Sufism, indeed, "extols the love of Allah, a love emotional and tender"; at the same time many of the Sufis, as we have seen, hold the doctrine of fana, the extinction of personality in Allah, combining it somehow with "continuance of the personality in or with Allah." This doctrine of absorption Professor R. A. Nicholson and others attribute—in part at least—to Hindu influences.[1] Professor Nicholson

[1] See Titus, *Indian Islam*, p. 149.

traces the source from which, in the case of Bayazid—a teacher of this type of Sufism who exercised a widely extending influence in Persia in the ninth century—fana was acquired, to Abu Ali of Sind who was acquainted with Indian Yoga. "He knew the Indian practice of 'watching the breaths' and described it as the gnostic's worship of God."[1] His pantheism even carries him to such an extreme of identification that he cries to God "O Thou I!" Certainly, whether this debt is proved at an earlier period or not, there is such an interchange of ideas in modern times between this pantheistic Islam and Vedānta teaching, especially when Theosophy is available to mediate between them.

While the influence of Vedānta is probably a factor, encouraging the growth within Islam of such sects as adopt what may be called Sufi beliefs and practices, at the same time it must be recognised that there are elements within the orthodox theology which promote Sufi modes of thinking, even if only by way of reaction against extremism. The exaltation and remoteness of Allah with the corollary of the impotence of the human will is not far removed in its implications from such a view as that of Hindu Advaita with its affirmation that the phenomenal world is illusion. Whether the sole reality is called Allah or brahman the consequences that follow are closely similar and the extremes of Transcendence and Immanence are able, if produced far enough, to meet. At the same time the removal of Allah to such remoteness is bound to accentuate in the case of some a sense of their need of the divine fellowship. What the official system refused to recognise had to find, by such a discipline as that of the Sufis, a means of satisfaction. Thus Islam was compelled to open its doors to a mystical pantheism, and to speak of matters so alien to its spirit as absorption in Allah and the divine love. The conflict that appears here within Islam between apparently irreconcilable aims

[1] *E.R.E.*, Vol. XII, p. 12.

we have found already to have arisen among the Hindu adherents of Bhakti, and the cause that has produced the conflict is closely similar in both cases. "While reason," writes R. A. Nicholson, expounding the Sufi doctrine, "is dualistic, love unifies by transcending thought."[1] The same authority on Sufism comments thus on the apparent contradiction in which the Sufi, like the Hindu bhakta, sometimes finds himself involved: "While Sufis who are pantheists often use language implying belief in a personal God, such belief is by no means inconsistent with the full theory of fana, or at least may be sincerely combined with it."[2]

How far these pantheistic doctrines have permeated the Islam of India and contributed to give it a character of its own cannot be estimated with any precision. No doubt Sufi mysticism has helped to create among the more thoughtful Muslims a spirit of tolerance which is not found to the same extent elsewhere. Sufism tends to the view, which pantheism finds it easy to maintain, and which is widespread among certain classes in India at the present time, that all religions are equally true. The syncretistic Behai movement leads to a similar hospitality of opinion but it does not appear to have had much influence in India.

A much more important modern movement, which must be reckoned with in any account of Indian Islam, is that which is represented by the Ahmadiyas. This sect had its origin, and still has one of its main centres, at Qadian in the Punjab, where its founder, Mirza Ghulam Ahmad, was born in 1839. The founder claimed to be the Mahdi-Messiah who came to the world in the spirit of Jesus. Jesus, it is affirmed, died and was buried in Kashmir where his grave is shown. This Mahdi, further, leads no jihad such as orthodox Islam recognises, but carries on a spiritual warfare. The sect divided in 1914

[1] *E.R.E.*, Vol. XII, p. 16.
[2] Titus, *Indian Islam*, p. 226.

into two sections, recognised as the Qadian party and the Lahore party. The Ahmadiyas claim to have half a million followers, but it is estimated that there are in India not more than 60,000.

The chief characteristic of this movement is the energy of its propaganda, not only in India but in many other countries as well. Its efforts are directed especially against Christianity, but also against the Ārya Samāj and against the modernists within Islam. The sect aims at working " not only for the reform of Islam, but for the regeneration of the Hindus, the Muhammadans and the Christians." The attitude of orthodox Islam towards the Ahmadiyas is distinctly suspicious and even hostile. How strong this hostility is in some circles may be indicated by the fact that when in 1924 four of the missionaries of this sect were executed for heresy in Afghanistan, orthodox leaders in India telegraphed to the Amir approving of his action.

The significance of the appearance of this sect at the present time is similar to the appearance of the Rāmakrishna Mission within Hinduism. Both are concerned to rehabilitate the religion they represent, before the world, in opposition at once to the rigidity of the orthodox and to the disintegrating influences of modern unbelief. Both seek to accomplish this by a bold policy which carries the war into the enemy's camp. Just as the Rāmakrishna Mission have invaded America in force, so the Ahmadiyas have established themselves in Great Britain and in Germany. In addition to their publications in many languages the Ahmadiyas carry on educational work and have a centre for the training of their missionaries.

The most significant enterprise, however, for the advancement of education among Muslims is that which derives its original impulse from Sir Syed Ahmad Khan and which centres in the Muslim University at Aligarh. The object that Sir Syed Ahmad had before him in his educational efforts, which resulted in the opening of the Anglo-Oriental College at Aligarh in 1875, was to promote social and religious reform. He was accused of introducing a spirit of rationalism hostile to Islam and was bitterly assailed. The College, which is now a University, is producing at the present time, it would appear, not so much "units in the army of Islam's missionaries,"[1] as enemies of all religion. With this danger, not to Islam alone, which the rising spirit of secularism is creating at Aligarh and elsewhere, we shall deal in the next section of our study.

The story of Islam in India is the story of an austere and rigid faith, exposed constantly to the subtle infection of the Hinduism which surrounds it on every side. Its defences are not always strong enough against these invasive influences, and when now to them is added the destructive forces of Western science and Western culture it seems inevitable that Indian Islam shall have to submit to radical transformation. What springs of spiritual life are still flowing within the religion we must now consider, and how it is adjusting itself to these new conditions which are affecting it so profoundly.

[1] Maulana Muhammad Ali, quoted in *The Muslim World of Today*, p. 106.

CHAPTER VI

ITS RELIGIOUS VALUE TODAY

The Muslim religion has always possessed within itself certain great and permanently precious elements. Its creed, so simple and so concrete, was admirably adapted to the intelligence of the primitive tribesman, and all the more so because it could so easily become his battle-cry. Muhammad was splendidly equipped for a great but limited achievement, binding together by his faith and his inspiration into one brotherhood the scattered clans and giving them an aim that appealed all the more to them because it was narrow in its scope and such that they could lay hold of it and be laid hold of by it. Of the Prophet's faith we may say, as has been said of another Semitic leader and judge, that it

> " Filled him with valour, slung him with a sword,
> Bade him go on until the tribes around him
> Mingled his name with naming of the Lord."

It filled his followers also with the same valour and sent them forth to conquer in a name and for an end that lifted them above what was selfish and tribal. As with Israel in the days of the great prophets, so with these Arabs, faith in a single, overruling Will gave them a confidence in themselves and in their cause, and, indeed, a scorn of the idol-worshippers, that helped to put iron into their blood and fitted them both to conquer and to command. The founder of the Mogul Empire in India, Babur, himself a worthy representative of much of the best in Islam, has described in his Memoirs the spirit in which he led his army through the northern mountains for the invasion of India. What he says applies equally to many another Muslim chief who went forth to conquer. "I placed my foot," he writes, "in the stirrup of resolution and my hands on the reins of confidence in God, and I marched against the possessors of the throne of Delhi and the dominions of Hindustan."

It is a spirit and temper that makes strong, and often chivalrous, leaders, but hardly one that arms men against the subtler temptations that life brings. The qualities of simplicity and austerity are natural accompaniments of such a religion, but when these are replaced by luxury and ease, decadence and corruption soon manifest themselves. The chivalrous Babur gives place to the voluptuous Shah Jehan. We can see still the nobility and majesty of the Muslim faith in the Jami Masjid in Delhi and the Pearl Mosque in Agra. Especially, when one passes into those places of worship from a Hindu temple, one is conscious how greatly it may exalt one's soul to bow before so high and so austere a God as Allah. To the Christian Puritanism and Calvinism have their place of honour in religion as—like tragedy—means by which the soul is cleansed and exalted; and one is aware of the same cathartic influences when one stands in one of the great mosques. So also we may well be moved as we listen to the voice of the muezzin calling the worshippers to prayer and reminding them that God is and that He is great.

These are the qualities in Islam that throughout all its history have given it strength and give it strength still. These springs are still flowing within the religion, creating in not a few of its children manliness and courage and dignity. Another central quality—that, indeed, which the name Islam itself suggests and signifies—is also, like those already named, an element in it both of strength and weakness. That quality is submission to the will of Allah. The history both of Islam and of Christianity demonstrates that such an impulse—the impulse of "abandonment" to God—may create strength for action quite as often as passivity in endurance. The fatalism that so often accompanies it is not approved as a general law of conduct by orthodox Muslim theology but "is limited to the outstanding accidents of human life and especially to death."[1] Baron Carra de Vaux quotes "a wise saying" of Khalif Omar, "which well represents the point of view of sound theology." "He who is in the fire should resign himself to the will of God; but he who is not yet in the fire need not throw himself into it." It is not difficult to see how such a doctrine might make a strong nature stronger while it might well eliminate initiative in the case of those of a more ordinary sort. Sir Muhammad Iqbal cites some instances of the "strong personalities" that have been capable of rising to this experience and quotes some of the phrases in which it found expression. "'I am the creative truth' (Hullaj); 'I am destiny' (Muawiya); 'I am the speaking Quran' (Ali); 'Glory be to me' (Ba Yazid)."[2] In these utterances we see once more how a doctrine of transcendence may pass over into pantheism and how the fatalism of Islam may utter itself with the same voice as Vedāntic monism. It is evident that we have here a powerful dynamic, but its moral quality must be determined by other factors. Sir Muhammad Iqbal is evidently conscious of this limitation when he adduces as an example of this "higher fatalism," as he calls it, a saying of Napoleon, "I am a thing, not a person." This is a fatalism that, as the same able exponent of modern Islam claims, "can make a man calmly offer his prayers when bullets are showering around him," but that, as he also frankly admits, "has prevailed in the world of Islam for many centuries" in "a most degrading type." He describes this type of fatalism as due in part to "the gradually diminishing force of the life impulse which Islam originally imparted to its followers." Others would make it rather a main reason

[1] Carra de Vaux in *E.R.E.*, Vol. V, p. 794.
[2] Iqbal, *The Reconstruction of Religious Thought in Islam*, p. 153.

why that life impulse has so greatly diminished. It may be that "Eastern peoples have a psychological tendency to fatalism," as Baron Carra de Vaux thinks; it certainly is the case that in India in both Hinduism and Islam a doctrine of fate lies heavy upon the lives of the common people and drains away their vital energy. We have seen how in modern times Hindus have been striving to correct this tendency. Muslims are equally aware of the need to set their religion also free from this hindrance to progress and achievement. The sense of the futility of effort and the vanity of all human purposes that hangs like a pall over most of the life of India is thus the creation alike of the Hindu and of the Muslim religious tradition.

All of those dominating conceptions that we have noted as fundamental to Islam combine to give to the faith its dignity and authority. It has achieved great things in its past history, and, if it has fallen in recent times upon less fortunate days, that should not lead us to ignore the splendour of its past. What is perplexing its leaders today is the problem of its future. How is it to adjust itself to modern conditions? Its mosques, so rigidly austere in their worship, and its Kalimah,[1] bearing its simple and stately testimony, call men away from idols to a loftier faith. The great commonplaces of human life—its brevity and at the same time the belief in a life beyond—are written deep upon its story and remain as of the essence of its message still. What Akbar carved over the great gate of the Mosque of his capital at Fatehpur Sikri is typical of much that Islam has taught through all its varied history. "So said Jesus," the inscription runs, "on whom be peace! The world is a bridge; pass over it, but build no house there. He who hopeth for an hour may hope for eternity. The world is but an hour; spend it in devotion; the rest is unseen. . . . Thy best traffic is selling this world for the next." This sense of the vanity of things is a natural inference

[1] The Muslim Creed.

from the teaching of the inexorable divine decrees and of the duty of submission which we have seen to be so central to Islam. This, too, approaches the Hindu doctrine of illusion, but with a difference, though the difference may seem small. "The world is but an hour; spend it in devotion" is an injunction that still bids men worship. But the Vedāntic "Thou art that" sets the enlightened free from all such occupations, as it sets them free from the hopes upon which they are built.

Another principle of Islam of a different kind is a source of justifiable pride to its followers. This is the sense of brotherhood which binds together into one all its members. Even in India, where in face of the Hindu system of caste the Muslim has sometimes, Sir Muhammad Iqbal says, "out-Hindued the Hindu himself,"[1] on the whole Islamic fraternity is a real achievement. "In the mosque," says Dr. Titus, "this ideal is triumphant; the beggar, the sweeper and the prince worship side by side."[2] There is, indeed, division and strife enough among Muslims, as their leaders are ready to admit.[3] At the same time the fraternity of Islam is a reality which overrides class distinctions and racial enmities.

Those doctrines of Islam which we have surveyed make up what we may call an elemental religion. But such simple and lofty conceptions do not comprise the whole of the Muslim faith. Its most earnest and enlightened adherents see Islam in India "lost in ritual and ceremonials, fitful superstition and fanatical passion."[4] It is this and not the abolition of the Caliphate that makes them fear for its future. It may be that the loss of such a centre of loyalty to Islam as the Caliph supplied will deprive the religion in some measure of its sense of solidarity and moral unity, but those whose interest lies in the spiritual vitality of the religion are inclined rather

[1] Quoted by Dr. Titus in *Indian Islam*, p. 171.
[2] *Indian Islam*, p. 171.
[3] See S. Khuda Bukhsh, *Essays, Indian and Islamic*, p. 273.
[4] *Ibid.*, p. 273.

to rejoice that this external support has been removed so that the real springs of life within Islam may now flow more freely. They see these springs being choked by formalism and insincerity both in the case of the peasants of the villages and the educated people of the cities. The conditions of the present time are influencing both these classes, weakening their allegiance to their inherited faith.

In the case of the village Muslims their circumstances as a small minority in the midst of a multitude of Hindus have always tended to lower the vitality and conviction of their religion. This, as we have seen, is especially so with those who have passed over from Hinduism—many of them outcastes—by mass conversion. There are large numbers who have never been more than half Muslim and whom the *suddhi* movement seeks, mainly from political motives, to win back to the Hindu fold. At the same time economic causes are operating to weaken the faithfulness of many to the precepts of their faith. As a result Muslims are frequently to be found following the profession of usurer in defiance of the injunctions of the Quran. Nothing has done more in some parts of India to embitter Hindu-Muslim relations than the fact that the Muslim is so often disliked and dreaded on this account. Further, the religion of the village Muslim had, in the past at least, been tolerant, whatever the motive-cause of his tolerance. Now, however, it appears that, in the Punjab, for example, " big Maulvies come from Lahore bidding Muslims not take food or drink from Hindus, and Hindus do the same."[1] This new hostility with all its possibilities of evil is due, it is said, to the influence and example of " the educated " and to their plans for obtaining political power. Where a religion is mainly made up of formalism and superstition it is easily perverted into fanaticism. The fear of bhutas on the one hand and the fear of jinns on the other do not create in Hindu and Muslim a spirit that tolerates and understands,

[1] M. L. Darling, *Rusticus Loquitur*, p. 284.

and mischief-mongers have their opportunity. Mr. Darling, who writes with an intimate knowledge of the peasantry of the Punjab, paints the village situation as it is today in sombre colours. "Hireling shepherds there are," he writes, "who in the name of religion and in the guise of education would set one community against another and put a stop to kindly offices and courtesies that for many years have bound Hindu and Muslim together in their common village life. But of real shepherds, men fitted to guide and protect, there are few. Yet never was guidance more sorely needed. The isolation of the village is fast disappearing; the explosive modern world is at its gates."[1]

It is evident that we have here, even among the Muslim peasants of the Punjab, two new forces disturbing what we may call either the old tolerance or the old torpor. The one of these, partly, but not wholly, political in its source, calls them to come out from among the Hindus and be separate and to return to the true faith of the Prophet. The other is the disturbing influence of "the explosive modern world." Even before the day of the political maulvie there were in the Punjab and elsewhere those who sought from worthier motives than move him to rekindle in these half-Hinduised Muslims the pure light of Islam. The Wahābi movement in Eastern Bengal, of which mention has already been made, is no longer in evidence there, but it has found successors who seek similar ends though with a more tempered zeal. Such are the Ahl-i-Hadith, "the people of tradition." They seek to recall those who have gone astray from the true doctrine to the original simplicity and sincerity of the faith. It is, we cannot doubt, the influence of a succession of what may be called "revival movements" that has brought it about that in Eastern Bengal, where the great majority of the Muslims were originally converts from among the humbler classes of Hindus, the faith is

[1] Darling, *op. cit.*, p. 339.

professed and followed with much more earnestness than among similar classes elsewhere. "Their religion," writes the census officer in 1921, "is a very real thing to the cultivating Muhammadan classes, especially in Eastern Bengal. Prayers are most punctiliously said by all of them at the appointed time." In some of the more densely populated areas "the 'tin mosque' is to be met with almost every mile." "It is everyone's ambition as he gets older to see Mecca before he dies." Not only is Islam zealously practised, but it is a faith that—unlike that of similar classes elsewhere—"has been to some extent purified of taints of Hinduism."[1]

These are indications of how Islam today affects the lives and thoughts of the village people. Among them it is an Islam largely corrupted from the dignified simplicity of its origin, but still able to lay a strong grasp upon the lives of its adherents. Other corrupting influences besides Hinduism are invading, as we have seen, even these peaceful scenes and dethroning the old authorities. A census officer in 1931 quotes as significant the statement of one of his correspondents that "with the spread of political knowledge almost all new or old religious movements have been shut out."[2] Political passions can be aroused even among these multitudes that seem so apathetic and resigned. When we turn to the educated classes we find much more evidence of a ferment than among the slowly-moving village people. "The explosive modern world" is in the midst of them, creating through a complex of influences disturbance both in their outward and their inward life. And we may be sure that, as Principal Zakir Hussain says, "the painful spiritual struggle which is going on in the educated Indian's breast will not leave the peasant's hut unaffected."[3] This struggle may be said to come first

[1] *C.I.R.*, 1921, Bengal, Vol. I, p. 159.
[2] *C.I.R.*, 1931, Bihar and Orissa, Vol. I, p. 247.
[3] In *The Student World*, Vol. XXII, p. 250.

to view in the efforts for educational and religious reform of Sir Syed Ahmad Khan.

This notable personality, who was the pioneer in the reform of Indian Islam, is associated mainly with the establishment of the Muhammadan Anglo-Oriental College which, as we have seen, was opened at Aligarh in 1875. It was his deliberate purpose and endeavour to bring the forces of Western science and of rationalism to bear upon the Muslim community. He was convinced that unless they were able to ally themselves with the new culture of the West and were willing to carry through radical reform of their customs and ideas they were doomed. He had, in consequence, to face relentless opposition. "He was excommunicated, slandered, and persecuted. He was called atheist, renegade, antichrist. Men threatened to kill him."[1] Even so it is said that he was never able to proclaim openly his views on religion, so fierce was the antagonism that his efforts for reform aroused.

The character of the movement that Sir Syed inaugurated is suggested by two of the names by which it has been called. Those who belong to it have sometimes been described by their co-religionists as neo-Mutazilites and sometimes as "Necharis." The latter name is a popular corruption of the more dignified name "Naturis" and is derived from the fact that they are viewed as advocates of "Natural Religion." One of Sir Syed's phrases, we are told, was "Reason alone is a sufficient guide," and he is said to have "quoted with approval the remark of a French writer that Islam, which lays no claim to miraculous powers on the part of its Founder, is *the* truly rationalistic religion."[2] The other name relates this movement of the nineteenth and twentieth centuries to a movement within Islam in the eighth century. A reform that was based mainly on reason and on natural religion would seem to be cutting itself loose from its

[1] Farquhar, *Modern Religious Movements*, p. 93.

[2] *Ibid.*, p. 97.

heritage and its history, but as neo-Mutazilites Sir Syed Ahmad and his followers can claim, as they do, that they are seeking to recover the true Islam and to purge the religion from the corruptions of the centuries.

The early Mutazilites rebelled against the bondage that a frigid predestinarianism and the claim of authority to control reason had imposed upon the followers of Islam. "Rationalists and Utilitarians," as Mr. Amir Ali, a neo-Mutazilite of today, describes his forerunners of the eighth century, "they based the foundations of the moral law on the concordance of reason with positive revelation. They walked in the footsteps of the Master and his immediate descendants. They upheld the doctrine of Evolution in regarding every law that regulates the mutual relations of man to man as the result and outcome of a process of continuous development."[1] That account of some of the views held by these early reformers may be taken as indicating the attitude of their successors in modern times. Of these the author of *The Spirit of Islam*, Mr. Amir Ali, is one of the most notable. He claims that "with the exception of the unity of God there was no dogma upon which insistence was placed" (in the original Islam) "in any such form as to compel reason to hold back its acceptance." On questions such as that of a future existence and moral responsibility "the words of the Teacher allow the greatest latitude of judgment."[2]

These quotations give some indication of the spirit that inspires the leading figures in this modern movement who are fully aware of the inadequacy of the traditional religion and the urgent necessity that it be given a new liberty and quickened with a new life. They are fully conscious of the depths to which the Faith has fallen. "Modern Islam," writes another of this group of reformers, Mr. S. Khuda Bukhsh, "with its hierarchy of priesthood, gross fanaticism, appalling ignorance and superstitious practices, is indeed a discredit to the Islam

[1] *The Spirit of Islam*, p. 421. [2] *Ibid.*, p. 423.

of Mohammad. Instead of unity we have Islam torn into factions; instead of culture we have indifference to learning; instead of liberal-minded toleration we have gross bigotry."[1] "The ancient tyranny of custom and routine," the same writer vehemently affirms, "must give way to the new order of things." If not, then he demands that "a kindly comet should sweep the whole affair into nothingness."[2]

This new rationalism betrays no desire to cut loose from the Muslim faith with its great record through the centuries since the days of its founder. The early Mutazilites "gave an impetus to the development of national and intellectual life among the Saracens such as had never been witnessed before,"[3] and their successors look confidently for a similar intellectual efflorescence in India today. They realise, as the Hindu reformers realise, that one hindrance in the way of a renaissance of the Muslim spirit is the lethargy that a belief in Fate creates. Another that has the same consequence is the formalism and insincerity which they denounce as characterising so much of their religion. "Sin as much as you may," says Mr. Khuda Bukhsh, describing this aspect of their decadence, "a visit to the *Karbalah*[4] or blessings from a *mujtahid* would whitewash and assure a secure passage to Paradise."[5] "The responsibility for the present decadence of the Moslem nations," Mr. Syed Amir Ali declares, "must be shared by the formalism of the Asha'ri and the quietism of the Sufi. Mystical teachings like the following:

> 'The man who looks on a beggar's bowl as a kingly crown
> And the present world as a fleeting bubble,—
> He alone traverseth the ocean of Truth
> Who looks upon life as a fairy tale,—'

---

[1] *Essays, Indian and Islamic*, p. 24. [2] *Ibid.*, p. 252.
[3] Syed Amir Ali, *The Spirit of Islam*, p. 415.
[4] This is a very holy place (in Persia) and a centre of pilgrimage for Shiahs. The *mujtahids* are the authorities on Muslim religion and learning.
[5] *Essays, Indian and Islamic*, p. 264.

can have but one result—intellectual paralysis."[1] The parallel is evident between the ills that, according to this diagnosis, the Indian Muslims are suffering from and those for which, as we have already seen, enlightened Hindus also are endeavouring to find a remedy.

It is difficult to judge how far this movement, apart from such outstanding personalities as have been named, has exercised a wide influence.[2] It is probably similar in this respect to the Samāj movement in Hinduism, and it may be that, as in the case of the Samāj leaders, its appeal has been somewhat narrowly restricted in its range. The College at Aligarh which Sir Syed Ahmad laboured so assiduously to establish has, indeed, grown to a Muslim University and has accomplished much for the enlightenment of the Indian Muslims. The ideal of its founder, however, and of those who have followed in his footsteps, of allying enlightenment with faithfulness to a reformed Islam that would still be truly Islam, is scarcely being realised. The new hostility to all religion which characterises so many of the educated youth of contemporary India possesses, it appears, one of its strongholds in Aligarh. One of the leading Muslim members of the staff of the University goes so far as to declare—though the view is probably exaggerated—that the spirit of secularism prevails more widely among young Muslims than among young Hindus. The fast of Ramadan is reckoned one of the pillars of Islam but few even of the staff of the University, it appears, observe it. In such Muslim strongholds as Lahore and Peshawar those who have received a Western education are said to have become aggressively irreligious. This does not, however, have the consequence of making those who no longer

[1] *The Spirit of Islam*, pp. 472 f.

[2] Writing in 1918 Dr. Farquhar quotes Mr. Syed Amir Ali as saying that there were few indeed who were ready to follow Mr. Khuda Bukhsh then. But the liberal movement has, no doubt, advanced since that date. Farquhar's *Modern Religious Movements*, p. 100.

believe in, or practise, the religion any less fanatical in upholding it than their fathers were. "While the true spirit of our religion has departed from us," wrote Mr. Khuda Bukhsh in 1912, "we are as fanatical as ever." If that was true then it is not less true twenty years later, when political and economic rivalry feeds more than ever the flames of Hindu-Muslim hostility. This enmity is commonly accounted religious, but many causes that are remote enough from religion are at work to create it. The ferocity of the communal conflicts cannot be taken as bearing witness to depth and reality of religious conviction. In the case of the Moplah outbreak of 1921 when thousands of Hindus are said to have been slaughtered and thousands more forcibly "converted" to the Muslim faith, the judgment of careful observers is that the rising, while inflamed by Khilafatist passions and Khilafatist propaganda, was in part a rising of poor Muslim landworkers against Hindu landowners. Religion supplies the battle-cry but in many cases political and economic influences have a larger share than religion in creating the whole complex of jealousy and suspicion from which these conflicts issue. Fanaticism is often remote enough from faith.

Apart from these invasions by unbelief on the one hand and by fanaticism on the other, the general direction of the life of Islam is on the whole towards the elevation of its ethical standards. This is shown by the growing sentiment against polygamy and by the part that Muslim women are taking in the movement for the emancipation of women that is so full of promise in India at the present time. A re-interpretation of the traditional views held on such subjects as jihad—which used to be taken as meaning a holy war—polygamy, slavery, is made possible by the application of the principle of ijtihad, which may be interpreted as the right of private judgment as to what the Quran teaches. This principle must also, according to Sir Muhammad Iqbal, be "reinforced and broadened by modern philosophical ideas."[1] The laws of the Quran were meant, it is pointed out, for a very different society from that of the present time. "A social system for barbarism ought not to be imposed on a people already possessing higher forms of civilisation."[2]

Sir Muhammad Iqbal, whose opinion has been cited more than once already, is a personality of considerable importance in Muslim India and represents a point of view that deserves careful consideration. He is a poet and a thinker of much insight as well as independence, and is deeply concerned for the future of Islam both in India and throughout the world. He sees how hostile to the central idea of his religion are both "the ideas set free by European political thinking" and also much of the pantheistic teaching that has found its way into Islam through the centuries, enervating it. Dr. R. A. Nicholson has translated one of his poems (Asrar-i-Khudi) into English under the title *Secrets of the Self*, and in his introduction he gives a brief account of the poet's message for his time. The theme of the poem itself is that self-abnegation is the way to death, while the way to power is by strengthening the self.

> "Do not abandon Self! Persist therein!
> Be a drop of water and drink up the ocean."

He prays thus for his Muslim fellows:

> "Give us the sleepless eye and the passionate heart,
> Give us again the nature of quicksilver."

Dr. Nicholson summarises the position of Sir Muhammad Iqbal as follows: "He sees that Hindu intellectualism and Islamic pantheism have destroyed the capacity for action. . . . This capacity depends ultimately on the conviction that khudi (self-hood, individuality, personality) is real and not merely an illusion of the mind. . . . Iqbal therefore throws himself with all his might against

[1] Quoted in *The Moslem World of Today*, p. 192.
[2] Maulvie Chiragh Ali, quoted in *The Moslem World of Today*, p. 309.

idealistic philosophies and pseudo mystical poets, the authors, in his opinion, of the decay prevailing in Islam, and argues that only by self-affirmation, self-expression and self-development can the Moslems once more become strong and free. He appeals from the alluring raptures of Hafiz to the moral fervour of Jalaluddin Rumi, from Islam sunk in Platonic contemplation to the fresh and vigorous monotheism which inspired Mohammed and brought Islam into existence."[1]

But not only is he an enemy of all "opium-eating";[2] he also sees the danger to Islam of a shallow acceptance of Western culture. The new education that the Muslim youth are obtaining from the West contents him as little as the old dead orthodoxy does. He has expressed himself with some violence in a verse which Dr. S. K. Datta quotes in his *Asiatic Asia*:

> "The father's at his pulpit, the son is in his school.
> The one is childish old, the other's spent in youth.
> Ye Muslims, I lament the curse of science and of art,
> For evil is cheap among us and good is hard to find.
> Revolution! Revolution! Revolution!"[3]

Sir Muhammad Iqbal's attitude to European culture is not really hostile. He himself is deeply indebted to its poetry and its philosophy. What he fears is that its "dazzling exterior" may fascinate the young Muslim and that he "may fail to reach its true inwardness."[4] He would use "the freedom of ijtihad" to rid Islam of fatalism and to recover its lost vigour. He would "tear off from Islam the hard crust which has immobilised an essentially dynamic outlook on life, and rediscover the original verities of freedom, equality and solidarity with a view to rebuild our moral, social and political ideals out of their original simplicity and universality."[5]

[1] *The Secrets of the Self*, by Sheikh Muhammad Iqbal. Translated by R. A. Nicholson, p. xiii.
[2] *Ibid.*, p. xxiii.
[3] *Asiatic Asia*, p. 180.
[4] *The Reconstruction of Religious Thought in Islam*, p. 9.
[5] *Ibid.*, p. 219.

This is an ambitious programme and demands a more powerful and enlightened leadership than Indian Islam as yet possesses. It will be all the more difficult to realise for the reason that Iqbal is too true a Muslim to range himself with the popular nationalism of the day. "It seems to me," he writes, "that God is slowly bringing home to us the truth that Islam is neither Nationalism nor Imperialism but a League of Nations which recognises artificial boundaries and racial distinctions for facility of reference only and not for restricting the social horizon of its members."[1] This puts him out of tune with Indian nationalism. What he aims at is a Muslim India within India, so that the principle of Islamic solidarity may be maintained through a league of Muslim nations. "The problem of India," he says, "is international, not national."

What influence Sir Muhammad actually exercises in India it is difficult to estimate. When his Asrar-i-Khudi appeared in 1914 Dr. Nicholson tells us, "It took by storm the young generation of Indian Muslims." His opposition to the idea of nationalism, however, shows him to be, as has been said of him, if "a man in advance of his age," at any rate, "a man in disagreement with his age." The realisation of his ideals will involve in Dr. Nicholson's opinion "a radical change in the Moslem mind."[2]

It is equally difficult to estimate the influence that is exerted upon Indian Islam by the Ahmadiyas. This influence is, of course, of a much more superficial character and for that reason produces results that are more obvious and wider in their range. The Ahmadiyas occupy a middle position between the rationalist reformers and the orthodox. Though orthodoxy bans them as rigorously as it does rationalism they may be said to have furnished in recent years the spearhead of Muslim propaganda. They occupy themselves mainly with an aggressive defence of Islam which takes the form frequently of an unrestrained

[1] *The Reconstruction of Religious Thought in Islam*, p. 223.
[2] *The Secrets of the Self*, p. xxxi.

attack upon Christianity. The general lines that their defence of Islam follows may be indicated by the fact that it claims that Islam is a religion of peace and toleration and that Muhammad was an apostle of peace. At the same time the purdah is defended as well as Muslim laws on divorce and polygamy. The fact that Christianity becomes almost inevitably the standard by which the religion is measured results in their describing the Quran as the Gospel of the Muslim and Muhammad as "the ideal Prophet." It is evident that, just as the educated Indian feels the necessity of moralising the Vedānta, so the educated Muslim is aware of the need of higher ethical standards within Islam. But while, to this end, the Hindu pantheist is ready to recognise Christian ideals and seeks to absorb them, the Muslim monotheist must remain, it would seem, a rival and an enemy.

An observer in Cairo writes in reference to the Ahmadiya movement, "It captures few Muslims with its propaganda outside India; the normal step for the critic is from orthodoxy to agnosticism and secularism." That is the normal step in India too. The fact that this is so serves to unite to a certain extent the aims of such modernising Muslims as Sir Syed Ahmad and Sir Muhammad Iqbal with those of conservatives of what may be called the Wahābi attitude of mind. Both, as Professor Gibb points out, "reject the accumulation of mediæval teachings which threatened to stifle the life of Islam and preach a return to the doctrines of the primitive community."[1] This agreement, however, is obviously quite unreal, and likely to prove very temporary. Will it avail to deliver the religion from the dangers that manifestly threaten it from the invasive forces of agnosticism and secularism? How formidable this invasion is and what effects it is producing one who stands outside of Islam can hardly estimate.

Principal Zakir Hussain of Delhi has described in

[1] *Whither Islam?* p. 372.

moving terms " the tremendous struggle " between faith and unbelief that he is aware of in the soul of educated India. He sees as the most active cause in bringing about irreligiousness religion itself—" the rigidity of religious dogma, the insistence on soulless formulæ, and hypocritical observance of forms that have lost their true meaning and significance." Writing of the educated Muslim, as one who knows him intimately, he tells us of " the bitterness of his soul " " and the tears of indignation that flow inwardly and scorch his being." Recognising, as Dr. Hussain does, the evils with which Islam has been identified and which orthodoxy still upholds, he and such as he believe, nevertheless, that the vital spirit of the faith can survive and adjust itself to the conditions of the modern world. " The spirit of the faith," he says, " that made out of barbarians civilised men, out of disbelievers believers, that gave to woman a status in a society where she had none, that set aside all distinction of caste and race and birth and recognised only an aristocracy of character in a brotherhood of men, that Islam shall remain and shall contribute its share to the future faith of men."[1]

[1] These passages are taken from Principal Zakir Hussain's article on " The Situation in India from the point of view of Islam," in *The Student World*, Vol. XXII, pp. 248 ff.

PART III

THE RELIGION OF THE JAINAS

CHAPTER VII

ITS HISTORY AND GENERAL CHARACTERISTICS

The religion of the Jainas does not derive its name—as in the case of Hinduism and Sikhism—from the people who profess it, nor—as in the case of the three other religions dealt with in this book—from the name of its founder. The word Jaina is derived from Jina (the conqueror) which is a title given, indeed, to Mahāvīra, the reputed founder of the religion, but shared by him with twenty-three other "Tīrthakaras," of whom, in the records of their mythology, he is the last. The Jainas are, accordingly, the followers of Mahāvīra, known as "the Jina" *par excellence*, but they are the followers as well of the others who belong to the succession of great, emancipated beings whom this religion venerates. Another name given in early times to this sect, but now no longer used, was the Nirgranthas, those "free from fetters," a word with a similar significance to the word Jina.

These names indicate that the central fact in this religion, governing its discipline and prescribing its goal, is the quest for deliverance from rebirth. The evidence would seem to indicate that in the period which we may call that of the early Upanishads, that is, the period centring round the sixth century before Christ, the quest for this deliverance absorbed the attention of many among the religious classes and often impelled them to adopt the life of the wandering ascetic. These mendicants in a large number of cases, then as now, must have been no better than idle beggars and charlatans. We know, indeed, of one such, named Gosāla, whose followers were called Ājīvikas, and who, according to both Buddhist and Jaina accounts, was a man of disreputable character. The anarchy that reigned among these professed seekers for emancipation and the confusion and contradiction in much of their beliefs and their discipline may well have been one of the causes that impelled some "men of commanding personality," such as Mahāvīra and Buddha, to organise them and direct their efforts towards a definite goal in accordance with a definite discipline. Another cause that was at work also would seem to have been resentment against the claims made by the Brāhmans that they alone possessed knowledge and could attain to moksha or deliverance. Thus both Jainism and Buddhism are unmistakably movements of revolt against Brāhman dominance. Jainism does not, however, represent—to the extent to which Buddhism does—a revolt against the Brāhman tradition either of the means to be employed or of the end to be sought. Nor were the Jainas or Nirgranthas apparently a new sect. They claim a long history before the days of Mahāvīra, who seems to have been an elder contemporary of Buddha. This teacher, the only one of their Tīrthakaras of whom we have definite knowledge, may be reckoned—along with Pārśva, who precedes him in this line and looms from the shadows as also a historical personage—to have, as far as can be judged, established, and given definite form to, a doctrine that was already very ancient. Thus the religion of the Jainas, while hostile to Brāhmanism, had then and has today, a very close relation with a tradition which, while it has always been much more comprehensive and more widely followed, cannot claim to be of greater antiquity.

The date of Mahāvīra, the last of the twenty-four Tīrthakaras, has been a subject of considerable debate. It would appear, however, to be now established that he was an elder contemporary of Buddha and is referred to in the Buddhist canonical books as Nataputta. He was a Kshatriya of the Jñāta or Jñātri clan and the name given to him by his parents was Vardhamāna. The fact that he was not a Brāhman is emphasised in the legend of his birth, and it seems fair to conjecture that at this time there was in Videha—the district in which he was born and died (just as there seems to have been in the contiguous district of Magadha where Buddha lived and taught)—a reaction against the priestly pretensions of the Brāhmans. This whole region, which corresponds to the modern Bihar, lies east of the centre where at that period Brāhmanism was most strongly established, Kurukshetra. Some scholars would indeed go further and maintain that even the brahman doctrine was the product of a Kshatriya revolt against Brāhman ritualism. It would certainly appear as though in the easterly provinces a new freedom of thought and a dissatisfaction with inherited solutions were agitating many minds. The tradition tells us that Mahāvīra attained Nirvāna in 527 B.C. at the age of seventy-two. Professor Jacobi, who writes with special authority on matters relating to Jainism, concludes that he died some years before Buddha, probably about 480 B.C.[1] It is not possible in the case of these two great figures to determine with certainty the exact year in which either died.

Mahāvīra's parents are said to have been followers of the sect of Pārśva, the Tīrthakara immediately preceding Mahāvīra, but actually, according to Jaina chronology, preceding him by two hundred and fifty years. At the age of thirty years he abandoned the duties of a householder and became an ascetic. Twelve years were spent in meditation and austerities. What through this discipline he then attained is thus described: "In a squatting position, with joined heels, exposing himself to the heat of the sun, with the knees high and the head low, in deep meditation, in the midst of abstract meditation, he reached

[1] *E.R.E.*, Vol. VII, p. 467. Dr. Jarl Charpentier places his death "ten, if not fifteen, years" after that of Buddha, namely in 468 B.C *C.H.I.*, Vol. I, p. 163. Professor Jacobi seems to have inclined to this view when he published his edition of the *Kalpasūtra* in 1879.

Nirvāna,[1] the complete and full, the unobstructed, unimpeded, infinite and supreme, best knowledge and intuition, called *kevala* (total). When the Venerable One had become an Arhat and Jina he was a kevalin, omniscient and comprehending all objects. He knew all conditions of the world, of gods, men and demons; whence they come, where they go, whether they are born as men or animals, or become gods or hell-beings; their food, drink, doings, desires, open and secret deeds, their conversation and gossip, and the thoughts of their minds; he saw and knew all conditions in the whole world of living beings."[2]

Though he is said then to have reached Nirvāna, he did not cease to live upon earth, according to the tale, but spent thirty more years instructing his followers until his final entrance into Nirvāna was accomplished. It was during these years of wandering and of teaching that he encountered Gosāla, who for a time attached himself to him. Later, however, the disreputable character of Gosāla's life and teaching brought the two teachers and their followers into sharp conflict. There was a similar antagonism—due to very different causes—between the followers of Mahāvīra and of Buddha. Though certain resemblances between the two doctrines caused scholars at one time to suppose that Jainism was an offshoot from Buddhism, it is now clear not only that they are wholly independent of each other in their history but that they are in fundamental contradiction to each other in some important respects. They agree in their monastic character and in their hostility to Brāhman claims. Both may be described as atheistic and both face toward the goal of Nirvāna. But in their teaching in regard to the soul, in regard to the way of deliverance, and in regard to the final goal itself the two religions are fundamentally at variance.

[1] "Not the final Nirvāna which is reached at the dissolution of the body, but that state which the orthodox philosophers call jivanmukti." (Note by Jacobi.)

[2] *Āchārānga Sūtra*, I, 15. *S.B.E.*, Vol. XXII, pp. 201 f.

Mahāvīra's relation to the tradition that came down from the twenty-third Tīrthakara, Pārśva, is indicated in one of the Jaina scriptures. There an adept of the older school maintains that between them there is no difference of any significance. "The two laws seek the same end. That of Pārśva prescribes four great vows and permits the use of clothing, while that of Mahāvīra adds a fifth rule and requires nudity."[1] The fifth rule was that of chastity. By this addition Mahāvīra, it is supposed, merely made explicit a requirement that had previously been taken for granted. Thus the two laws were really one and Mahāvīra was no innovator. That the addition of these two regulations to the inherited discipline was all that Mahāvīra accomplished for Jainism need not be supposed. From the specific requirement of nudity and chastity by the Prophet we may conclude that he called the members of the order to a stricter ascetic life. He was a reformer who set his stamp so deeply upon the Jaina Church that it is to him especially that all the later ages look back as their most notable teacher and example and the last of the Tīrthakaras.

The history of the Jainas for the centuries up to the Christian era consists of little more than the names of those who are supposed to have been their religious leaders. One of the most notable of these was Bhadrabahu, by whose influence according to Jaina tradition, the Maurya emperor, Chandragupta, shortly before his death became a Jaina ascetic and abdicated the throne. This tale is not generally accepted as true but there is evidence that the Jainas while sometimes persecuted, at other times exercised great influence. The fact that they are mentioned in one of Asoka's edicts indicates that their importance at that time was recognised. In the first century of the Christian era, however, there occurred a schism among them which resulted in the establishment of two rival orders which remain until the present time. Their names

[1] See *S.B.E.*, Vol. XLV, Introduction, p. xxi.

indicate that which chiefly distinguishes them from each other. The one section is called Śvetāmbara or "clothed in white," the other Digambara or "clothed with the sky," that is to say, unclothed. There is a legend as to the causes that brought about this division, but it seems probable that the difference in practice was an old one and represents two traditions, that of Pārśva and that of Mahāvīra, which only in the first century of the Christian era came to an actual rupture. The one section remained faithful to the primitive teaching of Pārśva; the other adopted the more stringent discipline of Mahāvīra and refused to wear any clothing. The differences between them in belief are said to be of little consequence.

Two matters on which the two sections differ deserve to be noted. The Digambaras maintain that no woman can attain Nirvāna. They also reject the books that the Śvetāmbaras recognise as canonical and maintain that the canonical scriptures were lost some centuries after the death of Mahāvīra.[1] The Digambaras are found mainly in the south of India, and in the view of some the difference in regard to clothing may be due to a difference in practice between those living in the south and those living in the colder north.

There is little to record in secular history of the achievements of the Jainas. The religion has few followers today in the province of Bihar where it had its headquarters in the days of Mahāvīra. The Jainas in the east of India are mostly immigrants from west and central India. One of their ancient sacred places is, however, in the hill of Pārasnāth in Chota Nagpur. The hill gets its name from Pārśva. Before the beginning of the Christian era Jainism had spread westwards to Mathura. Thence its influence extended to Rajputana and to Gujarat and in these two regions it has at the present day a large proportion of its

[1] "The date of the collection, or, perhaps more correctly, the composition of the Jaina canon would fall somewhere about the end of the fourth or the beginning of the third century B.C." H. Jacobi in *S.B.E.*, Vol. XXII, p. xliii.

followers. At Mount Abu in Rajputana one of the chief centres of its worship, notable for the splendour of its marble temples, was established in the eleventh century A.D. For five hundred years, up till the twelfth century A.D. the Jaina religion would appear to have been strongly established in southern India and to have come under the patronage of many kings. The conversion from Jainism of the Hoyshala king—who on his conversion took the name Vishnuvardhana—along with many of his people, early in the twelfth century, through the influence of Rāmānuja, may be taken as marking the beginning of the decline of the Jaina ascendancy in this region. It was, however, the growing strength of Śaivism that finally overcame it and caused it to disappear almost entirely from that region. There is evidence that even in Gujarat the Jainas suffered " a merciless persecution " under the rule of a Śaiva king of that province.[1]

As the reaction towards the Brāhmanical tradition and against Buddhism and Jainism asserted itself in the early centuries of the Christian era it was Buddhism, as the more irreconcilable enemy, that suffered most. Jainism had never wholly broken with Brāhmanism and was able to come to an accommodation with the claims of that capacious and adaptable system. " We find," writes Mr. Rice in an account of the Mysore State, " Jina described in 1151 as the Universal Spirit who is Śiva."[2] Such friendly relationship with Hinduism has continued until the present day. Thus among the members of the Bania caste, of which some sections follow Hindu and some Jaina practice, there is freedom of intermarriage whatever the form of religion professed. This illustrates the close affinity that has always been recognised to exist between Jainism and the main stock of Hinduism. It is less easy, however, for friendly relations to be maintained with

[1] *Archæol. S.W.I.*, Vol. IX, p. 16 (quoted in Vincent Smith, *Early History of India*, p. 191, note).
[2] *E.R.E.*, Vol. IX, p. 67.

Saivites, among whom the practice of animal sacrifice is common, than with Vaishnavites who are almost as careful of animal life as the Jainas themselves.

One reason why the Jainas are scattered so widely over India is that, almost as a necessary consequence of their strict views in regard to the taking of life, they have adopted the profession of merchants and especially that of money-lenders and bankers. They have by these means obtained great wealth and often exercise, no doubt largely because of their wealth, great influence. " If anyone doubts the influence [of Jainism]," writes Mrs. Sinclair Stevenson, " he has only to count up the number of edicts prohibiting the slaying of animals on Jaina sacred days that have recently been issued by the rulers of independent states."[1]

The Jainas in India, according to the census of 1931, numbered 1,205,235. This shows an increase of 2 per cent upon the total of the census of 1921. This is the lowest rate of increase of any religious community in India during the period, but the fact that Jainas are not always distinguished from Hindus makes these figures somewhat ambiguous. The total Hindu population according to the census returns shows an increase during the decade of 10 per cent. " The Jain Church," writes Dr. Jarl Charpentier, " has never had a very great number of adherents; it has never attempted—at least on any grand scale—to preach its doctrines through missionaries outside India. Never rising to an overpowering height, but at the same time never sharing the fate of its rival, Buddhism, that of complete extinction in its native land, it has led a quiet existence through the centuries and has kept its place among the religious systems of India till the present day, thanks to its excellent organisation and to its scrupulous care for the preservation of ancient customs, institutions and doctrine."[2]

[1] Mrs. Sinclair Stevenson, *Heart of Jainism*, p. 19.
[2] *C.H.I.*, Vol. I, pp. 169 f.

CHAPTER VIII

ITS DOCTRINE

Some scholars have hesitated to describe Jainism as a religion. It is certainly not a sect of Hinduism, for it has flowed alongside of that religious tradition, close to it but apart from it, all through the centuries. A designation that is sometimes made use of is that of the Jaina Church. That may serve to suggest the general character of the Jaina organisation. As with Buddhism, so here, the primary essential is the Sangha or community. This gathers around the four orders or tīrtha, monks, nuns, laymen and laywomen. (The Digambara Jainas, however, exclude women from their order.) The wandering monk, *sramana*, is expected to fulfil the whole duty of the Jaina and to strive to attain the supreme goal of moksha. He accordingly forms the centre of the system and sets the standard of life and of belief which the general body of the community seek in their measure to attain to. But what the practice of the community is issues from the doctrine, the body of beliefs upon which that practice rests, and to these doctrines we must first turn our attention.

The doctrines of the religion consist in large measure of certain primary principles which Jainism and, to a certain extent, Buddhism share with Brāhmanism, and which belong to what we may call the Hindu tradition.

Even Buddhism was not, of course, a wholly new religious discovery; but it was a new beginning, a structure built, on old foundations, but essentially the creation of its Founder's insight and inspiration. But the Prophet of Jainism stands on a lower plane. The religion may have owed much to Mahāvīra's personality, but what he achieved by his prophetic ministry was no more than the deepening and strengthening of a tradition that had come down from dim ages of antiquity and that he passed on, in its main characteristics unchanged. As an assertion of the rights in religion of those who were not of the priestly caste it probably represents a movement of reform, but even in this respect it is no revolution, and Brāhman teaching and Brāhman leadership in worship continued to be accepted within Jainism. In this religion we find a reassertion of the ideas implicit within Hinduism at its animistic levels, before as yet the speculations of the rishis had lifted it beyond the reach of the plain man. The soul, jīva—vital force—is the fact around which the religion centres and this is something belief in which has come down by direct inheritance to the Jainas from their primitive ancestors. According to their traditional faith almost everything that exists possesses a jīva—plants, fire, wind, water. Even particles of earth have "earth-lives." This conception—linked up with that karma rebirth doctrine which was probably obtained from the Hinduism of the higher level—constitutes the fundamental stuff of the Jaina religion though much ingenuity has been spent upon its elaboration in various directions.

"An account of the Jain absurdities in the way of speculation," Professor Hopkins writes, "would indeed give some idea of their intellectual frailty but . . . such an account has but little to do with their religion."[1] It is impossible not to agree with this judgment. The elaboration of their classification of physical and mental states and attitudes does a certain amount of credit to their ingenuity but has very little relation to the facts either of human intelligence or of religious experience. Thus we are told that "the inflow of karma into the constitution of the jīva can be classified into fifty-seven modes or types." The Jaina theologians from whom these words are quoted

[1] *Religions of India*, p. 285.

proceed with their exposition as follows: "A jīva desirous of salvation from the thraldom of the senses must make strenuous efforts to gradually stop the influx of fresh matter foreign to the soul. For it is these karma particles getting into the constitution of the jīva that blind its vision into the metaphysics of things and thereby prevent its right knowledge without which right conduct is held to be impossible."[1] This passage indicates the characteristic Jaina approach to metaphysical and moral problems. The teaching of its theologians is in large measure at the hylo-zoic level and need not therefore be considered here in any detail. A large part of its interest lies in the fact that so much of it is made up of vestigial remnants from the thought of primitive people. Its main principles alone and not the fantastic elaboration of them create the type of religious life and moral effort with which we are here mainly concerned. It is these things in Jainism that have kept it alive through the centuries and make it live still, especially its conception of the goal of life and the means by which that goal may be reached.

"As the vast ocean," said Buddha, "is impregnated with one flavour, the flavour of salt, so also this law and discipline is impregnated with but one flavour, with the taste of deliverance." This could be said not only of Buddhism but of Jainism and the religion of the Upanishads. In the time of Buddha and Mahāvīra very many thinking people—and that description would seem to mean, people who believed in the laws of karma and repeated birth—were apparently possessed by the desire to escape from what they had come to view as an intolerable bondage. Thus the religions that are Hindu or have Hindu affinities are in the main roads to deliverance, that is to moksha or Nirvāna. The means they prescribe differ, as do also the conceptions held as to the migrating subject and the character of the goal they hope to reach, but all of them draw upon a single reservoir of con-

[1] P. C. Nahar and K. Ghosh, *An Epitome of Jainism*, p. 583.

ceptions for the framework within which is set their scheme of salvation.

The differences that separate these religions from one another may be illustrated by a comparison of the Vedāntic doctrine of the Ātman and the Jaina doctrine of the jīva. The two words equally signify the soul, but the more elementary view of what the soul is that the Jainas hold is indicated by the word they use for it, a word which means "life." Further, these jīvas are infinite in number and are "beings individually embodied,"[1] not, as the Vedānta teaches, a single universal Soul. The Buddhists again deny the existence of any ātman, the individual being simply the union together of the five "Khandas" (the body, feeling, perception, the aggregates, and consciousness) which are united into one in the same way as the parts of a chariot make up the chariot. But whatever the basal character of the soul may be reckoned to be, all three are in agreement in holding that individuality journeys on endlessly from body to body with much weariness and suffering. How is an end ever to be reached? That is the question that absorbs them all alike.

The Jaina teaching answers this question by calling upon each one who is concerned to reach the goal of deliverance from this life of repeated sorrow to take up the life of the ascetic monk or nun. "Knowledge," says Professor Hopkins in a sentence that is epigrammatic but—as epigrams are apt to be—too exclusive to be accurate, "is wisdom to the Brāhman; asceticism is wisdom to the Jain; purity and love is the first wisdom to the Buddhist."[2] As a matter of fact ascetic practice was not, of course, by any means limited to the Jaina monks. All the three schools that we have been now comparing made use of it for the purpose that they all alike have set before themselves, but to the Jaina it is central in its significance and they have elaborated its

[1] *Āchārānga Sūtra* in *S.B.E.*, Vol. XXII, p. 3. [2] *Op. cit.*, p. 306.

requirements with an extravagance that is due to its being reckoned so important and also to the conceptions upon which their conviction of its importance rests. The Jaina ascetic discipline will, however, be considered later. We are concerned here with the view that Jainism teaches of the bondage in which the jīvas are held. It is karma which not only determines the kind of birth the jīva shall undergo but causes it to be reborn. When, therefore, the karma is exhausted deliverance is attained. To the Buddhist the impelling force that produces rebirth is craving, desire. Thus there is a conflict in this matter between the Buddhist and the Jaina, the one setting before himself as his ideal extinction of desire, the other extinction or exhaustion of karma. Buddha is recorded in the Majjhima Nikaya as enquiring from the Jainas (or Nirgranthas) whether their theory is "that by the extinction of old karmas through penance and by the non-performance of new karmas there is no outflow in the future"[1] and so moksha is attained. So the Jaina *Uttarādhyayana* says that "karman is the root of birth and death, and birth and death they call misery."[2]

Karma according to the Jainas, Professor Jacobi tells us, "consists of extremely subtle matter which pours or infiltrates into the soul, when worldly actions make as it were an opening into it." To these openings into the soul or *āsravas* and the material character of this whole conception reference has already been made. Buddhism accepts the word but re-interprets it in a higher sense, so that to it these "openings" are sensual desire, desire for existence, and ignorance. By the Jaina karma is conceived as consisting of atoms[3] "which fill the soul as sand fills a bag and act on it like a weight." The soul by itself has an upward gravity and is kept down during its worldly state by the karma-matter, which, like all matter, has a downward gravity. Therefore, if cleansed

[1] *Majjh*, ii. 214. [2] *S.B.E.*, Vol. XLV, p. 185.
[3] See *Uttarādhyayana*, XXXIII. 17 f. *S.B.E.*, Vol. XLV, p. 194.

of all karma, the soul, on leaving the body, will rise in a straight line to the top of the universe where the liberated souls abide forever."[1] In the words of the *Uttarādhyayana* the released soul " takes the form of a straight line, goes in one moment, without touching anything and taking up no space (upwards to the highest Ākāśa) and there develops into its natural form, obtains perfection, enlightenment, deliverance and final beatitude and puts an end to all misery." [2]

The stoppage of the inflow of new karma (samvara) and the dissipation of already existing karma (nirjarā) are two necessary means to the attainment of liberation. Materialistic as is so much of the framework of these conceptions the process by which these ends are achieved is highly ethical in its character. " The whole apparatus of monastic conduct is required to prevent the formation of new karma; the same purpose is served by austerities (tapas) which, moreover, annihilate the old karma more speedily than would happen in the common course of things." [3] " Experience has taught us," write two Jaina scholars, " that the karmic seeds—the root evolvent of miseries—could be burned up into naught in the glow of austerities (tapas).[4] Just as the fire consumes the combustible so do the tapas-austerities burn up the karma-bija of the jīva and set him free from the turmoil of samsāra." [5]

Thus Jainism prescribes the attainment of salvation by works and is opposed to the doctrine of inaction which follows from the Vedāntic doctrine of karma. " Exertion" (virya) is part of the monk's duty, but it must be right exertion. " Carelessness is called (the cause of) karma, carefulness that of the contrary (viz. absence of karma); when the one or the other is predicted (of a man he is

[1] Jacobi in *E.R.E.*, IV, p. 484.
[2] *Uttarādhyayana*, XXIX, 73. *S.B.F.*, Vol. XLV, p. 173.
[3] Jacobi in *E.R.E.*, Vol. VII, p. 470.
[4] *I.e.* heat.
[5] Nahar and Ghosh, *op. cit.*, p. 588.

called) either a fool or a wise man."[1] While the actions *par excellence* of the Jaina monk that bear him towards moksha are his austerities these must be undertaken in the right way and with the right intention. Many of the ascetic practices of other sects are "austerities of fools." By this would seem to be meant the magic practices by which, as the Brāhmanical legends tell, the ancient rishis obtained supernatural powers and inspired terror by their curses. The Jaina austerities, whether those distinguished as external or as internal, are of a higher class than these and are directed solely to the destruction of karma with a view to the liberation of the soul. Material and moral conceptions lie side by side in their exposition of their doctrine and seem scarcely distinguished from each other. Thus even modern exponents of Jainism describe "the crystallised particles of the soul's past experiences and unfulfilled desires, etc." as forming a subtle body which, at death, remains and "forms the very germ of physical life in future."[2]

Professor Jacobi is of opinion that this doctrine of release bears evidence of its primitive character and he adduces this as one of his arguments for the superior antiquity of Jainism to Buddhism. He believes the Jaina karma theory to be "a later developed metaphysical doctrine which was grafted on an originally religious system based on animistic notions and intent on sparing all living beings."[3] The duty of ahimsa, that is, of avoiding the taking of any life, is at the base alike of the theology and of the ethics of Jainism and its consequences in conduct will be considered later. It does not, however, take its rise from motives of compassion, but assumes that character in its later development in Jainism, as well as in its formulation as a principle of conduct in Buddhism. It is older as a metaphysical than as a moral principle

[1] *Sūtrakritānga*, I, 8. *S.B.E.*, Vol. XLV, p. 297.
[2] Nahar and Ghosh, *op. cit.*, p. 316 f.
[3] Jacobi in *E.R.E.*, Vol. VII, p. 472.

and as such is more fundamental in the religion than any other conception.

In the development of its metaphysics the religion seems to be mainly indebted to the Sāmkhyan philosophical tradition, whereas it takes from the system of Yoga much that reappears in the discipline and the ethics of its orders. These must, at the period when Jainism took form as an articulated doctrine, have been as yet little more than groups of unorganised speculations. The basal conceptions of the Sāmkhya, which are also maintained by the Jaina teaching, are, on the one hand, the reality of the material world (prakriti) and, on the other, of an infinite number, of individual souls, spiritual monads (purūsha). There are, however, some significant differences between the two systems. Thus, to take a single example, the purūsha of Sāmkhya philosophy is an inert spectator of matter, whereas the jīva of Jainism is itself active. The Sāmkhya and the Yoga both, however, agree with Jainism that the relation of soul with matter brings bondage and that emancipation comes when the soul is separated from its material bondage. The contribution of Yoga to Jainism lies in its system of ascetic contemplation by means of which the soul may be set free from its bonds. On the side of dhyāna (contemplation) and tapas[1] Jainism would seem to be indebted to the body of doctrine which is covered by the name Yoga. It seems highly probable that instead of holding that Jainism (and Buddhism likewise) is directly indebted to these two systems, we should rather maintain that the four currents of thought—Jainism, Buddhism, Sāmkhya and Yoga—developed simultaneously and made use of ideas and experiences which were the common property of the religious and philosophic teachers of that early age.

The Sāmkhya system is one in which a God is super-

[1] "This word (tapas) signified in the first instance 'warmth,' 'heat,' 'fervour' in the literal sense; then 'the sweat generated by self-mortification' and 'the condition of internal heat thus caused' *i.e.* 'ecstasy.'" Garbe in *E.R.E.*, Vol. XII, p. 833 (Yoga).

fluous, while Yoga, on the other hand, is usually represented as theistic. In the case of Jainism, as in the case of Buddhism, it is necessary to define what is meant by the terms used before one determines whether or not it is to be described as atheistic. It recognises gods and it recognises beings greater than the gods, and yet at the same time it quite definitely denies the existence of a supreme deity. " Those who on arguments of their own maintain that the world has been created do not know the truth. Nor will the world ever perish."[1] Just as with Buddhism and with Vedāntic Hinduism, the gods of the popular worship continue to have a place assigned to them in the scheme of things. They are beings that, like men and other living creatures, are in a state of transmigration. They have to submit to 400,000 successive rebirths, but all of these in the form of divine beings. Men, on the other hand, may be reborn, 1,000,000 times, and of these not more than eight births are in human form.[2] None of the gods are eternal, and to attain to moksha or Nirvāna, it is necessary to be born as man, for only from the human plane is such escape possible. Further, the gods can give no help to those who are seeking deliverance. What Professor Jacobi says on this subject may be quoted. He is describing the veneration of " the Jinas," and he goes on, " Prayers are addressed to them by the faithful, just as if they did, or would, bestow happiness or bliss on the devout adorer; but, of course, a Jina cannot show favour to anybody, as he is utterly indifferent to all that belongs to the world, and is entirely free from all emotions. He, therefore, does not reward the adorers or satisfy their wishes, but in his stead the gods who watch and control true discipline (śāsanādhishtayika devatās) hear their prayers; for the practice of the discipline taught by the Jinas is the best mode of worshipping them. In the case of spiritual gifts

[1] *Sūtrakritānga*, I, i. 3. *S.B.E.*, Vol. XLV, p. 245.
[2] Guérinot, *La Religion Djaina*, pp. 197, 204.

vouchsafed to the worshipper, the explanation given comes to this: the adoration of the Jina purifies and sanctifies the soul of the worshipper through his meditating on the perfection of the Jinas. In this sense the Jinas are regarded as the highest deity (parama devatā); temples are erected for their worship, and a kind of divine service is instituted in them on the model of that practised in Hindu temples."[1]

This worship is not conducted by Jainas but by Brāhmans. The Jaina community, in the words of M. de Guérinot, is "a Church without priests." The monks of the Jaina order keep jealously to themselves the teaching of the doctrine, but the cultus may be performed by the Jaina layman. The *pujaris* or performers of temple worship must in the case of the Digambara sect be Jainas, but the Śvetāmbaras allow Brāhmans and other Hindus to discharge this function for them. The daily ceremonial service of the images of the Tīrthakaras is performed in a similar fashion to that in which this service is rendered in Hindu temples to the Hindu gods.

But for the Jaina religion is not primarily the performance of such acts of worship. "To possess the faith, the true faith, is to believe in the Law revealed by the Tīrthakaras or prophets and taught each day by the authorised instructors. Thus may one understand the principles of the religion, know what is the nature of the soul and of material things, become aware of that in which merit and demerit consist."[2] His creed may be said to consist in the repetition of this formula of worship:

Reverence to the Arahantas (the enlightened ones),
Reverence to the Siddhas (the perfect ones),
Reverence to the Acharyās,
Reverence to the Upadhyayas,
Reverence to all the Sādhus (saints) of the universe!

[1] *E.R.E.*, Vol. II, p. 187 (Atheism).
[2] Guérinot, *op. cit.*, p. 96.

The first group in this catalogue of "The Five great ones" are emancipated souls, the great prophets, and next after them come those who have attained. To the remaining three groups belong those who, while still upon earth and among men, teach the doctrine and the discipline and who practise the ascetic life. To these the Jaina gives his veneration, but of all these he gives it especially to the Prophets, the Tīrthakaras, the twenty-four great personalities who, coming to earth in human form, established the Faith, and, having done so, each "cut asunder the ties of birth, old age and death; became a Siddha, a Buddha, a maker of the end to all misery, finally liberated, free from all pain."[1]

Many Jainas, however, it would appear, deny that they are atheists. They "believe in a God after their own way of thinking," but they "are not dependent on any almighty ruler for their being or beatitude here or hereafter." "We worship the Tīrthakara," two modern expositors of Jainism write, "the pure and perfect souls, merely for the sake of their purity and perfection, but not for the expectation of any reward in return." By following them as they dissipate their karma, "we shall be able," they go on, "to raise ourselves from the mire of the world and to attain to Nirvāna."[2] It may be doubted if the ordinary Jaina worshipper realises that the Tīrthakaras to whom he renders his worship occupy a position in regard to him so wholly detached and disinterested. Just as, in the case of Buddhism, the Buddha comes to be recognised as "the god beyond the gods" (devātideva), so also, as we have seen, the Jina is regarded as the highest deity (parama devatā) and is worshipped accordingly. The real ultimate, however, in the case of the Jaina, as of the Buddhist, is Nirvāna. This is not a condition of absorption into the Paramātman, a melting of the dewdrop into the silent sea. The soul maintains its identity though the character

[1] *Kalpa Sūtra*, Lives of the Jainas, *S.B.E.*, Vol. XXII, p. 264 f.
[2] Nahar and Ghosh, *op. cit.*, pp. 260, 264.

of the beatitude to which it attains is left indefinite. What Nirvāna signifies in the prospect of those who seek it has been described in one of the Jaina canonical books in simple and impressive language. "Do you, O sage," asked the young seeker, Keśi, "know a safe, happy, and quiet place for living beings which suffer from pains of body and mind?" The answer of the sage is as follows: "There is a safe place in view of all, but difficult of approach where there is no old age or death, no pain nor disease. It is what is called Nirvāna, or freedom from pain or perfection, which is in view of all; it is the safe, happy and quiet place which the great sages reach. That is the eternal place, in view of all, but difficult to approach. Those sages who reach it are free from sorrows, they have put an end to the stream of existence."[1] To the Buddhist Nirvāna is the extinction of craving; to the Jaina it is the destruction of karma. Perhaps we may say of Jainism what E. J. Thomas says of Buddhism, that in it also this is "the ultimately real." "It is not stated," says Dr. Thomas, expounding the Buddhist view, "in such a way that it can be identified with God, but it may be said to be feeling after an expression of the same truth."[2] No doubt this can be said also of the Jaina. This goal to which life is directed is a condition of beatitude in which the soul, purged of the pains and limitations of samsāra becomes infinite light.

It is noteworthy that in the development of the karma doctrine the Jaina thinkers are aware of a peril which it is difficult for them to avoid, that, namely, of fatalism. It may be that the tragic example of Gosāla, who made a rigid determinism one of the main tenets of his sect, the Ājīvikas, awakened Mahāvīra and those who followed him to the need of finding a way of escape from what seemed the inevitable consequence of the law of karma. They could not, and they do not, seek to escape the mechanical

[1] *Uttarādhyayana*, XXIII, 80 ff. *S.B.E.*, Vol XLV, p. 128.
[2] E. J. Thomas, *The Life of Buddha in Legend and History*, p. 208.

operation of the rule by which every act must bring its consequence through life after life. No prayer or worship, they recognise, can turn aside the course of this immutable law. But at the same time they desire to leave room for the resolute action of the free man to operate to counteract these consequences. The fatalists, they affirm, "have no knowledge and do not understand that things depend partly on fate and partly on human exertion." Thus, as we have seen already, the Jaina claims to have left room for free will in man and to leave room for the energy of action. "The sages," say Messrs. Nahar and Ghosh, "have devised means and methods whereby the seeds of karma could be so burned as to wholly neutralise their effects and leave the soul true and pure to soar up and up into the regions of the Siddhasila." "Jainism," says Dr. Thomas, "is the most extreme form of *kiriyavāda*, the doctrine that salvation is attained through works."[1] In this it is directly opposed to the Vedāntic doctrine of non-action, while between these two extremes Buddhism seeks to find the middle path. Jainism strikes a note which finds many echoes in other lands and in very different regions of belief when it says, "Man! Thou art thy own friend; why wishest thou for a friend beyond thyself."[2] And again it says in words which, we are told, "many devout Jainas repeat after their evening reading from the sacred books": "The soul is the maker and the non-maker, and itself makes happiness and misery, decides its own condition, good or evil, is its own river Veyarana."[3] Veyarana is a river of torment in hell—so that what the Jaina says is "Thyself art hell."

[1] *Op. cit.*, p. 207.
[2] *Āchārānga Sūtra*, I, 3, 3. *S.B.E.*, Vol. XXII, p. 33.
[3] Mrs. Sinclair Stevenson, *op. cit.*, p. 192.

CHAPTER IX

ITS DISCIPLINE AND ETHICS

JAINAS being adherents of the kiriyavāda doctrine and believing in the activity of the soul it follows that active endeavour directed towards the Jaina's *summum bonum* of release from samsāra will have a large part in their religion. We have seen that their great saints are prophets and teachers of the doctrine, and that for them the worship of the temple has an altogether secondary place. The ordinary adherents of the religion are accordingly Śrāvaka, that is, hearers of the law. But they hear in order that they may do; the Śrāvaka is one who submits himself to discipline. No religion in India indeed prescribes so severe a regimen for its devotees as does Jainism. It is, however, impossible that all who profess the religion shall be willing to submit themselves to so exacting a rule. Jainism is, accordingly, made up of two orders, the inner circle of monks and the outer community of lay persons. The discipline which the monks or ascetics accept cannot be exacted from the general body of the people who could not be expected wholly to renounce the world. These two orders were meant to be closely related to each other, the lay members of the community observing as far as they were able the five great vows of the monks. This close connection is emphasised by Professor Jacobi as one of the distinctive features of Jainism. "It is evident," he writes, "that the lay part of the community were not regarded as outsiders, or only as friends and patrons of the Order, as seems to have been the case in early Buddhism; their position was, from the beginning, well defined by religious duties and privileges; the bond which united them to the order of the monks was an effective one. The state of a layman was one preliminary and, in many cases, preparatory to the state of a monk." "It cannot be doubted," he concludes, "that this close union between laymen and monks, brought about by the similarity of their religious duties, differing not in kind but in degree, enabled Jainism to avoid fundamental changes within and to resist dangers from without for more than two thousand years."[1]

The bond that binds these two orders together is to be found primarily in the five vows. These are taken by the monks in their full strictness, while the laity are expected to observe them in so far as their circumstances and their secular avocations permit. These are the vows (1) to refrain from taking life, ahimsa; (2) to refrain from untruth; (3) to refrain from stealing; (4) to refrain from sexual intercourse; and (5) to renounce all worldly possessions. The first of these, ahimsa, is that which has the most far-reaching results, causing the monk to undergo the most extreme austerities. Many of the severest restrictions that he has to submit to follow inevitably from the care that he is required to take lest he should destroy life. He must examine carefully the ground on which he walks lest he should crush any small animal. Before eating or drinking he must scrutinise the food of which he is to partake. "He who lights a fire kills living beings; he who extinguishes it, kills the fire. Therefore a wise man who well considers the Law should light no fire."[2] It is obvious that this vow may well, when carried to its logical conclusion, lead to suicide, and this is probably one reason why religious suicide is, under certain conditions, sanctioned by the Jaina law.

So, again, the vow to abstain from stealing is to be understood as meaning that the monk must in all circumstances refuse to take anything that is not offered to him.

[1] *E.R.E.*, Vol. VII, p. 470.
[2] *Sûtrakritânga*, I, vii. 6. *S.B.E.*, Vol. XLV, p. 293.

Even then much care has to be taken as to what is received. "Seeing that to accept presents leads to hell, one should not accept even a blade of grass; only to preserve one's life, one should eat the food that is put in one's own alms-bowl." One argument for the custom of nudity required by the Digambaras is that clothes arouse in one pride of possession and the fear of being robbed of them, and so lead to evil. Thus in a multitude of ways that are detailed at great length in the canonical books the life of the monk is hedged about with restrictions. An instance of the extreme infliction of pain that they impose is the pulling out of the hair by the roots. This is required when the novice takes his vows as a monk and accepts initiation. The painful process is supposed to be repeated every year, but apparently shaving is frequently permitted. When taking his vows, the monk says, "I shall become a Śramana, who owns no house, no property, no sons, no cattle, who eats what others give him; I shall commit no sinful action; I renounce to accept anything that has not been given."[1]

It is scarcely surprising, when one considers the rigour of Jaina asceticism, that the way should be left open to the ultimate escape by suicide. This must not, however, be made use of as an easy deliverance from pain. Desire for death or non-existence—like any other desire—is evil for both the Buddhist and the Jaina. Nor is this end to be reached as the Vedantist may reach it by means of an insight that sees all transitory things to be unreal: the Jaina does not believe in māyā or in the philosophy of inaction that is a consequence of that belief. When death is chosen it must be as the crown of a life of asceticism resolutely adopted and fulfilled. The sage who has accomplished a twelve years' mortification of the flesh, should choose a place where he shall not lie "on sprouts of grass" but on bare ground and so "without any

[1] *Áchārānga Sūtra*, II, vii. 1. *S.B.E.*, Vol. XXII, p. 171.

comfort or food" he should await death.[1] The Tīrthakara, Pārśva, and the great scholar and statesman, Hemchandra, are among those who are said to have adopted this method of attaining moksha.

Women are admitted to this life of renunciation just as men are, and, except in the case of the Digambara Jainas who hold that no woman can obtain moksha, may enter the same kind of order as that of the Jaina monk. According to the Digambara doctrine a woman can only attain release from samsāra if she is reborn as a man. They give, as reasons for this, her physical weakness which cannot submit to the discipline and the austerities of the monastic life, and also the fact that she cannot be required to adopt nudity. Other sects, however, have orders of nuns who give a remarkable example of self-sacrifice.

The vows taken by the lay community are less severe than those of the monks and nuns. Thus the fourth vow does not in their case require a life of celibacy; nor is the layman required to give up all his possessions but, knowing that all things perish, he is to set a limit to the wealth he may acquire. The desire to avoid inflicting injury on living beings has excluded the Jaina layman from many of the ordinary occupations of life. In the case of monks the rule is that they are to wander continually so that they may form no ties of friendship. They are not, however, to travel in the rainy season when life is so prolific that it would be scarcely possible, while walking, to avoid destroying living creatures. A layman may approach in a measure to this ideal by setting limits within which he may travel, so as to avoid killing creatures that he might otherwise come in contact with.

These examples may suffice to indicate the character of the life enjoined upon the Jaina, and to show to how great an extent it is influenced by their doctrine of the jīva and of its sacredness. This has resulted also in such

[1] See *Āchārānga Sūtra*, I, vii. 8. *S.B.E.*, Vol. XXII, p. 75.

a strange custom as the feeding of ants and rats and noxious insects and in the establishment of hospitals where old and diseased animals are kept till they die a natural death. It also, of course, requires them to be vegetarians and to follow that rule with more thoroughness than the Buddhists, who allow meat to be eaten so long as he who so eats has not caused the animal to be hurt or killed. It is not the eating of flesh, they say, that defiles a man but the doing of sinful deeds. The Jainas undoubtedly looked upon the Buddhists as half-hearted compromisers. They often charge the followers of the rival sect with greed and luxury.

It would not be profitable to detail the interminable classifications of good and evil conduct, as of so many other aspects of life, that the Jaina teachers have enumerated. While for the most part these divisions and subdivisions belong to the type of unprofitable analysis that is associated with "scholasticism," it has to be recognised that in their ethical classifications they show discrimination. The Jainas certainly appear to be greatly concerned with questions of conduct. Thus they enumerate nine kinds of meritorious action and eighteen types of sinful action. But they go further and enumerate eighty-two ways "in which a jīva pays the penalty for his committing sins in the past."[1]

The ethical character of Jainism, in spite of so much that seems formal on the one hand and extreme on the other, is seen in the observance of such a sacred season as Pajjusana, which is the most important in their calendar. The period of the fast is occupied chiefly in the exposition of the scriptures by the ascetic teachers. "Lectures on the *Kalpa Sūtra* are delivered for the first seven days and on the last day fasting is observed and the text of the Sūtra is read out to the whole assembly of men and women who hear the same with great attention, respect and veneration."[2] "During this festival the annual

[1] Nahar and Ghosh, *op. cit.*, p. 517.
[2] *Ibid.*, p. 672.

confession is performed, in order to remove all ill-feelings over all living beings and to ask pardon from all living beings for any act done, knowingly or unknowingly, in the course of the year. This is considered to be an act of great merit and as imperative on all the Jainas."[1] Mrs. Stevenson tells us: "Letters must be written to friends at a distance asking their forgiveness also. The postal authorities can testify how faithfully this is carried out, for the mail of the Jaina community increases extraordinarily at this season of the year."[2]

The ethic of the Jaina is, however, centrally and in its whole character ascetic. This ascetic ideal—whether the extreme form which the Jainas follow or the middle way of Buddhism—seems to reach back to a period earlier than the time of either Buddha or Mahāvīra. It is believed by many scholars to have arisen in non-Brāhman circles and certainly the ahimsa doctrine which is an essential part of this asceticism is incompatible with the animal sacrifices that the Brāhman rites required. "It will be found," writes Professor Winternitz, "that the ideals and ideas of this ascetic poetry are organically connected with Sāmkhya and Yoga as well as with Buddhism and Jainism, while whenever they appear mixed up with orthodox Brāhmanism in Brāhmanical literature they appear as something foreign."[3] This ascetic tradition which has, it would seem, a close relation with folk-tales and the legends and ballads of the common people, has been maintained more fully by the Jainas than by any other of the religious developments within India.

[1] Nahar and Ghosh, *op. cit.*, p. 673.
[2] *E.R.E.*, Vol. V, p. 876.
[3] *Some Problems of Indian Literature*, p. 39 (Calcutta University Press).

CHAPTER X

ITS PRESENT CONDITION

ONE of the characteristics of Jainism is the conservatism which has governed the slow development of its life all through the ages. The Jainas have not neglected education—the standard of literacy by the census of 1911 was high, compared with that of the communities of a similar type in India. But the education they seek is not of the kind that brings the Jaina young man into contact with western science with its inevitably disintegrating effect upon the ideas upon which the religion is based. The Jaina seeks an education that will fit him for the business of finance and commerce with which he is mainly occupied. Few Jainas acquire an education such as will make them acquainted with the knowledge and culture of the west. As a result this religion has resisted to a considerable extent the process of erosion which threatens the stability of so many of its contemporaries. This resistance can hardly be maintained indefinitely. The Jainas claim that their religion has existed from all eternity. It certainly stretches back into the dimness of a very early past and travels through the centuries to modern times with little outward change in its principles or its practice. Now, however, even the Jainas are becoming aware of the need to reclaim their youth from "the perverted tendencies"[1] that Western ideas and modes of life are producing among them.

Another influence that has always been present to Jainism throughout its whole history, serving in a measure to protect it, but at the same time threatening to destroy

[1] Nahar and Ghosh, *op. cit.*, p. xvii.

it by a process of absorption, is that of Hinduism. Among the less instructed followers of the religion there may often be little to distinguish Hindu and Jaina, as the religious practices of both at these lower levels are mainly concerned with evil spirits and the means by which protection may be obtained from them. Jainism also approaches close to Vaishnavism in the emphasis that both lay upon the doctrine of ahimsa. This is seen, for example, in Gujarat and in the case of such a Gujarati Vaishnava family as that in which Mr. M. K. Gandhi was born. Thus the " family adviser " of the Gandhis who administered to the Mahatma in his youth the three vows of abstinence from wine, women and meat was " a Modh bania " who had become a Jaina monk.[1] More often, however, the Jaina adopts the simple designation of Hindu, and hence, no doubt, comes the steady diminution in the number of Jainas as these are given in successive Census Reports.

The fact that the latest enumeration (in 1931) shows an increase is probably a consequence of the increased self-consciousness that recent events in India seem to have produced in all the communities. It certainly is the case that Jainas have been awaking to a sense of the danger of their being disintegrated as a consequence of the two influences just noted, the greater strength and prestige of Hinduism and the subversive forces of Western culture. For that reason a movement has been set on foot to bring the various sections together in closer harmony. The All-India Jaina Association (Bhārata Jaina Mahāmandala), which was founded in 1911, takes for its motto the words " Maitribhava sarvān jayati " (" Love conquers all "), and has as its chief aims the unification and reform of the Jaina community and the spread of its doctrines. One of the most notable figures in the recent history of the religion was Rajachandra Raojibhai or Raychandbhai, a Sthanakvasi, born in Morvi State,

[1] Gandhi, *op. cit.*, Vol. I, p. 97.

Kathiawar, in 1868. He laid special emphasis on what has always been the chief strength of the Jaina Church, its ethical teaching. " He declared that neither *murti* (idol) nor *mumati* (mouth-cloth) led to *moksha* (release) but a good life."[1] The character of this man and of his teaching may best be indicated by the account of him given by Mr. M. K. Gandhi—who places him along with Tolstoy and Ruskin as " three moderns who left a deep impress on his life and captivated him." The qualities in this Jaina poet and saint that cast their spell over him, Mr. Gandhi tells us, were " his wide knowledge of the scriptures, his spotless character and his burning passion for self-realisation." " I saw," says Mr. Gandhi, " that this last was the only thing for which he lived. The following lines of Muktanand were always on his lips and engraved on the tablets of his heart:

> 'I shall think myself blessed only when I see Him in every one of my daily acts;
> Verily, He is the thread which supports Muktanand's life.'

" Raychandbhai's commercial transactions covered hundreds of thousands. He was a connoisseur of pearls and diamonds. No knotty business problem was too difficult for him. But all these things were not the centre round which his life revolved. The centre was the passion to see God face to face. . . . I have tried to meet the heads of various faiths, and I must say that no one else has ever made on me the impression that Raychandbhai did. His words went straight home to me. His intellect compelled as great a regard from me as his moral earnestness, and deep down in me was the conviction that he would never willingly lead me astray and would always confide to me his innermost thoughts. In my moments of spiritual crisis, therefore, he was my refuge."[2]

It is significant that this account has all the appearance of being an account, not of a Jaina but of a Hindu bhakta

[1] Farquhar, *Modern Religious Movements*, p. 328.
[2] Gandhi, *op. cit.*, Vol. I, pp. 208 ff.

who sought to enter into fellowship with God. So in another passage Mr. Gandhi quotes him as saying in reference to doubts regarding Hinduism that were disturbing Mr. Gandhi—" I am convinced that no other religion has the subtle and profound thought of Hinduism, its vision of the soul or its charity."[1] It is evident that Raychandbhai did not make any rigid differentiation between Hinduism and his own faith, and in this he probably represents a considerable body of advanced opinion among Jainas. It would appear that there is a movement on the part of modern Jainas towards theism and M. Guerinot quotes one of them as affirming that the only difference between Jainism and other theistic religions consists in the fact that Jainism refuses to attribute to God the power to create and to destroy, to reward and to punish.[2] To be sure these limitations are considerable, but the interest of the claim lies in its indication of a desire to come into line with the theism within Hinduism with which it has many affinities and which, as we have seen, has always struggled to maintain its character as theistic in spite of the constraint laid upon it, as upon Jainism, by some of those anti-theistic doctrines which it owes to the central Hindu tradition.

More and more as modern influences press upon it, Jainism is in danger of being absorbed by its powerful neighbour. In former days its kinship with, and outward resemblance to, Hinduism enabled it to escape the persecutions which finally drove Buddhism from India and this survival power may preserve it again from destruction. The fear of many Jainas, however, is that it may lose the separate identity that it has so long preserved. It is indeed the resolutely ethical character of this religion that has given it its strength in the past and commended it to those who have observed it. The ideal of ahimsa which Hinduism shares in a measure with it, has always been

[1] Gandhi, *op. cit.*, Vol. I, pp. 321 f.
[2] Guerinot, *op. cit.*, p. 276.

accepted with a seriousness which has attracted to it such a non-Jaina as M. K. Gandhi. No doubt many thoughtful Jainas today would agree with the young Jaina scholar, Mr. Chimanlal J. Shah, in claiming that this ideal is "the most important achievement of Jaina thought."[1] He adds that "towards this ideal, as the Jainas believe, the present world is slowly though imperceptibly moving." "The Jaina ahimsa," he writes elsewhere, "is not the ahimsa of a weakling but that of a brave soul which is, or wants to be, above all the evil forces of this world. Hemchandra rightly based it on the maxim: 'Look upon other beings as you would look upon yourself.'"[2] At the same time Mr. Shah is aware as everyone must be, of the dangers that threaten this ancient system in the modern world. As he says, though its conservatism has preserved it hitherto it is doubtful if it can do so now. He indicates an additional danger when he points to "the mutual distrust among the existing divisions in the Jaina community" and expresses his fear that these may cause the Jainas "to share the same fate as that of their brothers the Buddhists."[3] Whatever destiny may await it we can accept the judgment of Professor H. V. Glasenapp as we look back upon our study of this religion and as we consider its position still as a living religion directing many lives today. "The impartial historian," he writes, "will certainly affirm that Jainism is inferior to other religions in the profundity and the power of its religious life; but he will at the same time admire the incomparable vitality of this system which still today as in the distant past is able to bind to itself zealous and devoted followers and thereby proves ever anew its right to exist."[4]

[1] *Jainism in North India*, p. 1.
[2] C. J. Shah, *op. cit.*, p. 50.
[3] *Op. cit.*, p. 87.
[4] Glasenapp, *Der Jainismus*, p. 313.

PART IV

THE RELIGION OF THE SIKHS

CHAPTER XI

INTRODUCTORY

THIS religion like Jainism has a close affiliation with Hinduism and some would maintain—as indeed some would in regard to Jainism also—that it is properly to be regarded, not as an independent religion but as a sect of the ancient Hindu system and should still be reckoned as having its home within it. In the Punjab Census Report of 1881 a leading Sikh is quoted as saying that " a true Sikh, if asked whether he is a Hindu or a Musalman, will answer that he is a Hindu." The Census Officer himself, Sir Denzil Ibbetson, declares that both Sikhism and Jainism are " varieties of the parent Hindu faith." " They are probably wider departures," he goes on, " from the original type than are Vaishnavism and Śaivism, but not so wide as many other sects which, being small and unimportant, are not generally regarded as separate religions."[1] It is probable that if Sir Denzil Ibbetson was writing the Census Report for 1931 he would be less positive in his identification of the Sikh with the Hindu. Circumstances in recent years have caused Sikhs to affirm more definitely than was the case fifty years ago their separate religious identity. A reawakening of pride in the Sikh tradition on the one hand and political conditions on the other have combined to bring this change about. The competition for representation in the reconstituted Councils and Assembly has accentuated the communal consciousness in the case of the Sikhs, as in the case of other communities, and is causing them to emphasise more than formerly their separateness. But even in 1881

[1] *C.I.R.*, Punjab, Vol I, p. 130.

Sir Denzil Ibbetson recognises that Sikhism is "saved from being a Hindu sect by its political history and importance."[1] It can hardly be denied that Sikhism, whatever the attitude of its adherents may have been at particular times, was historically a movement of religious reform which went much further than was the case with most of the reform movements which have arisen within Hinduism and which have remained there. It might indeed—like so many other reform movements of a similar kind—have been reabsorbed, but circumstances and the instincts of those among whom it arose combined to give it a character of vigour and aggressiveness which has preserved it in its independence. Its history is well summarised in the words of the Census Report of 1921: "Sikhism," that Report says, "was an attempt to reconcile Hindu beliefs with a purer creed, which rejected polytheism, image-worship and pilgrimages. It remained a pacific cult till the political tyranny of the Musalmans, and the social tyranny of the Hindus converted it into a military creed."[2] Its interest thus lies, on the one hand, in the fact, that it is a movement for the reform of Hinduism, parallel to many others that have arisen and died down again in the long history of that religion, and, on the other hand, in the peculiar influences that entered into it, causing it to run a course altogether different from that of any similar movement and giving it an energy of life that was denied to them. In this case the history of the religion has a special interest of its own, an interest due to the characteristics of the people who profess it and to the relation it bears not only to Hinduism but to Islam. We have already seen how the Hindu saints who follow the way of Bhakti struggle to escape from the bondage in which the presuppositions of monistic doctrine hold them, but how seldom their struggles avail to set them free from these toils. In Sikhism we have an example of one

[1] *C.I.R.*, Punjab, Vol. I, p. 130.
[2] *C.I.R.*, Punjab, 1921, Vol. I, p. 114.

effort of this kind which attained a certain measure of success, to this extent at least, that it formally separated itself from Hinduism. It was strengthened to achieve and to maintain this exceptional independence by two factors that contributed greatly to reinforce the vigour of the faith which Bhakti had inspired in its adherents. These were the robust character of the Punjabi people among whom this movement of reformation arose, and the influence upon them of the religion of Islam which had come among them, with its teaching as to God and man, so much more concrete and rigid than the teachings of Hinduism.

CHAPTER XII

THE HISTORY

THE founder of this religion, Guru Nānak, was born at Talvandi, near Lahore, in A.D. 1469. He belonged to the Khatri caste, which is a trading caste, whose members possess exceptional qualities of manliness and of command. They are, we are told, " one of the most acute, energetic and remarkable races in India," " a very fine fair, handsome race " and " generally educated." One of the most notable of the caste was Todar Mal, the famous finance minister of the Emperor Akbar. " The Khatris are staunch Hindus, and it is somewhat singular that, while giving a religion and priests to the Sikhs, they themselves are comparatively seldom Sikhs." At the same time, " so far as the Sikhs have a priesthood, the Khatris are the priests or gurus of the Sikhs," and both the first Sikh Guru, Nānak, and the tenth, Govind, belonged to this non-Brāhman caste.[1]

Nānak's father was a farmer and a shopkeeper as well as a " land steward " in the service of " the feudal lord of the village," a Musalman. The story of his life is obtained from " Janamsakhis," one or two of which reach back as far as within fifty years of Nānak's death. It resembles the biography of many others among the Hindu saints in its main particulars. The indications that he had a higher vocation than that of a farmer or a trader are such as are told of others who belong to this

[1] These quotations, describing the Khatris, are from Sir George Campbell's *Ethnology of India* as quoted in the *Punjab Census Report* (1881), Vol. I, p. 295. This authority further suggests the quality of the Khatris by saying, " They are in fact in the Punjab . . . all that Marāthā Brāhmans are in the Marāthā country, besides engrossing the trade which the Marāthā Brāhmans have not."

assimilative powers of Hinduism is associated with the new temper awakened in them, and the new vocation manifested to them, by the tenth Guru, Govind Singh. It is true that he brought into Sikhism Hindu elements, such as the worship of the goddess Durgā, that had not been admitted before his time. But his purpose was to unite all Sikhs into a brotherhood, separate from and hostile to, its rivals—Hindus, but especially Muslims. "A Sikh is not even to salute one who is not a Sikh, otherwise he is an apostate and accursed by God."[1] Sir D. Ibbetson quotes the following passage as summing up the distinctive characteristics which Guru Govind enjoined upon them as the Khālsa, "the elect." "They should have one form of initiation, the sprinkling of water by five of the faithful; they should worship the one invisible God; they should honour the memory of Nānak and his successors; their watchword should be 'Hail Guru!' but they should revere and bow to nought visible save the Granth, the book of their belief. They should bathe from time to time in the pool of Amritsar, their locks should remain unshorn, they should all name themselves Singhs or soldiers, and of material things they should devote their energies to steel alone. Arms should dignify their person, they should be for ever encouraging war, and great would be his merit who fought in the van, who slew an enemy and who despaired not, although overcome."[2]

This militant brotherhood, as we have already noted, has kept the fervour of Sikh loyalty aglow and forms the central care of the faithful as distinguished from the Sahijdhari—"the easy-going," who are scarcely distinguishable from Hindus. In other respects the Sikhs of all types follow in the main the customs that they have inherited from Hinduism. They reverence the cow. They do not, indeed, practise ahimsa (non-killing), but the animal whose flesh is eaten must be killed by a single

[1] Trumpp, p. cxv. [2] *C.I.R.*, Punjab, 1881, Vol. I, p. 135.

stroke of the sword. Infanticide, which was so common in the Punjab before the days of British rule, was strictly forbidden by the Gurus. In spite of this fact the custom seems to have continued until recent times especially among some families of Sikh Jats. We learn also that, in spite of the fact that women are treated with more consideration than in the Hindu practice of that time, "among the Sikhs in the Punjab the suttee murders were atrocious."[1]

Of the Sikh sects the Akālis, to whom reference has already been made, carry on the militant tradition of Guru Govind Singh. Two other sects of some importance are the Nirmalas and the Udāsis. The former are an order which was said to be bitterly opposed to the Akālis. They appear to have become merged in the multitude of ordinary ascetic orders of Hinduism, but are described as "a well-disciplined and highly respected organisation."[2] The Udāsis formed one of the most important of the Sikh orders, but a breach with the Gurus early in their history placed them in an ambiguous position. They are also called "Nānakputras" or sons of Nānak, and revere the Ādī Granth and not the Granth of Guru Govind. We are told in the Punjab Census Report of 1881 that "they are hardly recognised as Sikhs."[3]

[1] Vincent Smith, *Oxford History of India*, p. 689, note.
[2] H. A. Rose in *E.R.E.*, Vol. IX, p. 376.
[3] P. 286.

But there were other causes of a deeper kind that were operating to produce this renaissance. The influences that were at work throughout the whole land opening men's eyes to the evils from which they were suffering and creating a desire for better things brought back again among them something of the reforming ardour of their gurus. A College, called the Khālsa College, was established at Amritsar with the object of promoting the higher education of the new generation of Sikhs, and there they obtain religious instruction. Other indications of this reforming spirit are to be found in new activity in education for girls and in the opening of a home for widows. The fresh life that is stirring in the Sikh community has expressed itself also in a measure in literature. One of their poets is Bhai Vir Singh who is described as "the representative poet of the old order of the Sikh poets." He is said to be able to make "unlettered men and women glow at the emotion of his verse," but in it, as translated, there appears to be little that is distinctive of Sikh teaching. His dominant religious note is that of a sense of inward thirst for God and of the satisfaction of that thirst in the divine love.

> "He speaketh not nor doth He smile!
> Enough for me is His presence!
> Enough for me these eternal desires and their eternal unfulfilment."[1]

Whatever the various elements may be that combine to create in the modern Sikh his sense of devotion to his Guru, it is evident from the verses of this poet that it is an intense emotion which does not halt this side of worship. It is noticeable that this devotion is given to the great warrior Guru, Govind Singh. "O beautiful sun wearer," he cries, "the sun is in thy crest."

> "I have nor beauty nor art,
> By thy favour I am;
> Thou madest me!
> Thou art God."[2]

---

[1] Nargas, *Songs of a Sikh*, translated by Puran Singh, p. 64.
[2] *Ibid.*, p. 63.

Religious devotion is present here as well as the clan loyalty of a fighting race. The bhakti ardour of Kabīr and Nāmdev is still alive in this modern Sikh and evidently finds its response in those who listen to his songs. What marks off the expressions of his worship from that of the educated Hindu is no more perhaps than the heritage of courage and manliness that come down from the warrior Gurus of an older day.

This distinction is still fainter in the case of the ordinary village Sikh. As we have seen, it is often very difficult for the onlooker to tell in what he differs from his Hindu neighbour, and he appears not infrequently to have difficulty himself in drawing any line of demarcation. The pressure of economic need, as we have noted, sometimes even constrains the Hindu to sell his cow to the butcher: the same necessity causes the Sikh to cultivate tobacco and so to break what probably in many cases is the only law that he is aware of as giving him a right to the name of Sikh. The Granth Sahib may be read to him from time to time but it " is as difficult for a peasant to follow as Chaucer would be for an English rustic."[1] " Beyond the observance of a few rites mainly on special occasions religion hardly enters into his daily life. And even these rites are more the concern of women than of men."[2] Mr. Darling gives as a typical expression of the religion of the poor Sikh cultivator in the Punjab, who has to wage an unremitting war with poverty and hunger, this passage from Kabīr which he may sometimes sing in the evening when the day's toil is over:

> " A hungry man cannot perform Thy service,—
> Take back this rosary of Thine.
> I only ask for the dust of the Saint's feet.
> Let me not be in debt.
> I beg for two seers of flour,
> A quarter of a seer of butter and salt.
> I beg for half a seer of pulse

---

[1] Darling, *Rusticus Loquitur*, p. 338.
[2] Darling, *op. cit.*, p. 34.

sense. In the narrow understanding of the name it is applied to those who have submitted to the baptism of initiation, instituted by Guru Govind. Thus no one is born a Sikh if the name is understood in this sense. These Sikhs are the Singhs. On the other hand "the vast majority of those who profess only the tenets of Nānak call themselves Hindus." These two groups, we learn, are tending to separate, though a Sikh of the former class may still marry a girl of the latter.[1] The Nānakpanthis or Sahijdhari ("easy-going") Sikhs "are distinguished by no outward sign, have no peculiar customs or observances, and, though they reverence the Granth and, above all, the memory of their Guru, have but little to distinguish them from any other Hindu sect except a slight laxity in the matter of caste observances."[2] This ambiguity makes it difficult to determine with confidence the actual numbers of those who ought to be described by the Sikh name. It is evident that Hinduism would have in time, as in so many other instances, subdued this movement and reabsorbed into itself the reformers, had it not been that the spirit of religion was reinforced by the passion which persecution aroused. The spirit of patriotism and the fighting instinct, so strong in this northern people, rekindled the dwindling religious fervour and transformed the character of the movement.[3] Similarly in the more peaceful days of British rule, when the sword was being replaced once more by the ploughshare, other influences, notably those of nationalism and political ambition, are arousing the Sikh spirit from its stagnation and causing them to reaffirm their separation from Hinduism. These facts suggest, what is evident in the case of other religions as well as Sikhism, how many elements besides those that can be described as strictly religious

[1] Rose in *E.R.E.*, Vol. XI, p. 510.
[2] *C.I.R.*, Punjab, 1881, Vol. I, p. 136.
[3] "In times of war converts to Sikhism are much more numerous than in times of peace." *C.I.R.*, Punjab, 1881, Vol. I, p. 140.

may unite for the creation and the maintenance of a religious movement.

The Sikh religion became more and more militarised as its struggle for existence against the Muslims continued. Sikh kingships were established and by 1767 they had "made themselves masters of the Punjab from the Jamna to the Indus."[1] Mr. Rose considers, however, that with this achievement the religious development of Sikhism may be said to have ended. "In 1768 a national council held at Amritsar proclaimed the Khālsa the supreme religion and minted coins" bearing in Persian the legend, "Guru Govind Singh received from Nānak the degh (the world), the sword, and unfailing victory." Their character as a Warrior religion is signalised by the power among them during all this period of struggle of the sect Akālis (that is, "immortals" or "worshippers of the Immortal"). This was a fighting sect similar to the sects of armed ascetics, such as Nāga sannyāsis, that were formerly (especially in the sixteenth and seventeenth centuries) numerous within Hinduism.[2] It is said to have been founded by Guru Govind himself.[3] "They wear blue chequered clothes, bangles of steel on the wrist and quoits of steel on their conical blue turbans, together with miniature daggers, knives and an iron chain. Their headquarters used to be at Amritsar where they assumed the direction of religious ceremonies and the duty of convoking the council of the Khālsa. They were dreaded even by the Sikh chiefs for their fanaticism and turbulence and often levied offerings by force."[4] These Akālis seem to have formed the spear-head of Ranjit Singh's conquests early in the nineteenth century, but, realising the danger to his rule of their growing power, he set himself to limit their importance. Their importance, accordingly, dwindled through the period following the conquest of

[1] H. A. Rose in *E.R.E.*, Vol. XI, p. 510.
[2] See J. N. Farquhar, *The Fighting Ascetics of India*.
[3] Farquhar, *op. cit.*, p. 15.
[4] *C.I.R.*, Punjab, 1881, Vol. I, p. 287.

the Punjab by the British until the recent revival of Sikhism brought them, as the champions of the true faith, once more into prominence.

When the long Sikh struggle came to an end in 1849 we are told that "the Sikh population were soldiers almost to a man." More than ever was the case even with the Muslims this was a religion in arms. At that time their historian, Sir William Cunningham, wrote of them: "The Sikhs do not form a numerous sect, yet their strength is not to be estimated by tens of thousands, but by the unity and energy of religious fervour and warlike temperament. They will dare much and they will endure much for the mystic Khālsa or Commonwealth; they are not discouraged by defeat and they ardently look forward to the day when Indians and Arabs and Persians and Turks shall all acknowledge the double mission of Nānak and Govind Singh." That description of the warlike ardour of the Sikhs in the early days of struggle is quoted by Sir Denzil Ibbetson in his Census Report, and he immediately appends an account of the condition of this same sect in 1853 by Sir Richard Temple, who wrote of them from a personal knowledge of the change five years of peace had already wrought in them. "The Sikh faith and ecclesiastical polity," he says, "is rapidly going where the Sikh political ascendancy has already gone. Of the two elements in the old Khālsa, namely the followers of Nānak, the first prophet, and the followers of Guru Govind, the second great religious leader, the former will hold their ground and the latter lose it. The Sikhs of Nānak, a comparatively small body of peaceful habits and old family, will perhaps cling to the faith of their 'fathers,' but the Sikhs of Govind, who are of more recent origin, who are more specially styled the Singhs or lions, and who embraced the faith as being the religion of warfare and conquest, no longer regard the Khālsa, now that the prestige has departed from it. These men joined in thousands, and they now depart in equal number. They rejoin the ranks of Hinduism whence they originally came and they bring up their children as Hindus. The sacred tank of Amritsar is less thronged than formerly, and the attendance at the annual festival is diminishing yearly. The initiatory ceremony for adult persons is now rarely performed."[1]

But such sweeping and confident prophecy, whether foretelling, as in the case of Sir William Cunningham, unflagging ardour, or in the case of Sir William Temple, a final failure of their early zeal, is scarcely borne out in either case by the facts. The spirit of the Sikhs ebbs and flows, waning in times of peace and stirring again to life when any call to conflict summons them. That this is so was proved in the time of the " Mutiny," and it is being proved again, as we shall see, in the midst of the new influences that today are awakening them once more.

[1] Quoted in *C.I.R.*, Punjab, 1881, Vol. I, p. 140.

Which will feed me twice a day.
I beg for a bed with four legs to it,
A pillow and a mattress.
I beg for a quilt over me;
And then Thy slave will devotedly worship Thee.
I have never been covetous,
I only love Thy name."

There is a simplicity and sincerity about that confession of faith that links its author and those who through it utter their aspirations with the Hebrew psalmists. But, as Mr. Darling goes on to remark, "the times are changing and a more acquisitive spirit is in the air." No one indeed can tell when conditions may change and the old battle cries ring out again and summon them to leave the plough as well as their tasks of trade and colonisation and to gird on the sword again. There are signs that they would be quick enough to do so, but no one can desire that any such occasion should arise. A religion that is in the main a call to battle and to clan loyalty does not find the same opportunity in the India of today as in the India when Aurangzib was Emperor. The glow of Nānak's faith burns more dimly in the Sikh peasant's breast when the winds that fan it are no longer those of persecution but merely those of poverty. Yet it was originally to a spiritual warfare that Nānak called his followers; the spirit of his Bhakti, like that of the Hindu saints, was a spirit that craved divine fellowship and sought it by the road of self-purification.

"A well without water, a cow without milk, a shrine in darkness,
So art thou without Him, O my soul!
Renounce anger and passion: forsake illusion and pride:
The Lord alone is thy salvation; love Him with adoration." [1]

Rather let that call be heard again by the Sikh peasant than the call to battle, even if it be to as bloodless a battle as that of the ballot-boxes.

[1] *Temple Bells*, p. 28. (Translated from Nānak by Cyril Modak.)

course through a jungle of superstitious fears and lofty aspirations; no single personality appeared powerful enough in inspiration and conviction to cut a clear way through the undergrowth. That is what Zoroaster accomplished for the Iranian faith when the divine revelation came to him, making him a prophet.

When Zoroaster (or Zarathustra, to give him his proper Persian name) lived is a subject of much dispute among scholars. It is enough to state here that the traditional date—660–583 B.C.—is accepted as the latest period to which he can be assigned. There is, however, a considerable weight of scholarly authority in favour of placing him about 1000 B.C. or even three centuries earlier. With his date goes the date of the Gathas, seventeen poems, the majority of which are utterances of the Prophet himself. The triumph of the new faith which he proclaimed came with the conversion, after the years during which his message was unheeded, of a chieftain, Vishtaspa. Thereafter his message obtained many converts and spread widely throughout Iran. In one of the Holy Wars, however, the prophet himself perished.

All the reliable knowledge that we possess of the prophet's personality is obtained from the Gathas, seventeen psalms that form the earliest portion of the Zoroastrian sacred scriptures, the Avesta. The simplicity and naturalness of these utterances convince most scholars that they give, as they claim, actual messages from the Prophet's own spiritual insight, not unlike in their lofty tone those granted to the prophets of the Hebrew people about the same time. Whether he belonged to a priestly caste or not, he was in spirit a prophet, bringing a message of righteousness to his people. He was at the same time a peasant, calling his people to the simplicity of the pastoral life. Righteousness and pastoral simplicity are linked together in his oracles. "Whoso is most good to the righteous man . . . or with diligence cares for the cattle, he shall be hereafter in the pasture of Right and good Thought."[1] "To learn the straight paths by the Right" and "to practise husbandry" are the two poles of his message of reform, calling his people to the worship of the Right and the practice of a simple pastoral life.

What is, however, central to his whole reform is his message of Ahura Mazda (the wise Lord) as Right and as Supreme. He is "creator of all things through the holy spirit."[2] The question how far the religion that he proclaimed is a monotheism or is rather, as it is so often represented, a dualism of the hostile forces of good and evil, is one that has been much disputed. "The two primal spirits who revealed themselves in vision as Twins are the Better and the Bad."[3] The questions that arise in this connection cannot be discussed here. In the view of Dr. A. V. Williams Jackson it was Zoroaster who made dualism "in its moral and ethical aspects" "a typical unit in his great system."[4] At the same time in this scholar's view "Zoroaster's dualism is monotheistic and optimistic," postulating the ultimate triumph of good. "The god," says Dr. Moulton, "who takes his place at the centre of the Reformer's religion had lost, if he ever possessed, all real traits of an elemental deity."[5] "Ahura is wholly spiritual and surrounded by spirits."[6]

The lofty spiritual character of the Wise Lord with his attributes, one of which is Asha or Right—the Rita of the Vedas—has its consequence in the inwardness of the ethical qualities required of the worshipper. There is, it is true, the promise of those concrete temporal gifts, which the soul of the herdsman longs for, such as "ten mares with a stallion and a camel,"[7] but the eyes of men are to be lifted beyond these uncertain rewards to a judgment that is to come after death. Thus the irregularities and injustices of life shall be finally redressed. "In immortality shall the soul of the righteous be joyful, in

[1] Yasna, 33. 3. [2] *Ibid.*, 44. 7. [3] *Ibid.*, 30. 3.
[4] Jackson, *Zoroastrian Studies*, p. 30.
[5] Moulton, *Treasure of the Magi*, p. 95.
[6] *Ibid.*, p. 292. [7] Yasna, 44. 18.

that behind its worship a single God who is personal looms up. The belief in Karma and transmigration was, however, retained by Nānak and is universally acknowledged by the adherents of the religion. When to this is added belief in māyā it is difficult to see how there can be room in the conceptions of this religion for the worship of a personal God in the sense in which such worship is usually understood. The word māyā, however, in the poems of Kabīr seems to have often an ethical implication that differentiates it from the ordinary Hindu usage. Macauliffe, accordingly, in his translation of the Granth uses " mammon " to convey its significance. It seems to revert in this usage to its older meaning of magic power, and is represented as a woman " who is in collusion with the five evil passions."[1] Here also, however, the Granth speaks with a double voice and it is impossible to reduce its doctrine to consistency.[2]

In other regions than theology we find more definiteness of conviction. Nānak does not directly attack the caste system but he says of one who is " a beggar at the gate ": " Thou acknowledgest the light (that is in him) and dost not ask after (his) caste. For in the other world there is no caste." [3] " Nānak," says Trumpp, " received all men as his disciples without any regard to caste recognising in all the dignity of the human birth and laid thus the foundation of a popular religion." [4] In this matter, however, as in others the good example of the founder has not proved strong enough to overcome deep-seated prejudice and ancient Hindu custom. This is so even in the case of those who from among the Chuhra or scavenger caste have become Sikhs and who are called Mazhbi

[1] Keay's *Kabīr and his Followers*, p. 77.
[2] To indicate how varied are the interpretations of the theological position even of Guru Nānak himself we may take the following passage quoted as " the words of a Sikh scholar," in the *Punjab Census Report* of 1911 (Part I, p. 155): " From Dualism (Dwait) he (Nānak) lifted the people to Monism (Adwaita) through the intermediate grades of qualified non-Dualism (Visishtadvaita)."
[3] Trumpp, p. 494.
[4] *Ibid.*, pp. cxii. f.

Sikhs. They are said to have a special claim upon the Sikh community as having been admitted to the faith because of their devotion in bringing from Delhi the mutilated body of Guru Teg Bahadur after he had been executed there. They are described as good Sikhs who take the pahul, wear their hair long, and abstain from tobacco. In spite, however, of these facts "the taint of hereditary pollution is upon them, and Sikhs of other castes refuse to associate with them even in religious ceremonies."[1]

It may, indeed, be maintained that as a reform movement within Hinduism which was strong enough for a while to establish itself in a position of separation, Sikhism has only been able very imperfectly to maintain its independent and distinctive character. Two facts in regard to it have preserved it from that complete re-absorption into the old religion which has been the fate of so many other similar upsurgences of the Protestant spirit. One of these is emphasised by Trumpp in his comments upon the effect of the strong pantheism which he finds pervading the teaching of the Gurus. "With precepts of this kind," he writes, "the disciples of Nānak would have sunk into a state of dull apathy to the world around them, or they would have led a contemplative life in monasteries, as the Buddhists did, if Nānak, cautioned by his many disputes and contentions with the Jogis, and convinced by practical experience of the wickedness and hypocrisy of the erratic Faqirs, had not enjoined to them, to remain in their secular occupation and not to leave the world. It is owing to this sound principle that the Sikhs have not become a narrow-minded sect of Faqirs, but that they developed themselves by degrees into a political commonwealth." [2]

The other fact which—as we have already noted—has given the Sikhs the resolution and the *esprit de corps* that have enabled them to stand together and resist the

[1] *C.R.I.*, Punjab, 1881, Vol. I, p. 319.

[2] Trumpp, p. cxi.

tradition, such as Tukārām and Kabīr. Like them he caused his friends much anxiety and was even supposed to have become mad. He neglected his secular duties, kept company with holy men, and would spend nights in singing praise to God. About this time a wave of religious emotion was passing over North India and it is evident that the influence of this movement was carried from province to province by wandering preachers and singers. Thus it came about that Rāmānanda brought his gospel from South India to the north, while Kabīr is said to have travelled with his message as far as Balakh and Bokhara, and Tulsi Dās also a little later did the same in other directions. These wanderings brought about contacts among these men of insight and inspiration, not only Hindu but Musalman also, and the exchange of tales and traditions and experiences provided a university of spiritual culture for a wide variety of students and seekers.

Thus to Nānak there came a crisis in his life when he, too, submitted himself to the power of the religious impulse and received miraculously the prophetic initiation and the injunction "to proclaim the name of Hari on earth." He accordingly became a wandering ascetic, accompanied in his journeys by Mardana, a Muslim musician, who played on the rebeck accompanying Nānak's songs. He is said on these journeys to have met Kabīr and to have treated him with great affection and respect. Undoubtedly whether he actually met him or not Kabīr was one of the influences that determined his career and from him he learned some of the basal principles of his religion.

When the call to become a teacher came to him his message was summed up in the words, "There is no Hindu and there is no Musalman." One of the tales told in his janamsakhi—and it has, indeed, parallels in other legends of the saints[1]—describes a visit to Mecca

[1] For example in the legendary tales told in relation to the Marāthā saint, Namdev. See my *Indian Theism*, p. 124.

when he lay down to sleep with his feet towards the Ka'bah. When he was blamed for this he replied, "Where the house of God and the Ka'bah is not, drag my feet to that direction." But to whatever direction they turned his feet, the Ka'bah turned with it.[1] Nānak's relation to the two great religions of his time is also emphasised in the legend that tells of his death. In this case also, however, an almost identical tradition is preserved in the popular account of the death of Kabīr. When the guru died a dispute arose between the Hindus and the Musalmans, the former demanding that they should burn his body, as that of a Hindu, the latter that they should bury it, since they claimed him as theirs. But when the sheet that covered the body was lifted, there was only a heap of flowers.[2]

From such tales as these we learn at least what the impression was that this saint produced by his life and teaching upon the people of his time. He is believed to have died in 1533 at the age of sixty-four. Before his death he appointed as his successor in the line of gurus which he established his disciple Angad, also, like himself, a Khatri. There followed in the religious succession eight other gurus of whom the most notable and the one who impressed upon the Sikh community and the Sikh religion qualities and characteristics that are second only in their significance to those contributed by the founder himself, was Guru Govind. Circumstances and, perhaps, the natural disposition of those among whom this new religious influence was at work tended to make the religion more and more aggressive in spite of the comprehensiveness and tolerance of the teaching of Guru Nānak. As the numbers of the adherents of the Sikh faith increased and their power and influence spread they became drawn into political intrigue and the fifth guru was imprisoned by the Mogul Emperor for his share in a rebellion. From this time onwards the relation of the

[1] Janamsakhi in Trumpp, p. xli. [2] *Ibid.*, p. xlv.

CHAPTER XIV

SIKHISM TODAY

THE position of the Sikh religion at the present time is difficult to estimate with any confidence. If one were to judge of it simply by the number of its adherents as recorded at each successive census during the past fifty years the conclusion must be that there has been steady and remarkable growth. Between 1901 and 1911—a period during which there was a decrease of 2 per cent in the total population of the Province—the Sikhs according to the census returns increased by 37 per cent. Again between 1921 and 1931, when the percentage of increase of Hindus was 10 per cent, the percentage of increase of Sikhs was 33 per cent. In 1911, the Sikh population was given as 1,706,165; in 1931 it is 4,306,442. Part of this remarkable increase in recent years may, no doubt, be attributed to a more careful attempt on the part of the census officers to distinguish Sikhs from Hindus. In 1891 for census purposes a Sikh male was "one who wears the hair long and refrains from smoking." In 1911 the census entry was not made in accordance with this rule; it was left to the individual to decide how he desired to be designated. In view of the fact that very often "the line between Sikhs and Hindus is vague in the extreme,"[1] neither method can be considered to be quite satisfactory. How indefinite was the character of the Sikh religion as practised and how difficult it was in consequence to demarcate the boundaries between it and Hinduism is indicated in a statement on the subject prepared by Mr. H. A. Rose who was intimately associated with the

[1] *C.I.R.*, Punjab, 1911, Part I, p. 153.

P

Sikhs in his service in India. Writing in the Census Report of 1901, Mr. Rose gives an account of Sikh religion as it appeared in the Punjab at that date. "It is not easy," he writes, "to say what is the distinctive creed of Sikhism. It is nearly always difficult to state a religious creed, and in the case of Sikhism there is the great difficulty that the Gurus, from first to last, strove, like the modern Hindu reformers, not to break away from the ancient beliefs but to reconcile them with a purer creed. Unfortunately this resulted, as probably it always must result, in a medley of beliefs, so that within Sikhism we find many religious ideas at variance with its ideal creed. That creed involves belief in one God, condemning the worship of other deities: it prohibits idolatry, pilgrimages to the great shrines of Hinduism, faith in omens, charms or witchcraft: and does not recognise ceremonial impurity at birth or death. As a social system it abolishes caste distinctions, and, as a necessary consequence, the Brāhman supremacy and usages, in all ceremonies, at birth, marriage, death and so on. But this creed is probably accepted and acted up to by a very small number even of those who call themselves true Sikhs."

This account suggests that at that time Sikhism was in danger of becoming submerged in Hinduism. Already, however, even then there must have been the stirring of a new life among them and certainly in the years that have followed there has been a remarkable accentuation of the Sikh self-consciousness and a revival of fading loyalties. Thus in 1911 the Census Officer confidently affirms that the increase then indicated is due mainly to "accretions from the Hindus." "Singh Sabhas," he writes, "have been very active in enforcing the tenets of Guru Govind Singh on all followers of Guru Nānak, whether Sikhs or Hindus, and they have been assisted greatly in their efforts by the fact that only Keshdhari Sikhs are enlisted in the army."[1]

[1] *C.I.R.*, Punjab, 1911, Part I, p. 153.

There can be little doubt that, whatever the causes behind it may have been, there began, perhaps about 1910, and continued right up to the present time what the Census Report of 1911 described as a "Sikh Revival." It showed itself in the fact that Keshdharis, who had formerly freely intermarried with Sahajdharis now refused to do so until the latter took the pahul. Also, the Report notes "the Singh Sabhas and their teachers have been doing a great deal towards the reclamation of the depressed classes."[1]

Among the influences that were at work bringing this about were, undoubtedly, the political aspirations that at that time and during the succeeding decades have stirred so many from lethargy and seem to have, among the Sikhs especially, reawakened slumbering passions and ambitions. No doubt one cause of this was the fact that in August 1914, events had aroused in them the spirit of war and evoked once more that call to battle which always seems to stir the blood of the followers of this warrior faith. The summons brought them back from the ends of the earth. Thus we learn that from October of that year onwards "thousands of Sikhs from abroad were pouring into the Punjab."[2] Unfortunately they did not come with the single aim of rallying once more to the support of the British cause which they had served so loyally for two generations. The enterprise of the Sikh had sent him forth as a colonist to other lands and he had not always found a welcome there. Thus it came about that in 1915 a serious situation was created in the Punjab by the return of Sikhs "driven away from Canada and bitterly estranged from British rule by the anti-Asiatic immigration laws inexorably enforced against them in British Columbia."[3] To these causes of embitterment were added others that resulted from the wild passions

[1] *C.I.R.*, Punjab, 1911, Part I, p. 154.
[2] O'Dwyer, *India as I knew it*.
[3] Valentine Chirol, *India* (*The Modern World*, Vol. V), p. 296.

aroused by the political agitations of the time. A new spirit had been kindled which flamed up, now against one wrong, now against another. The old reformist faith of the Gurus came to life once more and called them to separate themselves from the Hindus and the idolatry that Nānak had condemned.

Already forces had been at work to this end and some action had been taken by the leaders of the community. In 1905 the Golden Temple at Amritsar had been cleansed and the idols that had been installed even in that shrine had been flung into the temple tank. A fresh impetus was given to that movement of reform by the new temper that had now awakened. The lead in this reformation was taken by the sect of the Akālis, the zealots of the faith, the Sikh Ghazis as they have been called. A few years before they were "fast dwindling away,"[1] but the circumstances of the time stirred in them new life and ardour. In March 1921 a hideous incident occurred when one of the corrupt and Hinduised priests, the Mahant of a wealthy Sikh shrine, caused a company of these zealots to be massacred within the very temple courts. This sent a thrill of horror through the Punjab and aroused to still greater vehemence the religious fervour of the true Sikhs. Religion and politics combined to produce a dangerous and highly explosive situation. For there was also—to quote Sir Valentine Chirol again—"the bitter memory of many inoffensive Sikhs shot down in the crowd at Jallianwala Bagh."[2] Some years of bitter hostility and estrangement had to pass before a way of reconciliation was found and by means of the "Sikh Shrines Act" the desire of the Sikhs to have the right as a community to control their religious houses and carry out their reforming aims was fully secured to them.

These, it cannot be doubted, were some of the circumstances that explain the remarkable increase in the Sikh community as recorded in the recent census returns.

[1] Sir D. Ibbetson in *C.I.R.*, Punjab, 1881.

[2] *Op. cit.*, p. 298.

Sikhs with the Mogul power became definitely hostile and Har Govind, the sixth guru, "rejected for good the tokens of a *faqir* and wore two swords, one denoting *faqiri* or spiritual, the other *amiri* or secular, authority." Under the bigoted rule of the Emperor Aurangzib those circumstances continued to develop which were to transform Sikhism from a message of peace to a message of war and the Sikh brotherhood from a farming and trading community to a military confederacy. The ninth guru was seized and executed at Delhi in 1675. When in 1707 Aurangzib died the tenth Guru Govind Singh had completed the transformation of the quietist faith of Nānak and welded together his disciples into a powerful weapon of warfare and aggression.

He did this by a ceremony of initiation through which his followers became the Khālsa, the "pure." This is the "Khandeki pahul" or "initiation by the two-edged dagger." All who desired to be his disciples, he said, must have always with them five things which were to be the distinctive marks of the Sikhs. These five "K's" are the uncut hair (Kes), the comb (Kangha), the sword (Kripan), the iron bangle (Kara) and the breeches ending above the knee (Kachh). They are forbidden also to smoke tobacco. Within this closely knit order there were to be no caste distinctions and the Brāhman's thread must be broken.[1] In consequence of this many of his disciples who were of high caste left him, while many members of lower castes, especially Jats, entered the Khālsa. There thus arose a division within the community, those who called themselves Singhs, as the Guru did, and those who preferred to be known simply as Sikhs. This distinction extended further to the book, the Granth, from which the followers of this faith had hitherto drawn much of their inspiration. Guru Govind was not content with the Ādī Granth, the original collection of hymns, and the spirit of meekness and humility that it inspired. He accordingly

[1] *C.I.R.*, Punjab, 1881, Vol. I, p. 135.

produced the Granth of the Tenth Reign which includes an account of his own warlike deeds and a poem in praise of the Hindu warrior goddess, Durgā. This Granth has not the place in the Sikh religion that is held by the Ādī Granth, and its authority is recognised only by the extreme sections of the community. Guru Govind did not, indeed, displace the original *Granth* from its central position of authority. On the contrary he installed the sacred book itself as his successor in the position of the Sikh Guru—the Granth Sahib, the venerable Book, the embodiment of all the gurus. He died in 1708, the last in the succession of the ten Gurus who may be recognised as the joint founders of the Sikh religion.

In the Punjab Census Report for 1881, Sir Denzil Ibbetson sums up the change in the character of Sikhism that Guru Govind sought to bring about. "His religious creed," he writes, "was in many respects the same as that of Nānak: the God, the Guru and the Granth remained unchanged. But while Nānak had substituted holiness of life for vain ceremonies, Govind demanded brave deeds and zealous devotion to the cause as the proof of faith; and though he retained the tolerance which his predecessor had extended to the Hindu gods and worship, and indeed showed a marked inclination in their favour, being himself a votary of Durgā, he preached undying hatred against the Musalman persecutors. The religious was entirely eclipsed by the military spirit, and thus for the second time in history, a religion became a military power, and for the first time in India a nation arose, embracing all races and all classes and grades of society and banded together in the face of a foreign foe."[1]

It is necessary to make clear before proceeding further what constitutes a Sikh and how they are related to the people among whom they live and especially to their Hindu kinsfolk. The name means disciple, and may be used in a stricter or in a vaguer and more comprehensive

[1] *C.I.R.*, Punjab, 1881, Vol. I, p. 135.

CHAPTER XIII

DOCTRINE AND PRACTICE

As we have seen Sikhism belongs in its origin to the context of Indian devotional theism or Bhakti and is part of that general upsurgence within Hinduism of the devout heart which reached its climax in various parts of western and northern India between the fourteenth and the sixteenth centuries of the Christian era. It derives primarily from Hinduism, but has been powerfully affected by the example and not less by the later hostility of Islam. Its teaching can best be realised by the relation it bears to the doctrines of Hinduism, from which it was in its origin in the main a revolt. One of Guru Nānak's biographers describes the popular worship of the time, against which the Guru protested and which he sought to reform, in the following terms: "Some worshipped the sun or moon; others propitiated the earth, sky, wind, water or fire; and others again the God of death; while the devotion of many was addressed to cemeteries and cremation grounds." Guru Govind in his turn is said to have called his Khālsas to forsake the worship of "idols, cemeteries or cremation grounds." Nānak seems to have been a man with a simple message who made no high claims for himself[1] but who sought to bring men back to a purified religion, to faith in one God and to repentance and righteousness. These continue to be the chief notes of the religion in so far as the influence of the founders has remained living and operative. Nānak was no system builder, nor did he aim at establishing a new religion.

[1] "I am not chaste nor learned; foolish and stupid I was born. Nānak says: I flee to the asylum of those by whom thou art not forgotten." Trumpp, p. 505.

When he went forth with Mardana and sang to the music of his companion's rebeck, he was undertaking the unambitious task of an evangelist, echoing the truths that he had learned from others, rather than proclaiming any new doctrine of his own.

What the doctrines of Sikhism are can best be discovered from the Scripture of the religion, the "Granth Sahib" or "Venerable Book" into which the Guru Arjun collected the sources from which the religion drew its inspiration. This Scripture contains not only the messages of the Gurus but also those of fourteen of the Bhakti saints (one of them a Sufi) whose songs had been sung all over the north and had thus obtained a certain religious authority. Of these saints the one to whom this movement, and its founder Nānak in particular, owed most is believed to be Kabīr, the weaver poet whose influence in India at that period was so great that in Trumpp's opinion he is to be reckoned "the author of the whole reformatory movement going on in India during the Middle Ages."[1] Whether Nānak came directly into contact with his elder contemporary cannot be determined but the debt he owes to Kabīr is indicated by the large place given to his songs in the collection of the Ādī Granth. These are, in the opinion of Trumpp "far superior in form as well as in originality of thought to the versifications of the Sikh Gurus."[2] It may, indeed, be said that in this collection which comprises within itself the creed, the prayer book, and the hymn book of the Sikh religion, the dominant note is that which is struck by the weaver of Benares in whose person Hindu and Muslim strains seem to have mingled.

The place that the Granth holds in the veneration of the Sikhs is important not only as revealing the character of the beliefs that they profess but also because of their attitude to the book itself. This collection—called the Ādī Granth—was made by Guru Arjun, in order that the

[1] Trumpp, p. 93, note 1. [2] *Ibid.*, p. cxix.

PART V

THE RELIGION OF THE PARSIS (ZOROASTRIANISM)

CHAPTER XV

THE EARLIER HISTORY

Of all the ancient religions which have a continuous history through the ages and survive as living faiths today, there is none that has so small a company of adherents as the religion which looks back to Zoroaster as its founder and is professed by the Parsis in India and their co-religionists in Persia. But few though the number of Zoroastrians in the world today may be, the position that the Parsis of India have attained by reason of the high level of their education and intelligence, the remarkable influence they have in public affairs, as well as their wealth and generosity, gives a special importance to the study of the faith they follow. In addition there is the interest that attaches to this religion because of the high moral dignity of the figure of its prophet and founder and of the message that he proclaimed so early in the world's history. The nobility of the ancient form of the religion may be indicated at the outset of our study in the words of Professor A. V. Williams Jackson, one of the most authoritative of the scholars who have studied this subject. " The sacred books of but few peoples," he writes, " contain so clear a grasp of right and wrong, or so ethical a conception of duty, as the Zoroastrian scriptures. Few creeds inculcate more strongly than that of Persia the need for purity of body and soul. Outside of Judaism and Christianity it is impossible to find in antiquity so true, so noble, so ideal a belief in the resurrection of the body, the life everlasting, the coming of a Saviour, and the rewards and punishments for the immortal soul as is to be found in the scriptures of ancient Iran which are illumined by the spirit of the great teacher Zoroaster (Zarathustra)."[1]

The study of this religion has an additional interest for one who, as is the case in the present survey, sets it side by side with Hinduism. Both spring from the same Aryan stock and their adherents once worshipped together the same Aryan gods. It would even appear, if we judge by an inscription discovered in the north-east of Asia Minor, as though the gods of the two branches of the Aryan family still in 1400 B.C. bore the same names, Mitra, Varuna, Indra. However this may be, what is of peculiar interest to us is the wide distance that presently separated from each other two interpretations of life and God that once had dwelt together within the same tents. There could hardly be a greater contrast in idea than that which is presented by the almost Semitic monotheism of Zoroaster when set side by side with the speculative pantheism of the Upanishads. It is not possible to discern clearly the causes which brought about this great intellectual cleavage, by which the devas or "bright ones" of India become the daevas or demons of Iran. It must have been Zoroaster himself, when he appeared, who gave the religion, which had been up till his time a nature worship, like that which the Vedic Hymns reveal to us, its impetus towards an ethical monotheism and passed sentence upon the false deities of the popular worship. The modern Parsi scholar, Dr. Dhalla, describes the change thus effected in words with which most students of the subject would agree. "The pre-Gathic religion of Iran," he writes, "is the evolution of the religious thought of many men and many ages; Zoroaster's is the creation of one man and one age. The prophet of Iran establishes a new religion."[2] The religion of Hindu India on the other hand continued the earlier evolution "of many men and many ages." It struggled onwards on its tortuous

[1] A. V. Williams Jackson, *Zoroastrian Studies*, p. 3.
[2] Dhalla, *Zoroastrian Theology*, p. xxx.

Sikhs might have a sacred code, "to unite them more closely and separate them from the mass of the Hindus."[1] It displaced the Vedas and Purānas and was able to do so because it was largely made up of religious songs which had already won the hearts of the people and which, being in the vernacular, could be understood and used by them. The whole Bhakti movement, indeed, represents in a measure a break away from the organised Hinduism of the Sanskrit scriptures and the Brāhman priests and Nānak's reformation emphasised this tendency and went beyond it. The need, however, for some concrete centre for the religious life soon made itself felt and to correct this "unchartered freedom" the authority of the Guru or spiritual teacher inevitably increased. The *Bhaktamāla* which records the history of this type of religion in North India enumerates as its essentials "faith, a faithful devotee, the Adorable (Bhagavanta) and the Guru."[2] The Sikhs had their ten Gurus, but each of the nine that followed Nānak was supposed to be another embodiment of the first Guru. Then the tenth Guru, Govind, installed as his successor the Granth itself, as the final and permanent guide.

Thus it came about that, in place of the worship of the living Guru which is widespread among many branches of the movement to which Sikhism has so close a relation, worship of the book in which the wisdom of the gurus was stored up, became established. In the Golden Temple at Amritsar, which is the headquarters of Sikh worship, the sacred book is installed in the place of deity and the ceremonial of Hindu worship is rendered to it. "It is looked upon as a living person," and "a *granthi* stands behind it all day waving a *chauri*, or yak's tail, over it as a servant does over the head of an Indian Prince."[3]

It is very difficult, indeed, to make any definite state-

[1] Trumpp, p. cxxx.
[2] Grierson in *E.R.E.*, Vol. II, p. 546.
[3] G. D. Maclagan in *E.R.E.*, Vol. I, p. 399.

ment as to the theological tenets of the Sikh faith, as one has to distinguish between the original beliefs of its founder and the faith and practice of those who in varying degree from the time when the faith was first proclaimed until today, have separated themselves from the Hinduism of their neighbours and followed a way of their own. Nānak himself declares unequivocally:

> "Whom shall I call the second? There is none.
> In all is that One supreme."

Further on in the same poem he affirms the second primary truth of his religion:

> "Know that there are two ways, (but) only one Lord."[1]

The worship of this one God must be worship of the heart. Thus Kabīr says:

> "By performing devotion he is obtained.
> By sincere love they are united with King Raghu (=Rām)."[2]

But there can hardly be consistency in the teaching of a miscellaneous group of bhaktas, whose beliefs are nebulous and only united by their emotional reality. It is always difficult to determine the extent to which a Hindu is a polytheist and whether or not he is fundamentally monotheistic all the time. The word monotheism has a different connotation when it is used by those—such as most Hindus are—who inherit a radical pantheism which colours every aspect of belief. "No Hindu god," writes one Western student of the popular Bhakti sects, "is an entirely separate independent deity, as Western thought would suppose him to be. In every case, every Hindu god is believed to be a manifestation of some sort of God Supreme (Devadhidev)."[3]

The most we can say accordingly of the theology of Sikhism is that it is turned in the direction of theism and

[1] Trumpp, pp. 320, 321. [2] *Ibid.*, p. 461.
[3] J. E. Abbott, *Stotramāla*, p. xii. This is a volume in a series of translations entitled, *The Poet Saints of Maharashtra*.

perpetuity shall be the torments of the Liars."[1] There is no trace in this eschatology of anything that bears relation to the Hindu conception of liberation from rebirth and absorption into the All. "The Mazdean ideal is quite simple and singularly like the Christian—the delivery from evil, moral and physical in this life, and the securing of eternal happiness in a conscious individual life of bliss after death."[2] "When creation shall reach its goal" Ahura Mazda will come with his holy angels to judge the world.[3] "As the great shepherd, Ahura Mazda will bring back into the fold of righteousness all those persons who, led astray by the archtempter, had left his flock."[4] Zoroastrianism, according to M. Meillet and Archbishop Söderblom is in its origin the religion of an oppressed peasantry in rebellion against their aristocratic oppressors. "The prevailing religion was the religion of the predatory upper classes. Zarathustra brought about a revolution. . . . The once despised care for the pastures and the cattle is exalted to be the service of the All-wise Lord."[5]

"The Avesta," says Bishop Casartelli, "treats the whole life of man and the whole history of the world as a 'spiritual combat.'"[6] Life is a free choice between good and evil and the individual is called to make the same decision as the Prophet himself made when, according to a later story, he was tempted by Angra Mainyu, the Spirit of Evil, and said, "I shall not renounce the good Religion, not though life and limb and soul should part asunder."[7] One of the most precious elements of the ancient faith that passed down the ages to become a living part of the religion of the Parsis today is that which recognises the significance in man's life of good word, good thought, good deed. "Every Zoroastrian

[1] Yasna, 45, 7.
[2] *E.R.E.*, Vol. XI, p. 137 (Casartelli).
[3] Yasna, 43, 5, 6.
[4] Dhalla, *Z.T.*, p. 61 ; cf. Yasna, 47, 6.
[5] Söderblom, *The Living God*, p. 186.
[6] *E.R.E.*, Vol. XI, p. 563.
[7] *Vendidad*, 19, 8, quoted by A. V. Williams Jackson, *Zoroaster*, p. 53.

child," says Dr. Dhalla, " imbibes this triad at its mother's breast."[1]

The contrast between this ancient spiritual message so lofty and so simple and that which, springing from the same root, presently cast its sombre shadow over India, is almost startling. Central to Zoroastrianism are Piety and the " Ox-Creator," both children of God, that is to say, the life of duty and the life of common labour among the cattle. Central to Hinduism is knowledge, speculation on the mystery of things and ascetic discipline. Neither mysticism nor asceticism is encouraged within the Zoroastrian system. It was the wail of the " Ox-Soul " that aroused the Prophet first and his revelation centres around human injustice and the vindication of the rights of the humble. Fasting and austerities have no place in this religion. Zoroaster was an optimist holding confidently the faith that good will be the final goal of ill. " Zoroastrianism," in the words of Dr. Dhalla, " is active, practical and militant." " The tone that runs through the Gathas " he sums up in the sentence, " The sun will never set upon the Kingdom of righteousness."[2]

This was the treasure of spiritual inspiration that Zoroaster received from the Wise Lord, Ahura Mazda, and bequeathed to the generations that succeeded. It was too lofty to be fully understood and accepted by the uninstructed multitude without other interpreters and teachers who might have renewed the first prophet's witness. But Zoroaster had no successors; there was no such prophetic line in Iran as there was in Israel. The result is that the jungle of superstition presently reinvaded the territory that Zoroaster had subdued to righteousness. Ahura Mazda could not retain the solitary pre-eminence that Zoroaster had given him. The gods of the pre-Zoroastrians returned to their thrones; and the divine righteousness no longer has the prominence that it had in the earlier scriptures. Mithra who had

[1] Dhalla, *Z.T.*, p. 32. [2] Dhalla, *Z.T.*, p. 17.

been expelled by Zoroaster, according to Dr. Moulton, "because he was too warlike," returns. The whole religion tends increasingly, under the influence, perhaps, of the powerful priestly caste of the Magi, to become the elaborately ritualistic system that priests are likely to make it. Dr. Moulton considers that this tribe, whose influence was undoubtedly very great in all the subsequent development of the religion, brought into it a "non-Aryan stratum." They may be taken to represent the indigenous people of Media who now assert themselves and import large non-Persian elements into Zoroastrianism. To them is apparently due the transformation of the spiritual faith of the founder into ritual formalism.[1] Offences against ritual are reckoned to be as serious as moral transgressions, and much of the concern of the worshipper is to guard himself against the demons of disease and death. It is obvious that we have here a lapse back to those fears from which an ethical monotheism delivers men and a return to the terrors of an animistic religion. "Zarathustra," says J. H. Moulton,[2] "never allowed men to cringe before the devil with offerings and prayers, hoping to turn aside his malignity." The manthra, "by which Zarathustra meant a word of prophetic inspiration,"[3] now, however, resumes the meaning of an incantation, a meaning which it, no doubt, had in pre-Zoroastrian times and which it has always had in India.

Parsis have often been called "fire-worshippers" though they repudiate strongly what that name implies.

[1] L. H. Gray sums up the history of the development of Zoroastrianism as follows: "The system consists of at least five strata: to the religion of Persis were due aniconism, animal sacrifice and nature worship (=the system described by Herodotus); to extra-Persian, pre-Zoroastrianism Mithra, Haoma, and other elements common to Avesta and the Veda; to the teachings of Zoroaster himself monotheism and the war against evil (=the ethical element); to Magianism, dualism, exposure of corpses, marriage with near kin, horror of mountains and ritual prescriptions; to Babylonia oneiromancy, astrology and certain myths." (Quoted from Gray, *Harvard Theological Review* (1922), p. 88, by Baynes, *Israel Among the Nations*, p. 286.

[2] *The Teaching of Zarathustra*, p. 6.

[3] Moulton, *The Treasure of the Magi*, p. 60.

Zoroaster speaks to Ahura Mazda of "the gift of adoration to thy fire,"[1] and recognises it as the emblem of deity, sacred also as being "the instrument of the eschatological 'Regeneration.'"[2] It was to him no more than that. It may have been the Magi, as Dr. Moulton suggests, that introduced the more formal tendance of the sacred flame, its maintenance in the fire-temple and on the domestic hearth, certainly this seems to have been through many centuries a significant ceremonial of this religion. The utmost care has always been taken to preserve fire, as also earth and water, from defilement by anything impure, especially by the bodies of the dead.

Today, as in the days of Strabo, a bundle of twigs is held before the face of the priest who approaches the Sacred Fire, and today as in these early days, he wears when he comes into that presence a covering over his mouth.

Whether or not it was the Magi that gave so central a place in the religion to this cultus, two of their peculiar practices seem to have been the exposure of the dead to be devoured by vultures and the strange enjoinment of marriage with the nearest of kin. The former custom was accepted by the religion at an early date, but the latter was emphatically rejected. To the Magi also is attributed the increasingly dualistic character of the religion in post-Zoroastrian times. The antithesis between good and evil becomes more and more sharply outlined, until the Vendidad, the third section of the Avesta, shows itself as definitely dualistic. The war with evil continues right to the end but it ends in the final defeat of Angra Mainyu or Ahriman. The time shall come at last when "the Sovereign of Evil, bereft of power, will bow to his bitter fate and will hide himself forever in the bowels of the earth."[3]

These developments of the original doctrine continued through successive periods of Iranian history down to the

[1] Yasna, 43, 9. [2] Moulton, *E.Z.*, p. 200. [3] Dhalla, *Z.T.*, p. 159.

crisis that came with the conquest of Persia by the Muslim power in A.D. 651. An earlier catastrophe that had befallen the religion was the invasion of Alexander the Great followed by the rule of the Seleucids from 330 to 250 B.C. The Zoroastrian tradition is that the conqueror burned the Avesta and wrought so much ruin to their religion that he is known by them to this day as "the accursed Sikander." A lightening of the darkness that enveloped them through succeeding centuries came when the Sasanian empire was established in A.D. 226. Ardashir, who founded this dynasty, was a Magus, an ardent propagator of the faith, one "whose fame is writ large in the history of Zoroastrianism."[1] For four centuries, that is, until the overthrow of the House of Sasan, in 651, by Islam, the Zoroastrian faith flourished as the state religion of Iran. During this period of prosperity there were, however, some hostile influences at work within the religion, especially the religion of Mani which, according to Jackson, "came near to shaking the throne just at the moment when the second Sasanid ruler, Sapor, entered upon his reign." This religion resembles Zoroastrianism in its dualistic character, but while "the aim of the Zoroastrian is to banish evil from the world, the aim of the Manichaean is to extract from the world that which is good."[2] The difference between the two religions is seen in the pronounced asceticism of the Manichaean "elect," in contrast with the Zoroastrian rejection of all asceticism. The conflict of the religions culminated when in the year A.D. 274 Mani was put to death with cruel tortures by the Sasanian king, Bahram I.

The turn of the Zoroastrians themselves to endure persecution came when in A.D. 652 the Sasanian dynasty was overthrown by the Arab invasion of Persia. Among the calamities that this invasion brought upon them was the destruction of their culture. This catastrophe,

[1] Dhalla, *Z.T.*, p. 191.
[2] A. A. Bevan in *E.R.E.*, Vol. VIII, p. 400.

following upon the destruction wrought according to the Zoroastrian tradition by Alexander the Great, was fatal to Iranian scholarship. Darkness descends upon this unhappy race and what glimpses we obtain of their life show them to be crushed and oppressed. This was not altogether undeserved; the intolerance of the Zoroastrian priesthood to such sects as the Manichaeans had caused them to be hated. On the other hand the Magians seem to have been treated, at least at times, with the tolerance that the Muslims professed to show to "people of the Book." Great numbers of them yielded to persecution and accepted Islam. But even this did not preserve them from oppression for "the non-Arab Muslims were regarded by the Arabs as no better than slaves."[1] Those who still clung to their ancient faith had to pay the jizya tax. Their chief occupation was that of agriculture which had traditionally been the occupation of their ancestors. Now, as "Gabars" or infidels, they were debarred from more profitable callings which might bring them into contact with those who regarded them as outcastes. "They had to bear the same vexations," writes Mademoiselle Menant, "as those experienced in India by the Mahars (outcastes) at the hands of the high-caste Hindus."[2] "Writing to their co-religionists in India in the fifteenth century," says Dr. Dhalla, "they complain that ever since the overthrow of the Empire they are living under such troublesome times that the atrocities of a Zohak or an Afrasiab or an Alexander pale before what they have been suffering for nine centuries."[3]

When the darkness that had enveloped them for so long lifts and we are able to take note of their religious condition it is to find companies of very poor and ignorant people living by themselves, aloof from non-Zoroastrians, with a scripture that they could read but could not under-

[1] D. Menant, *E.R.E.*, Vol. VI, p. 148.
[2] *Ibid.*, p. 150.
[3] Dr. Dhalla, *Zoroastrian Theology*, p. 298 f.

stand. In the eighth century A.D. a band of exiles had fled to India and had prospered there. Others had fled, they say, to other lands but all traces of them have vanished. Only with their countrymen in India was occasional intercourse maintained, and from them, as more learned in the Pahlavi language of their holy books, help was requested. "The faithful," one letter from Iran declares, "have little help to perform meritorious actions in the path of Hormazd." The communications that passed between Persia and India from the fifteenth to the eighteenth century—called Rivāyats—form, we are told, "our most precious source of information in the customs of the two communities, and through them old works, fragments of the most precious books of sacred literature, found their way to India, jumbled up with questions of pure ritualism or social life."[1] The Zoroastrians in Persia were poor, depressed and mostly illiterate; the Parsis, as they were called in India, were prospering, indeed, but bestowed little thought or care upon the religion of their fathers. A new era came in the history of Zoroastrianism when a French scholar Anquetil du Perron came upon some pages of the Avesta in Paris and in his determination to find out their meaning travelled to India and found there a priest who had been taught Avesta by another priest who had come to India from Persia. Du Perron's translation was published in 1771.

From that time onwards the Avesta became a subject of devoted study by a succession of Western scholars, French, German, American and British, and simultaneously in India a new interest awakened among Parsis in their ancient religious inheritance and was accompanied by a new realisation of its spiritual treasures and some recovery of faith in its spiritual values. By the middle of the nineteenth century this new spirit was aroused among them and their renaissance had begun. For twelve centuries their history is wrapped for the

[1] D. Menant, *E.R.E.*, Vol. VI, pp. 152, 153.

most part in obscurity and little more is known of it than that it must have been a history of almost continuous subjection and suffering. We must at this point review in its most general aspects the changes that that long martyrdom had brought about in a religion that had once been so lofty and so austere.

The greatest possession of ancient Zoroastrianism had been the ethical monotheism that would appear to be due to the religious inspiration of its great Prophet. When the barrier of that powerful personality was removed and he had, as seems to have been the case, no prophetic successor, the fears and superstitions that his influence had restrained reasserted themselves and the old gods and the old machinery of nature-worship obtained control once more over the minds of the multitude. The abstractions, such as Asha, the Divine Order and Vohu Manah, Good Thought, which Zarathustra had associated with Ahura Mazda, not as personal beings but as divine attributes, could not satisfy the hunger of men's hearts. "The cold, pure splendour" of the monotheistic deity, according to Dr. Moulton, "gave their opportunity to the old gods," and Mithra, for example, was restored to honour and retains his place in the worship of the Parsis even now. "The general tendency," writes Dr. Dhalla, "of drifting towards the concrete and material in religion endures throughout the Younger Avestan as well as the subsequent Pahlavi period, in which it reaches its climax." "To think of Zoroastrianism," he adds, without the pre-Zoroastrian divinities, "is inconceivable."[1]

It is true that Ahura Mazda (or Ormazd as his name appears in the Pahlavi scriptures) continues to hold nominally the position of supreme godhead. He is omniscient, omnipotent, and "whatever is good in the world proceeds from him." "All light proceeds from Ormazd. In the moral sphere Ormazd is eternal truth."[2] At the same time, as Dr. Moulton says, "monotheism

[1] *Z.T.*, pp. 76 f.

[2] *Ibid.*, pp. 222, 223.

is submitted to a severe strain"[1] when Ahura Mazda himself offers worship and sacrifice to such angels as Tishtrya, "the star genius that directs the rain," and Anahita, "the angel of waters."[2]

On the other hand, in the words of Dr. Moulton, "the old nature gods have been well purged of former taints before being allowed to enter the ranks of Zoroastrian angels."[3] A far more serious fact in the later Avestan religion is the place of a mechanical cultus in the religion and the prominence of the use of spells or manthras. The Gathic hymns now fall to the rank of incantations for protection against disease or the evil eye. It is not surprising that even in a religion which possessed the tradition of Zoroaster's ethical monotheism the dark shadows of persecution and unhappiness should drive men to resort to practices of magic. So Dr. Williams Jackson found that scriptures were read by the priests at Yezd in Persia for protection against evil influences. The fact that the language of these scriptures was unintelligible even to the priests no doubt served to make them be reckoned all the more potent for such purposes. Even the Parsis of today continue practices, some of which those who are enlightened among them recognise as "survivals of the magic ritual of primitive times." "One correct repetition of the Ahuna Vairya," writes one of the modern leaders in reform, Professor P. A. Wadia, "without any omission is worth the chanting of a hundred Gathas and will enable the devout to reach Paradise. The credulity of a later age describes how the chanting aloud of this formula by Zarathustra brought about the flight of the demon Buiti. The careless soul that commits mistakes in the intonation and recital of the formula is debarred from Paradise."[4]

At the same time it remains true of Zoroastrianism even in its later phases that ethical interests continue to

[1] *The Treasure of the Magi*, p. 87. [2] *Z.T.*, pp. 129, 137.
[3] *The Treasure of the Magi*, p. 88.
[4] P. A. Wadia, *Zoroastrianism and our Spiritual Heritage*, p. 24.

have a chief place in the practices of the religion. "The characteristics of the godly life are the absence of any ascetic means of bringing the soul into mystical communion with God and the legalistic spirit that pervades it."[1] This legalistic spirit which now pervades the religion, replacing the prophetic insight of Zarathustra, creates new sins, as it creates new ritual. Thus among sinful actions are included walking with only one boot or barefooted, and eating while talking.[2] This confusion of ethical values is seen in such a claim as that of the Rivāyats that "bull's urine makes man's inner nature as bright and pure as the sun and is the very life of religion,"[3] and in the list of punishments included in the Vendidad, "the Leviticus of the Parsi Canon." The penalties there enumerated are elaborated in ridiculous detail so that, as Dr. Moulton puts it, "the tariff of stripes is a matter of comic opera." The Hell of Zoroastrianism has held even up to the present time an important place in the religion as "a hangman's whip" for the discipline of its adherents. The Book of Arta-i-Viraf, a vision of the world beyond the grave, has had a wide popularity both in Persia and in India for centuries. Eighty-three of its 101 chapters are occupied with a description of hell. If such restraints as the Vendidad and this Zoroastrian Inferno furnish could preserve men from committing sin, the Parsis should be models of good conduct, for the whole Vendidad is solemnly read through at the Nirang ceremony and the Book of Arta-i-Viraf when similarly read to Parsi audiences is said to move them deeply.

In one respect the development of the religion after the time of Zoroaster has been a real advance from what was in the main an individual eschatology to a conception of the final destiny of the world as a whole. The Prophet's conviction of the final triumph of good is elaborated into an affirmation of an eternal moral order and the ultimate

[1] N. Söderblom in *E.R.E.*, Vol. III, p. 776.
[2] *E.R.E.*, Vol. XI, p. 565. [3] Dhalla, *Z.T.*, p. 309.

destruction of hell itself when Ormazd shall reign and "humanity attune its will to his."[1] The importance of this great theodicy as differentiating the religion that proclaims it from most of the other world religions can best be indicated by a quotation from Archbishop Söderblom's article on the subject in the *Encyclopædia of Religion and Ethics*. He writes: "The Mazdayasnian (*i.e.* Zoroastrian) scheme expresses in a somewhat scholastic way the idea implied in the word history: that is to say, 'something happens in what happens' (G. J. Geijer), so that the intricate mass of events has a meaning and a goal beyond the actual combinations and situation. The real kernel of history is a 'forward,' not a 'see-saw' and not a 'backward,' although it may seem so to human eyes. This profound conception has arisen only twice in the history of human thought—in the only two ancient prophetic religions, one Aryan, one Semitic—in Zarathustrianism and in Mosaism. Neither seems to have borrowed it from the other. Christianity inherited it from Mosaism, and it has become prevalent in the Western civilisation in the form of a belief in a divine purport in history, in progressive evolution or in a redeeming crisis, and constitutes one of the most significant features and influential factors in the civilisation of Europe and America, as distinguished from the great civilisations of India and of the Far East." "To have originated," Archbishop Söderblom concludes, "faith in the significance and purpose of history may fittingly be called Zarathustra's greatest gift to mankind."[2]

The parallelism in this particular between the religion of Zoroaster and the religion of Israel is not, it is generally agreed, due to any indebtedness on the part of the religions to each other but to the fact that both are deeply rooted in an ethical monotheism.[3] The kinship of these

[1] Dhalla, *Z.T.*, p. 293. [2] *E.R.E.*, Vol. I, p. 210.

[3] For an examination of some of the questions that arise in this connection see Edwyn Bevan's survey in his lecture *The Hope of a World to Come* (Allen & Unwin).

Recently two scholars, Pettazzoni and L. H. Gray, have supported the

two faiths, the one Aryan in origin and the other Semitic, is as striking as is the contrast and divergence that we have already noted between the Aryan religion that migrated to Iran and the Aryan religion that migrated to India. There is much in the history of the Zoroastrian people, as well as in their religious beliefs, that resembles the tragic history of Israel. Both were crushed beneath the yoke of the conqueror and the oppressor: both suffered exile. The followers of Zoroaster were for more centuries than the Jews "a people scattered and peeled," and, like the Jews, have, even now, no land that they can call their own. Neither people throughout all the period of their martyrdom forsook the faith of their fathers and they both preserved tenaciously their national identity. The Zoroastrians never appear to have possessed the source of strength for endurance that came from the Jewish conviction of God's election of them to fulfil a mission to the world. As a consequence they seem at an early period to have abandoned the belief, which is in accord with the lofty theism of Zoroaster, that they should open the gates of their faith to the world outside their borders. The fact that they were not as successful as the Jews in maintaining in its purity their monotheistic conviction, no doubt lowered the vitality of the religion and helped to weaken in its adherents that fervour of conviction which glowed in Israel all through the period of their oppression. Thus it comes about that when we find the Zoroastrians in India they have become the Parsis, a rigidly exclusive community, almost indeed, as Dr. Moulton describes them, "a caste, compassing sea and land to frustrate the making of a proselyte."[1]

view that "the reform of Zarathustra" arose in the seventh century B.C. as a result of contact with the exiled Hebrews settled "in the cities of the Medes" after the fall of the Northern Kingdom of Israel. See Baynes, *op. cit.*, pp. 276 f.

[1] Moulton, *The Treasure of the Magi*, p. 128.

NOTE.—The quotations from the Gathas are from Dr. Moulton's version in his *Early Zoroastrianism*.

CHAPTER XVI

THE ZOROASTRIANISM OF THE PARSIS

THE word Parsi means "an inhabitant of Pars, the old Persian province of Pārsa, or Persia Proper."[1] This is the name by which the Zoroastrian inhabitants of India are called. They number, in the Indian census of 1931, 106,972 and form the great majority of surviving adherents of the religion of Zoroaster in the world. The number of their co-religionists in Persia was estimated in 1902 as 11,000. The Parsis are the descendants of the Zoroastrian fugitives who found in India a haven of refuge from their Muslim oppressors in Persia. Their headquarters are in the district of Gujarat in the Presidency of Bombay. By their business ability, their wealth and their zeal for the progress of their community they have acquired an influence in the West of India, and indeed throughout the whole sub-continent that is far greater than their numbers would suggest. Since 1849 when they began, in the words of one of them, "to put their house in order" and took in hand the education of their children they have steadily advanced to their present position of authority and respect.

In this way the descendants of those worshippers of the same Aryan gods who parted from each other in Central Asia, perhaps five thousand years ago, have come together again and live in close contact as members of the same Indian nation. But the religious practices of each of these kindred Aryan people seem now to be in large measure in direct antithesis to one another. Dr. Dhalla, a learned priest of the Parsis, describes the contrast

[1] Jackson, *Zoroastrian Studies*, p. 181.

between them in striking sentences. "The Hindu rises in the morning to begin his day's work with the devout utterance of devas on his lips; the Parsi leaves his bed cursing them. One seeks their help, the other does battle with them. One invokes them with his uplifted hands, the other lashes them with his sacred girdle. The Hindu anathematises the asuras as infernal beings, the Parsi pays his homage to the ahuras as celestial beings." Thus, he goes on, "these two friendly peoples, living close together incessantly revile each other's gods without in the least impairing their friendly relations."[1]

It cannot, indeed, be alleged that fanaticism is in any respect a characteristic of the Parsis. At the same time their loyalty to their community is deep and intense. The social ties that unite them seem unbreakable. They are able to combine a narrow racial and communal exclusiveness with great breadth of cultural interest and generous service of their fellow-men of every race and religion. They adhere with the utmost tenacity to their own ancient faith, but how far they practise it as a faith by which they live, rather than a body of traditions which make them and keep them a united family, is more difficult to determine. It is, no doubt, true, as Dr. Dhalla claims, that "the Zoroastrian virtues have made the modern Parsi great."[2] We have to try to find out how these still operate in the life and the convictions of the members of this community and how far Zoroastrianism ministers to the spiritual needs of a people so remote in time and circumstance from the great founder of the religion which they profess to follow.

It must be recognised that that ancient inheritance has in large measure contributed to create those virile qualities that are characteristic of the Parsi people. Their industry and their integrity can be claimed as the fruit of the ethical religion that has come down to them from their fathers. At the centre of their profession of faith and

[1] Dhalla, *Z.T.*, pp. 304 f.

[2] *Z.T.*, p. 370.

continually held up before them as their ideal is the triad of "good thought, good word, good deed." At the ceremony of initiation, when the child is invested with the sacred cord (kusti) and shirt (sudrah) the child repeats a creed which contains the words, "Righteousness is the best gift, and happiness. Happiness to him who is righteous for the (sake of) the best righteousness."[1] In spite of the fact that Zoroastrianism has become, as the Parsis received and practise it, almost entirely a system of ceremonial, and in spite of the fact that those ancient formulæ which bear down to them the ethical kernel of their faith is hidden from them in an ancient and little-known tongue, this ethical emphasis has never been wholly lost and has stamped its impress upon the people. "In the individual life this ethic appreciates industry, self-control and veracity; in social life—righteousness, regularity and social accord." These are qualities that are characteristics of the Parsis at their best and make them the good citizens that they so often are.

"The Zoroastrian religion," writes Darmesteter,[2] "was a religion of life in the noblest sense of the word; it brought two things of which the old Aryan religion, in the midst of which it rose, had no idea or only a dim apprehension; these two things were morale and hope." These are the proper fruits of an ethical theism and are fruits that Hindu monism cannot bear. Fatalism has never had a place in the true Zoroastrian tradition though in the Sasanian period the sect of Zarvanites sought to create a place for it within the religion. "Fatalism," says Dr. Dhalla, "never came to be employed among the Zoroastrians as an excuse for cloaking man's indolence." "The ever active spirit of Zoroastrianism," he goes on to say, "saved the nation from its baneful influence." This active spirit which the modern Hindu is striving, in opposition to the spirit of his ancient religion, to win for

[1] J. J. Modi, *Navjote Ceremony of the Parsees.*
[2] J. Darmesteter, quoted in *E.R.E.* article, "Parsis," Vol. IX, p. 647.

himself, is part of the heritage brought by the Zoroastrian faith to the Parsi and is bred in his bones. He has learned that every man must freely choose between right and wrong and that by his choice is determined his destiny in the world to come.

Parsiism is thus, in its traditions a religion of morality and of activity. We see its virtues exhibited in the public spirit and the benevolence that so honourably characterise the leaders of this community. They have learned by the resolute doctrine that has come down to them from their great Prophet not to succumb to evil but to do battle against it. Though they have ceased to believe that they possess a message of religious truth that they should share with the world, they are generous in sharing other gifts that they possess with all who are in need. The great Wadia Charities, founded by one of their generous sons, are at the disposal of all sufferers from calamity the whole world over, unconfined by bounds of race or of religion. In Bombay Presidency in the struggle for social reform, though it was the need of the Hindu population that was greatest, it was a Parsi, Mr. B. M. Malabari, who showed the way to the Hindu reform leaders; and so also in the political movement it was Dadabhai Naoroji, who was the pioneer not for his own Parsi people only but for all India. There are other qualities besides vigour and resolution that are needed to make either a great saint or a great servant of the state, but these two qualities at least are to be found among the Parsis, needing only a divine fire to cleanse and illuminate them for the highest ends, and these qualities they owe in great measure to a religion which, even after the vicissitudes of nearly three thousand years moulds the characters of those who profess it. It moulds their character as a race even though today it is a living faith only to a few.

These qualities of character have come down to the Parsis of today as part, one might say, of their racial inheritance. They are the creation of the religion, but rather its creation in the past than in the present. The old Zoroastrian faith is losing its influence it once had as a living force upon the thoughtful members of the community. The language of its sacred books has long ago ceased to have any meaning for them, and the prayers, repeated in that language, which even the priests can no longer pronounce correctly, convey no meaning at all to those who are supposed through them to confess their sins and utter their thanksgiving. The ceremonial which now constitutes almost the whole of the religion can no longer satisfy the religious needs of the thoughtful people. One or two enlightened priests endeavour to supplement these ritual performances by sermons which may instruct the people in the lofty tenets of their faith, but those among the Parsis who realise the need of religious belief for the nourishment of the soul are discovering with dismay how unfitted is a religion that is mainly made up of an obsolete ceremonial to resist the destructive influence of Western science and Western philosophy. The Parsis are, indeed, today, divided into three classes, the orthodox who blindly follow the traditional practices and accept the traditional beliefs, those who hold by the Zoroastrian faith in its central principles but would abandon what is unessential and obsolete, and those—an increasing number—who, from indifference or from positive unbelief, neither practise nor profess the religion of their fathers.

1. An orthodox religion need not, of course, be a dead religion, and there are Parsis, as there are adherents of other faiths, who find comfort from walking in ancient ways, just because they are ancient. Nor has one a right to say that a religion that is mainly cultus has no living spring within it. One educated Hindu—and there may be many like him among both Hindu and Parsis—recently complained bitterly of the absence, in the arid and rationalist doctrine he had adopted, of a ceremonial,

such as the old Hinduism had, that in times of bereavement brought comfort, just because it provided something to be ritually executed. So such ceremonies as those of initiation when the child takes up the duties of his religion, and those at the time of death and when the body is carried forth to be exposed in the "Tower of Silence," as well as the ritual relating to the tending of the sacred fire in the temple, all have their contributions to make, in the case of many, to the moulding of their character and the cleansing and comforting of their hearts. On all these occasions prayers are repeated and formulæ used which, if they were understood, might well lift the thoughts of those who hear them to what is worthy of reverence. We have seen how this is so in the case of the investiture with the sacred cord and sacred shirt at the time of initiation. The kusti or cord is "held to be a symbol of obedience to God closing the door against sin and breaking the power of evil."[1] The daily knotting of the kusti is also meant to be associated with pious resolutions.

The tending of the sacred fire is an important part of the religious ritual and has often caused the Parsi to be mistakenly described as a fire-worshipper. But fire is no more than a symbol of the sole God whom they worship. They venerate, however, the angels presiding over such elements as fire, the sun, the waters. Symbolism has a large place in the interpretation of the ritual of the religion, and by this means, no doubt, it edifies those who devoutly perform it.

The Dakhma or "Tower of Silence," as it is generally called nowadays, is the place around which the ceremonial for the dead is centred. There the dead bodies are exposed to be devoured by vultures. Their doctrine of the sacredness of fire and of earth forbids either cremation or burial, as a dead body is to them peculiarly a source of evil contagion. For that reason the "corpse-bearers"

[1] J. J. Modi in *E.R.E.*, Vol. VII, p. 325.

are a class by themselves who remain perpetually unclean. Some of the ceremonies that are followed in this connection can be explained today as possessing a sanitary value and are defended on these grounds by many Parsis. An interesting comment that Dr. Moulton makes on this funeral ritual is that " there is no trace anywhere of that almost universal fear of the ghost, which has determined the usages of so many peoples."[1]

It is indeed the case in all this religion that the object of dread is evil, and evil, especially, as embodied in the demon emissaries of Ahriman. Sin produces demons, and " the impurity of death is the worst of all, the fiend who inflicts and strengthens himself by it the deadliest enemy." For that reason the utmost care must be taken in carrying out the funeral rites of purification. Hell also has a large place in the religion of the orthodox Parsi and the fear of hell and its torments must be a powerful deterrent against evil-doing. A Parsi who became a greatly honoured Christian in Bombay, Rev. Dhanjibhai Naoroji, used to tell of the deep and abiding impression made on him as a boy by the harrowing description he once listened to of the terrors of hell as these were described by a wicked Parsi woman. " The Book of Arta-i-Viraf," which gives a description of the sufferings of those in hell, has been translated into Gujerati and " is a favourite work with all classes of the Parsi community." As they listened to it, we are told, " they used to weep." " It was a most affecting spectacle," one of their Dasturs (priests) writes, " to witness the awakening conscience exhibiting itself in trickling tears."[2]

2. It is not surprising that to many educated and enlightened Parsis much of the ritual that is crude and meaningless, and many of these strange beliefs in demons and in the tortures of hell are no longer acceptable and that among those of them who still cling to the ancient

[1] *The Treasure of the Magi*, p. 151.
[2] Quoted in *E.R.E.*, Vol. XI, p. 847.

faith a movement has arisen to cleanse it from such relics of ancient superstition or legacies from the gross nature worship of the ancient past. Such a piece of ritual is that of the *sag-dīd*, when a "four-eyed" dog is brought near the corpse as it is being borne out to be exposed. This dog is supposed to be able to frighten away the demon of the dead body by his look. Nor can the modern Parsi be expected to join in the washing of a corpse in *gomez* (bull's urine) even if it is justified on the ground that it "is believed to possess some disinfecting properties."[1] The truly religious Parsi is not content with prayers "mechanically droned, according to instruction, in an archaic tongue, unintelligible to the large majority." Even if the prayers were understood, one of the most earnest and able of the representatives of this point of view, Professor P. A. Wadia, writes,[2] "these prayers are a propitiation and invocation of nature deities, in whom (the Parsi's) ancestors three thousand years ago may have vainly trusted for help and guidance, but who have now ceased to exercise that influence over his life and who have passed into mythical products of primitive fancy. Whilst this old world of the sun god and the moon god, the water sprite and the wood sprite has ceased to have living contact with him, a new world has been steadily opened to him, requiring new adjustments in his spiritual life, new expressions for this changed outlook, a new set of prayers and a new ritual."

Those like Professor Wadia who are calling for a new birth of religion among their Parsi fellow-countrymen have met with bitter opposition. Some of these reformers would reduce their creed, apparently, to something that would satisfy "a unitarian or a rationalist."[3] Some indeed would appear to have adopted a completely agnostic attitude. It is not easy to retain the power of a religion

[1] Moulton, *op. cit.*, p. 152.
[2] *Zoroastrianism and our Spiritual Heritage*, p. 24.
[3] So H. J. Bhabha, quoted by Moulton, *op. cit.*, p. 174.

while rejecting its traditions and its ceremonial usages. For that reason Dr. J. H. Moulton, as a Christian who had made a profound and reverent study of the teaching of Zarathustra, strongly urged the Parsis, in meetings that he held with them in Bombay, not to think only of their narrow interests as a community but to realise that their possession in the Gathas of a pure and ethical monotheism constituted a call to preach, and that such "a passion for sharing the good things of their ancient faith was the one certain way of bringing a new springtime of life to themselves."[1] No doubt it is the intensely conservative social instincts of the Parsis that have prevented this controversy, while it has aroused intense feeling, from causing an actual schism in the community. In the words of Dr. Dhalla, one of the more cautious reformers, "the battle goes on, still to be won."[2]

3. There are indications, however, that the battle may end in the extinction not only of orthodoxy but of the spirit of religion itself. The religion the Parsis inherited, in spite of its ethical nobility, lacked certain elements without which it could not retain its hold, in the changed circumstances of the modern world, of the hearts of its adherents. Dr. E. Lehmann has indicated what some of these were. "The Persians," he writes, "cared little for the emotions of disinterestedness; even in the religious feelings we feel too often the lack of lyric elements; on the contrary we always feel the burden of the juristic spirit."[3] In some respects the strength of the old Zoroastrian tradition lay in its avoidance both of the perils of mysticism and of the extravagances of asceticism. "The whole fabric of the ascetic and unworldly view of life," Dr. Dhalla claims, "is in direct antagonism to the active, and in the best sense, worldly spirit of the Mazdayasnian faith."[4] But in this lay a source of weakness also. When

[1] Moulton, *op. cit.*, pp. 176 f.
[2] Dhalla, *Z.T.*, pp. 35 f.
[3] Dr. Edv. Lehmann in *E.R.E.*, Vol. V, p. 516.
[4] Dhalla, *Z.T.*, p. 318.

there comes to men what one anthropologist[1] calls "a wave of asthenic emotion," and another[2] "a failure of nerve," the religions that do not plumb the depths of human need, religions of law and not of grace are apt to prove insufficient. "Zoroastrianism," says Dr. Dhalla, "stands for self-assertion." But probably Dr. Moulton is right in his suggestion that it is "the absence of a strong call to sacrifice which lies at the root of the failure of Parsi religion today."[3] These defects are, no doubt, among the causes that have led so many, disappointed in the resources of their own religion, to betake themselves under the influence of their fears and their unsatisfied longings to "the Hindu augur and the Moslem diviner." "The Zoroastrian priest ruled in the fire-temple but the non-Zoroastrian priest had a powerful sway over the hearts of the Parsi populace."[4] In the seventeenth century there were, we learn, those "who found consolation in the teachings of the Hindu Yogis and became their willing disciples."[5] In the twentieth century such persons are still to be found. Dr. Moulton found them following the Vedāntist teaching of the Radhasaomi sect; and later than his time a Parsi sannyāsi gathered disciples about him in Ahmadnagar, teaching the traditional Hindu doctrines that lead men to release.

By the testimony of Dr. Dhalla, "Zoroaster had partly ceased to be a living force in the spiritual life of the community."[6] These circumstances—the weakening of the old defences of Zoroastrianism in face of the assaults of modern thought and, alongside of that, the longing for some deeper, or at least more mysterious, explanation of the universe than their traditional religion supplied—caused many Parsis to turn to the Theosophical Society which in 1879 had transferred its headquarters to India. This Theosophy was, indeed, fundamentally in contra-

[1] Marett, quoted in Gilbert Murray's *Four Stages of Greek Religion*, p. 105.
[2] G. Murray in *op. cit.*, p. 103.
[3] *Op. cit.*, p. 196.
[4] *Z.T.*, pp. 342, 343.
[5] *Ibid.*, p. 313.
[6] *Ibid.*, p. 344.

diction to the central teachings of the faith of Zarathustra. Mrs. Besant has defined the aim of the Society as "the strengthening and uplifting of the ancient religions—Hinduism, Zoroastrianism, and in Ceylon and Burmah Buddhism." This was, however, understood by her to mean the reinterpretation of them in conformity with that Hinduism which she had adopted as her own belief. The service that she has rendered in India has been, accordingly, a service primarily to Hinduism. It is difficult to see how any true Zoroastrian could co-operate in an attempt to assimilate his religion to its direct contrary. Their antagonism is revealed in the case of those elements in the religion of the Parsi which have contributed so much to his character and energy. His acceptance of the karma law which is so central to Theosophy would inevitably lead to that fatalism which Zoroastrianism has always repudiated. This had been an old heresy in Iranian religion from the time when it was held that both Ahura Mazda and Ahriman were sprung from an impersonal "Endless Time" or Fate. The very life of Zoroastrianism lay in what Söderblom calls Zarathustra's defiant "No" to evil. There was all through the later history a fear lest the seduction of Hinduism would prevail over the intransigence of the ethical tradition. Mr. B. M. Malabari, one of the most resolute of fighters against moral evils, whether in Hinduism or among his own Parsi people, tells us how his Hindu associations taught him a tolerance towards his erring brother which he sometimes felt to be too easy. "Now and again," he says, "I break away from this beneficent restraint."[1] "The spirit of protest against wrong," it is evident, could not be silenced in this loyal Zoroastrian. But when pantheism and fatalism came to them under the ægis of the Western Theosophists there were many who accepted its easy accommodations. Mrs. Besant would have them believe that the original duality

[1] Dayaram Gidumal's *Life of B. M. Malabari*, p. 176.

of their faith was " not of good and evil, but of spirit and matter, of construction and destruction," and so the ethical Protestantism of the Zoroastrian was resolved.

Not only accordingly was Ormazd dethroned and Zervan Akarana set up in his place, as the monistic principle that is ultimate in Theosophy. They proceeded further to introduce into Zoroastrianism the Hindu doctrine of transmigration which theosophy accepts but to which the Parsi traditional faith is wholly opposed. As compensation for these radical transformations of their ancestral beliefs the Parsi receives from the Theosophist, as the Hindu also may receive from him, such a defence of the cultus, even when it seems irrational and repulsive, as may persuade him that he may still perform it. Thus the use of " manthras " or spells is vindicated on the ground that they " set up certain vibrations " which produce peace and calm; or references to the power of the dog, which naturally enough are found in the sacred literature of a pastoral people, are explained as giving " an allegorical description of conscience and its workings." Again, the segregation of Parsi women at certain periods is explained as due to the fact that " the aura of a woman in her menses is spiritually diseased," while the urine of cattle is invested with mysterious occult powers. " They preach to the less educated classes of people that there is high efficacy in offering flowers and milk and cocoa-nuts to the waters; they preach to the people, as an act of special religious merit, to fall prostrate before and kiss imaginary pictures of their prophet; they exhort people to make a show of penitence by vigorous slapping of cheeks."[1]

Not by that road lies hope for the renewal of Parsi religion. To many besides Dr. Dhalla it is plain that their " enlightened faith " will not obtain salvation by " cultivating credulity," " losing their grip of common sense and deceiving themselves with fond delusions."

[1] *Journal of the Iranian Association*, quoted by Farquhar, *Modern Religious Movements*, p. 344.

Theosophy has indeed ceased to attract such people and instead, we are told " the present-day Parsi grows cold and apathetic towards his creed and ritual and feels that the only things worth living for are the things that belong to his daily avocation, the things that bring him material ease and comfort, that religion is cant and hypocrisy and that the priesthood is a selfish hierarchy of men interested in preserving their own domination."[1] There are still many among Parsis who cherish the ancient ideals of their faith and have not sunk to that enslavement by material things. One of these is the High Priest of the Parsis of North Western India, Dr. Dhalla, who defines in the last chapter of his book, *Zoroastrian Theology*, the religion towards which they still look with hope. " Zoroastrianism will live by its eternal verities," he writes, " of the belief in the personality of Ormazd, an abiding faith in the triad of good thoughts, good words and good deeds, the inexorable law of righteousness, the reward and retribution in the life hereafter, the progress of the world towards perfection, and the ultimate triumph of the good over evil through the coming of the Kingdom of Ormazd with the co-operation of man. These are the truest and greatest realities in life. They are valid for all times. They constitute the lasting element of Zoroastrianism."[2]

[1] P. A. Wadia, *Zoroastrianism and our Spiritual Heritage*, p. 55.
[2] *Z.T.*, p. 371.

PART VI

INDIAN CHRISTIANITY

CHAPTER XVII

ITS HISTORY

It cannot, of course, be said of Christianity, as of so many other of the religions we have been considering, that it is indigenous to India, but no other immigrant has had so long a history within the land and none accordingly may claim more confidently the rights of citizenship. The Parsis came as fugitives, driven by persecution, to seek a haven and a refuge among hospitable strangers. The Muslims came as warriors and conquerors, not that they might impart Islam to India, but that they might obtain power and wealth by their arms. In the case of the Christians, if we accept the ancient legends that tell of their earliest entrance into the land, they came in the lowliest guise, their first leader indeed becoming a slave in order that he might establish a kingdom that was to be wholly spiritual. It is true that in later times the aims of the western immigrants often appear more equivocal; Portuguese and French and English were usually conquerors or traders or empire builders first and only secondarily Christians. In reality there have been two wholly separable streams of "Christian" invasion, one that might profess religious zeal but was really inspired by greed of gain and power, the other seeking the ends of the Kingdom of God. Francis Xavier and Bartholomew Ziegenbalg and Henry Martyn and Alexander Duff gave themselves indeed as truly to serve India for Christ's sake as St. Thomas when, according to the legend, his Master sold him to King Gudnaphar. But sometimes the two streams mingle and the turbidity of the one infects the other. St. Francis Xavier in bitter and disappointed hours calls on John III of Portugal to reinforce with his authority the ineffectual forces of the Spirit.[1] Others were ready at least to believe that projects for the attainment of wealth and power might advance in co-operation with those that sought to bring the Kingdom of God. Some, probably, in India would be willing to subscribe to what John Williams wrote in 1837 in his dedicatory preface to William IV that "in prosecuting the one great object to which their lives were consecrated the missionaries will keep in view whatever may promote the commerce or the science as well as the religious glory of their beloved country."[2] Facts such as these have often caused Christianity to be viewed in India as elsewhere as a stranger and even as an enemy and have made the process of its naturalisation in the country slower than in the case of other immigrants. That process has, however, been in large measure accomplished. We may claim that those who call themselves Christians are no longer accounted aliens in India but partners with the Hindu and the Muslim in the national heritage of this ancient land.

(a) *Syrian Christianity in India*

If we reckoned merely by numbers the Christians have a stronger claim than any except the Hindus and the Muslims to be recognised as forming a significant element in the Indian population. They occupy the third place among the religions of the land, coming next to the Muslims—though at a long interval behind them—with 5,961,794 adherents. But further, and more important, they are no new-comers to the land. No other religion indeed that entered from without did so at an earlier date than Christianity or can rival it in the long record of its history within the borders of India. If it were possible

[1] "You must declare as plainly as possible . . . that the only way of escaping your wrath and obtaining your favour is to make as many Christians as possible in the countries over which they rule." Letter to the King of Portugal from Cochin, 20th January 1548.

[2] Ogilvie, *Our Empire's Debt to Missions*, Chapter II.

to accept as historical the legend that is recorded in the apocryphal *Acts of Judas Thomas* (dated by Harnack in the third century), the Christian religion was first preached in India by the Apostle Thomas about A.D. 50. Similarly the tradition preserved by the Syrian Church in Travancore claims St. Thomas as its founder and dates his arrival in India in the year 52. It is not possible to examine here the arguments for and against the acceptance of this tradition as historical. This tradition and the legend of the *Acts*, enshrined amid many miraculous tales and obviously designed as propaganda in behalf of an ascetic doctrine, were accepted as no more than fairy tales until the discovery of proof that Gudnaphar did indeed rule at that time in Northern India caused the evidence to be re-examined. Dr. J. N. Farquhar has sifted fact from legend with the utmost care and has constructed a narrative of the Church's origin which he believes may be authentic. His view is that St. Thomas preached first in North India where Gudnaphar or Gondopharnes reigned, that he later proceeded southwards and continued his work there first in the west in Travancore and later on the east coast where, according to the tradition, he suffered martyrdom. Dr. Farquhar has stated the case for the tradition with much elaboration and learning, fitting it skilfully into the context of history, as far as the history of these times has come down to us.[1]

However this may be, there is no doubt that by the fourth century a Christian Church was in existence in the south-west of India, that its affiliations were with Syria and that its parent city was Edessa. This Mesopotamian city which seems to have become Christian at a very early period is associated in the Eastern Church with St. Thomas as in the Western Church Rome is with St. Peter. It was Judas Thomas, according to the legend, who sent Addai to Edessa to teach its King Abgar the

[1] See J. N. Farquhar's two papers, reprinted from the Bulletin of the John Rylands Library, on St. Thomas in North and in South India.

Christian faith. And while the Apostle is said to have been martyred in India, his bones, it is claimed, were transferred later to Edessa. From this centre Christianity was carried to Persia and, in the opinion of many scholars, the Syrian Christian Church is in the main the fruit of the missionary activities of the Persian Church. Another view that is maintained is that when in the fourth century the Sassanid Emperor of Persia began a cruel persecution of the Christians "a number of them, with Bishops and Clergy, fled to the more tolerant Hindu princes on the western coast of India."[1] This need not mark the first appearance of Christians in that region of India. It is probable that at an earlier date, perhaps in the second century, a church had come into being, whether through the labours of St. Thomas or of some later evangelist. There is indeed a Malabar tradition of a merchant called Thomas Cannaneo or Thomas of Jerusalem who drew the attention of the Edessan Church to this neglected outpost and caused succour to be sent to it in the year 345. It is even possible, some think, that it is to this benefactor and not to the Apostle Thomas that the Church owes the ancient designation which it still bears of "Thomas Christians." The connection of this Christian community with Persia is confirmed by the testimony of the Alexandrian merchant who is known as Cosmas Indicopleustes. He testifies that in the land called Male "where the pepper grows" (by which he is understood to mean Malabar) there was in the middle of the sixth century a Christian Church to which priests ordained in Persia were sent. The fame of this far-off company must have spread widely, for King Alfred, the Anglo-Saxon Chronicle tells us, in fulfilment of a vow when the Danes were defeated in an attempt to capture London, sent gifts "to India to St. Thomas."[2]

[1] Adrian Fortescue, *The Lesser Eastern Churches*, p. 358.

[2] "He sent Sighelm or Suithelm, Bishop of Shireburn, with the gifts. Sighelm came to Rome and then went on to the Malabar coast. He made

The question as to whether this ancient Indian Church owes its origin to the preaching of the Apostle Thomas or to the activities of Persian missionaries may not appear to have any great significance, but as a matter of fact it has always had considerable importance in the minds of the Syrian Christians. Perhaps this significance became all the greater in the course of their long struggle with the Latin Church, represented by the Portuguese conquerors, who at the beginning of the sixteenth century brought the Malabar coast under their control. The Portuguese report their discovery there of about two hundred thousand Christians with fifteen hundred churches. What the ecclesiastical relationship of the Church was is not altogether clear. Apparently they normally recognised as their spiritual guides the Nestorian Church of Persia, but they also at times would seem to have sought for Bishops from the Monophysites, who were a dissentient minority in that country. This oscillation between two opposite and hostile views, of which the one placed a one-sided emphasis on the humanity, the other on the divinity, of Christ, seems to us strange. Perhaps their attitude was more traditional than theological and is best represented by what some of the Persian Christians are reported to have said to the Nestorian Katholikos, "We are the disciples of Thomas the Apostle and have nothing to do with the see of Mari."[1]

The Jesuit ecclesiastics whom the Portuguese brought in their train could not permit a continuance of such heresy and schism. At the Synod of Diamper in 1599 the Malabar Church, in the words of a Roman Catholic historian, "was made to renounce Nestorianism and all connection with the Katholikos in Mesopotamia, to accept

his offerings here and brought back from his long journey jewels and spices. Strange to see an English Bishop in India in 883." Fortescue, *op. cit.*, p. 361.

It has to be remembered, however, that "India" was a word of somewhat vague connotation in these days.

[1] The legendary founder of the Nestorian Church in Persia. See Fortescue, *op. cit.*, p. 360.

the Catholic faith and the Pope's authority."[1] This involved not only the abandonment of the Nestorian heresy in respect of its failure to affirm a true Incarnation for Christ, but also the acceptance of the term "theotokos" for the Virgin Mother and of the Roman doctrine of the Mass. What followed may best be described in the words of the Catholic historian already quoted, who cannot be charged with bias against the methods of his Church. "There begins," says Dr. Fortescue, "a line of Uniat Metropolitans, dependent to some extent on the Portuguese Latin hierarchy. As long as the Portuguese were masters, that state of things continued. . . . The Inquisition was set up; prison and in some cases death were the penalties of relapse into schism. But the Inquisition rarely succeeded in securing hearty affection from its victims." This failure to secure hearty affection resulted in a return on the part of a large section of the Church to their Syrian allegiance as soon as the Portuguese power was broken. In 1665 Gregory, Monophysite Bishop of Jerusalem, came to India and ordained a Metropolitan for India. Henceforward the Syrian Church, whatever its theological character had previously been, was divided between the Uniat[2] Section, dependent upon Rome and the Jacobite[3] Section, which acknowledged the Patriarch of Antioch as its spiritual director.

To what extent the somewhat tortuous road by which the Malabar Church has travelled through the centuries has been determined by theological convictions it is not easy to determine. Dr. J. N. Farquhar suggests that it was the apostolic doctrine that he believes may have been in truth sown in their hearts at first by St. Thomas that

[1] Fortescue, *op. cit.*, p. 363.

[2] "The name 'Uniat' is applied to those Eastern Christians who have been united to Rome but are allowed to keep their own liturgical language and ecclesiastical customs, especially as to the marriage of their clergy." *E.R.E.*, Vol. XII, p. 174.

[3] "The Syrian Monophysites are called Jacobites from Jacob Baradai . . . a monk of a monastery near Edessa who came to Constantinople A.D. 540 to plead the cause of Monophysitism." *Ibid.*

gave this Church the steadfastness that enabled it to live on, while the seed which others sowed in neighbouring lands withered away. However this may be it can hardly be questioned that theological conviction was not the only influence, probably not the strongest, in shaping their course. Just as the Church in Syria was largely influenced in its formation by nationalist feeling, so certainly was this daughter Church also. We can agree with Dr. Adrian Fortescue that the one point that mattered to what he calls " the schismatical party " was " to be independent of Rome, represented to them by the hated conqueror."[1] The Jacobites to Dr. Fortescue are " schismatical " and the Uniats " as a matter of historic continuity are the original Church which accepted union with Rome at the Synod of Diamper." This he holds would be the case even if the union was brought about by force. It is impossible to agree with that claim. The Syrian Church of Malabar remains a Syrian and not a Latin Church and clings still with the utmost tenacity to its ancient characteristics. For the quarrels and contentions, of which their history has so largely consisted since 1599 when they " were made to accept the Catholic faith," a share of the blame must be borne by those who sought by force to deprive them of their great tradition and to mould them into a new form.

The Romo-Syrian section of the Malabar Church is the largest of the fragments into which it has broken up, but the Church as a whole remains in the main Jacobite in its character and outlook. The disputes and excommunications which make the later history of this Church so obscure and perplexing are due as much to the efforts of those who are striving to attach it to one particular branch of the Christian Church as to the inherent quarrelsomeness of its own members. The Papacy, the Patriarch of Antioch, the Nestorian Katholikos are rivals in the struggle to capture and control this little company of

[1] *Op. cit.*, p. 364.

Christians. The distance that separates the Patriarch from India and his ignorance of the actual situation of those of whom he has spiritual charge inevitably create misunderstanding and conflict. The coming among them of missionaries of the Protestant Churches of the West has produced further complications, though the Church Missionary Society has sought not to detach the Syrians from their traditional allegiance, but to rekindle their Christian faith and loyalty. One result of their efforts has been, however, the formation of another section of the Church, a Reformed body, called the Mar Thoma Christians. The chief sections are now the Uniat or Romo-Syrian body, to which the largest number of Syrian Christians belong, the two sections into which the Jacobites in recent years have broken up, the Mar Thoma Christians and the little group of Nestorians under the direction of their own Bishop.

How much need there was for these isolated and almost forgotten Christians to obtain spiritual renewal, whether it came from a Roman or from an Anglican source, can be judged by the description of their condition that is given by Jordanus, a Dominican friar who was sent out about 1330 by Pope John XXII to be Bishop of Columbum, a town which is identified with Quilon, the ancient port of Malabar. "In this India," he writes (that is, apparently, in Malabar), "there is a scattered people, one here, another there, who call themselves Christians, but are not so, nor have any baptism, nor do they know anything else about the faith. Nay, they believe St. Thomas the Great to be Christ!"[1] Four hundred and twenty years later, in 1757, the French Zend scholar, Anquetil du Perron, visited Malabar and reports that at that time the Christians were said to number two hundred thousand. Of these 50,000, according to this estimate, were Roman Catholics, 100,000

[1] Friar Jordanus, *The Wonders of the East* (*Mirabilia Descripta*), p. 23. Translated by Colonel Henry Yule, Hakluyt Society.

"Catholiques Syro-Malabares," and 50,000 "Syro-Malabares-Schismatiques." These figures cannot, of course, be accepted as more than a rough estimate. He goes on to give an interesting description of them. "The Christians of St. Thomas are well made, have fine features, a distinguished air and are rather difficult to control. However poor any of them might be he would not demean himself so far as to serve the Fathers. They estimate their nobility by the antiquity of their possession of their religion."[1] When one considers the circumstances in the midst of which this little company of Christians has lived on throughout the centuries, the darkness that has surrounded them, and the harassment to which they have had to submit even more from professed friends than from professed enemies, the tenacity with which they have held to their faith must win our admiration. If its witness has been for the most part a smoking flax, yet it has never been wholly quenched.

(b) *Latin Christianity in India*

The Syrian Church of Malabar stands by itself in its history and its characteristics among the Christian Churches of India. No full account can be given here either of it or of the other Churches which along with it make up what we have designated as Indian Christianity. All that can be attempted is to present some aspects of the development of each religious type, selecting those which may best illustrate the process of its acclimatisation in the Indian environment. The Syrian Churches have passed through the storms of the centuries to obtain a secure place in the States of Travancore and Cochin as representative of a religion that is not merely tolerated but honoured by the non-Christian Governments of these States. When we turn from them to consider the Christians of the Roman communion there are two Jesuit

[1] Anquetil du Perron, *Zend-Avesta, Ouvrage de Zoroastre*, Vol. I, pp. 157 f.

missionaries that may be selected as suggesting some of the main avenues along which this type of Christianity has won its way in India and done so with such effectiveness that it, too, is now established in similar security and honour. These are St. Francis Xavier and Robert de Nobili. Both were members of the Society of Jesus and both were heroic in the devotion of their service, but they adopted widely differing methods and directed their religious appeal to widely differing constituencies. They may be said to represent two rival roads of approach which have been used by many since their time—and these not Roman Catholics only—to bring to the Indian people the message of Christ. We cannot be content with the hasty conclusion of Dr. Gustav Warneck who describes the one method as " the mere outward admission to the Church with which since Xavier's time the Roman Mission has contented itself," and the other as " the refined accommodation by which De Nobili sought to filch the introduction of Christianity."[1]

No one indeed can claim that Francis Xavier's missionary methods were above criticism. He laboured under the great disadvantage of preaching a Christianity which was all the time being travestied and blasphemed by the policy and acts of the representatives of the Christian power which had established itself in that region of India. No doubt it is true, as his biographer, Edith Anne Stewart, says, that " the contrast between the outward authority of the representative of Portugal and of Western civilisation, and the personal appearance and bearing of the Saint, must have been a strangely moving one and may account for much of his success." In 1496 Pope Alexander VI had assigned the whole Eastern world to Portugal and accordingly when Francis Xavier went out to India in 1542 he went out as an emissary not only of Christ but of John III of Portugal. " He puts us," says

[1] *History of Protestant Missions*, p. 248. Translated by Dr. George Robson.

the young missionary, " under an obligation, *for God's sake*, to be his perpetual servants."[1] Christianity was part of the political equipment of the Portuguese Government. Francis Xavier, no doubt, hoped much from that relationship and he repeatedly appeals for the support of the temporal authority in his task of evangelism. " If the Governors," he writes to the King with great frankness in 1548, " understand as a certainty that you mean what you say and will fulfil your oath, the whole of Ceylon will be Christian in a year, and many Kings in Malabar and Cape Comorin and many other places. But so long as the Governors have not this fear before them of being dishonoured and punished you need not count on any increase of our holy faith."[2] But instead of the co-operation that he desired he found the king's own officers everywhere, as he puts it, conjugating the verb *rapio*. " I am terrified to see how many moods and tenses and participles of this wretched verb those who come here can invent."[3]

Had it not been for these adverse influences, we can believe that the results from the labours of this " whirlwind of love " would have been even greater than they actually were, amazing as they appear to have been. Jordanus had found in the fourteenth century that the people of Travancore were remarkably accessible to the Christian messenger. " If there were two or three hundred good friars," he said, " there is not a year that would not see more than ten thousand converted to the Christian faith." This result Francis Xavier was able to see within not a year but a month. His own account of what he achieved in Travancore and how he achieved it will indicate his ardour and the methods he employed. " In a month," he writes, " I baptized more than ten thousand persons. . . . Here is how I baptize: I give to each his Christian name in writing. Afterwards these men go home and

[1] E. A. Stewart, *St. Xavier*, p. 135.
[2] *Op. cit.*, p. 258. [3] *Op. cit.*, p. 219.

send their wives and families, whom I baptize in the same way as I baptized the men. When the baptisms are finished I command that the houses where they have their idols are to be thrown down and I arrange that after they are Christians they are to break the images of the idols into the smallest pieces. . . . In each place I leave the prayers written in their language, ordering that each day they shall teach them once in the morning and again at the hour of vespers. When this is finished in one place I go to another."[1]

The work of Xavier was essentially that of an evangelist, but even from this account of it it cannot be described as "the mere outward admission to the Church." We have an example of what he taught to "the newly converted, children, and simple folk," in the exposition of the Apostles' Creed which he composed and wrote down for the Malays some years later. And at the same time he continually urged upon those to whom he committed the further charge of his converts that they should "behave very lovingly with these people," as he assuredly did himself. One of his fellow-workers who lived with him six months in Travancore, describes for us how he appeared as he toiled from day to day among the humble fisher-folk. "He went barefoot with a poor torn gown and a kind of hood of black stuff. Everyone loved him dearly. He so gained the heart of a King that this Sovereign made a proclamation that the people were to obey his brother, the *Great Father*, as they did himself: he permitted all his subjects to become Christians if they wished to do so, and he gave him large sums for the succour of the poor. The *Great Father* has caused forty-four or forty-five churches to be built along the coast where the new Christians are."[2]

It was among the people of the Fishery Coast and Cape Comorin, as well as in Travancore, that Xavier's few years of service in India were spent. He could say

[1] E. A. Stewart, *op. cit.*, pp. 189 f. [2] *Op. cit.*, p. 190.

of the poor Paravas, whom he brought to Christ, as truly as St. Paul could of the Philippians, that he had them in his heart. His eagerness for their nurture in the Christian faith is shown in many letters written to those who had charge of them. These "mass movements" of which he was the centre were mainly among the same classes of people who came in similar multitudes into the Church in South India through the later preaching of Protestant missionaries. "Xavier," writes St. Francis's Protestant biographer, "found those primitive Paravas living in a state of perpetual terror, haunted and harassed by demons, night and day. He gave them a perfunctory enough version of the Gospel of Jesus Christ, and a version with many defects. . . . But one thing he undoubtedly did, he brought an immense peace and joy to the generation that knew him personally; he came to them like a friendly voice and a friendly hand to children lost in a dark night."[1]

St. Francis left India in 1552. The Jesuit historian Polanco tells us that at that date there were 60,000 Christians in the neighbourhood of Cape Comorin and thirty churches. How far this ignorant and isolated company, as well as those whom he had won by the fervour of his zeal in Travancore, continued to be cared for through the years that followed it is difficult to discover. The power of Portugal withered. The Society of Jesus was suppressed in the Portuguese dominions in 1755. In spite of these vicissitudes, however, the work of Francis Xavier has remained and the number of Christians has increased. In 1921 a member of the Parava caste was elevated to the Episcopate as the first Bishop of the diocese of Tuticorin.[2]

The work that St. Francis did in India was among the humblest and most ignorant classes. Their necessity was

[1] *Op. cit.*, p. 173 f.

[2] For this information I am indebted to Rev. Stephen Neill who is engaged upon a history of Christianity in India.

so great that in a despondent hour he writes of them as "the filth of the human race." But what caused him even deeper despondency was the spectacle of the lives lived by their Portuguese rulers. Goa, which still exhibits to us in its ruins a multitude of Christian churches, was to him when he landed there, he says, "a sight for sore eyes."[1] It soon showed itself to him as a sight of a different sort. The "cruelty and cupidity"[2] of the foreigners and the degradation of the ignorant outcastes may well have had their influence in driving him to seek a field where his eager hopes might be more speedily realised. It was probably also these two factors in the situation in which he found himself that caused Robert de Nobili to adopt a policy that contrasts strongly with that of St. Francis. He was an Italian, of a family not less noble than that of his predecessor. Like him also he was a Jesuit. He landed in Goa in May 1605, fifty-three years after St. Francis's death off the Coast of China. From Goa he proceeded to Madura, the capital of a Hindu State and an important stronghold of Brāhmanism. He was within some sixty miles of the Fishery Coast that had been the scene of so many of St. Francis's triumphs. But he has to report that the fathers had not succeeded in making a single conversion though they had been there for twelve years.

De Nobili, accordingly, adopts a new policy. He will denationalise himself and so divest himself of the odium that attaches to the name, Pharangi or Portuguese, by which all Europeans were described; he will identify himself instead with the Indian people; and he will give himself to the task of winning, not the despised outcastes but the arrogant and intellectual Brāhmans.

In carrying out this policy, de Nobili followed courses which have caused him to be charged with practising deceit and perpetrating an elaborate literary forgery. He called himself a "Roman Brāhman," adopting the

[1] *Op. cit.*, p. 160. [2] Quoted from Correa's *Lendas* in *op. cit.*, p. 162.

Brāhman dress and the Brāhman mode of life. That does not mean that he lived a life of ease. It was rather, in the words of a Protestant missionary who himself laboured later in South India, " a life of indefatigable austerities."[1] His " forgery " was the production of what was called a fifth Veda which, it is alleged, he claimed as an ancient Indian scripture, discovered by himself. It is not possible to investigate at this date the facts upon which this charge, and others brought against him, are based. It is not even certain that this book should be attributed to him and not rather to his successor, de Britto. In any case we know that about twenty years earlier another Jesuit, Thomas Stephens, an Englishman, produced in Marāthi in another part of India, a Christian Purana, and yet no charge of forgery or deception has been brought against him. These two works bear remarkable witness to the thoroughness with which these early missionaries assimilated to themselves the language and the culture of the people among whom they lived. The Christian Veda is said to have held its place among the ancient Indian scriptures for one hundred and fifty years. The Christian Purana appears to have obtained a permanent position of honour—foreign though its authorship has always been known to be—in Marāthi literature. In both cases they demonstrate the learning as well as the zeal which their authors were employing with a view to nationalising the Christian religion within the Indian spirit.

What certainly, however, demands censure in the missionary policy that de Nobili inaugurated is his acceptance within the Christian Church of the distinction of caste. " The holy spiritual law which I proclaim," he declared, " does not oblige a man to renounce his caste." His view that caste was merely a social distinction and had no religious significance has been largely accepted in the Roman missions in India, though not always in as extreme a form as that which de Nobili maintained. In

[1] W. Robinson, *Robert de Britto*.

1623, in de Nobili's lifetime, Pope Gregory XV placed some limitation upon the recognition by the Church of emblems of caste superiority. The conflict, however, continued and undoubtedly in the years that followed it weakened the Church. The extreme caste policy which separated so rigidly Brāhman and pariah converts had the effect that the pariahs were left uncared for. A double system of priests, one class of them for Brāhmans and another for pariahs, was continued by the Jesuit missionaries, who resisted interference with their policy even by the Popes. In 1744, however, Pope Benedict XIV directed that pariahs must not be left without the sacraments and placed definite limitations upon the Jesuit policy of accommodation. Robert de Nobili and his successor, John de Britto had, however, given a direction to the policy of Roman missions in India which, for good or evil, they retain still. A considerable amount of accommodation to heathen practice has been permitted by Roman tradition in all periods of the history of the Roman Church and its influence is seen in all parts of the Roman Catholic world. In India it is seen in various directions, and, among others, in the recognition in considerable measure of caste distinctions among Christian converts.

This long-continued dispute over concessions to Hindu usages was, in the opinion of a Catholic historian, one of the causes of the serious decline in the latter part of the eighteenth century in the number of Roman Catholics in India. Other causes were the decline of the Portuguese power and the total suppression of the Jesuits in 1773. Further, we are told, " the Sultan Tipu Sahib of Mysore between 1782 and 1799 put 100,000 Christians to death, forced 40,000 into apostacy, and sold 30,000 as slaves to Mohammedan dealers." " Thus," this Roman Catholic writer continues, " the missions in India which in 1700 numbered some 1,500,000 or even 2,500,000 Roman Catholics were only ruins and wreckage (500,000 or even less) in 1800."[1] The break-up of Portuguese power made it necessary for vigorous measures to be taken if the position was to be restored. Accordingly Gregory XVI "took matters into his own hands without consulting the interests of Portugal." "India was opened to all Roman Catholic missionaries irrespective of nationality or religious orders."[2] The century that has elapsed since then has shown a remarkable recovery in the position of the Roman Catholic Church in India and a remarkable growth in the number of its adherents.

(c) *Protestant Christianity in India*

Of the three types of Christianity which have established themselves in India, the latest comer was Protestantism, but it has made up in some measure for this tardiness by the energy with which since its arrival it has gone about its task. No individual Protestant can rival St. Francis Xavier in the passion of his zeal and sacrifice but by their disciplined and sustained ardour, supported by the steadfast faith of the Churches behind them, the missionaries of the non-Roman Churches of the West have achieved results that seem to give promise of a Church fully rooted in the life of India and in consequence powerful to renew and to transform it. They have been faced with the same problems as their Roman fellow-workers and have by no means always avoided their mistakes.

In this case also it was to South India that the first missionaries found their way and to a region not far removed from some of the scenes of Xavier's and de Nobili's labours. At Tranquebar on the south-east coast Denmark owned a tiny territory, and there first Bartholomew Ziegenbalg and later Christian Friederich Schwartz kindled the flame of Protestant Christianity. They were the fruits of the German Pietism that was then so influential in the University of Halle, both of them not

[1] Maternus Spitz, O.S.B., in *E.R.E.*, Vol. VIII, p. 715. [2] *Ibid.*, p. 716.

only men of deep devotion and noble character, but at the same time wise architects of the missionary enterprise which they inaugurated. Between 1707 when Ziegenbalg landed and 1798 when Schwartz was laid to rest in the land of his adoption, it is estimated that over 40,000 had been baptised into the Church. The influence of Schwartz's long life of service was not limited to the Danish settlement but extended over a wide area of South India, Trichinopoly, Tanjore and Tinnevelly. What St. Francis, as we have seen, was to a Rajah in Travancore, Schwartz was—and more—to the Rajah of Tanjore, and he also was, as was his great Roman Catholic predecessor, the beloved Father of the people.

The most serious error into which these pioneer missionaries fell was one which they shared with the Jesuit mission that had preceded them in this area. They, too, recognised and tolerated caste. That may well have been one of the reasons why, after their time, the work they had done proved, as in the case of the work of de Nobili and his successors, to lack stability and permanence. But another reason undoubtedly was that these successors, as in the case of those who followed de Nobili, proved to be ill-fitted for their great spiritual task. They were, we are told, "good rationalists" who held that "missions must cease to be an institution for conversion."[1] The result was that fifty years after Schwartz's death a Christian community of 20,000 had dwindled to 5000.[2]

The Tranquebar pioneers had, however, furnished an example of what faith and ardour can accomplish and it was not long before others appeared who were inspired by the same spirit. Not in the south alone but all over India signs appeared that the eighteenth-century distrust of enthusiasm was passing away. William Carey may be recognised as the inaugurator of the era of the organised mission activity of the Protestant Churches, an era which

[1] Warneck, *op. cit.*, p. 250. [2] Ogilvie, *Apostles of India*, p. 289.

may accordingly be dated as beginning in 1793 when he landed in Calcutta. In our survey of what has been achieved since then for the growth of Indian Christianity we may distinguish two main methods of operation that have been followed, the one that of the widespread dissemination of Christian ideas, the Christianisation, let us say, of the Indian psychological climate, and the other the more direct presentation of the Christian message to individuals, resulting not infrequently in "mass conversions." We may choose as typical representatives of the former method, William Carey and Alexander Duff. The latter type of Christian activity can more easily be studied in its effects upon the character of the multitudes who become Christian than through any individuals selected from the great number of devoted men and women who have ministered to them.

There is at least this point of contact between Carey and de Nobili that they were both pioneers in the Western study of oriental learning. Carey's conception, however, of the benefits that he could convey to India was immensely the wider of the two. He took an eager part in bringing about the abolition of "suttee." He is credited with having translated the Bible or parts of the Bible into thirty-four languages. But his publications were not limited to any narrow purpose of evangelisation. He is said by his printing press and his own writings to have done much to create a renaissance of Bengali literature. "Culture and utility were rarely divorced from one another in his life. As literary adviser and translator to Government, as grammarian and lexicographer, as joint keeper of the horticultural gardens—for he was a keen and scientific gardener—as member of the newly founded Royal Asiatic Society, he proved that he was not only indefatigable but indispensable."[1]

Thus in a multitude of ways Carey was winning for a religion, hitherto so widely misunderstood and mis-

[1] Mayhew, *Christianity and the Government of India*, p. 68.

represented[1] in India, a new position of respect and consideration. The authorities who had refused to admit him into India found themselves constrained to invite his co-operation. He sought no privileged position as a representative of Christianity and he obtained none. "We must justly congratulate ourselves," writes Mr. Mayhew, "on the good sense of John Company in refusing from its earliest days to countenance any kind of pressure, and on the wisdom of the missionaries in our territories who abstained from advocating them."[2] It was by the value of the services rendered to the life of the community that missions won acknowledgement from the Government. This service was specially notable, as time went on, in the sphere of education. By the year 1818 the Serampore Mission possessed 126 vernacular schools and in that year also Carey and his colleagues launched a scheme for the establishment of a "College for the instruction of Asiatic Christian and other youth."

The name of Alexander Duff is, however, that which is especially associated with the initiation of a new system of higher education in India and its use as a missionary agency. In 1830 he began his work in Calcutta. His life was given, like that of de Nobili, though in very different circumstances and by very different methods, to the presentation of Christianity to the higher classes of Hindus. But the medium that he used was not Sanskrit, as it had been in the case of de Nobili, but English. It is true that no great influx of Brāhmans into the Christian Church has resulted from the work that the Christian Colleges have carried on through the century since Alexander Duff landed in India. Robert de Nobili apparently baptised a larger number from among this class than he. The number who declared themselves to be Christians,

[1] "The Indian conception of Christianity, quoted by the chaplains to Sir Thomas Roe's embassy: 'Christian religion devil religion : Christians much drink, much do wrong, much beat, much abuse others.'" Mayhew, *op. cit.*, p. 47.

[2] *Op. cit.*, p. 40.

Duff himself wrote in 1844 in reference to his own College and the Colleges in Bombay and Madras, "has been comparatively small." "But," he went on, "the amount of general influence excited must not be estimated according to the number." An Indian Christian peculiarly qualified to speak with knowledge and authority on the subject of that diffusion of the Christian spirit throughout India which we are here seeking to estimate, Dr. S. K. Datta, has described the situation as it appears after a hundred years of such work as that of Carey and Duff. "A study," he says, "of the autobiographies of eminent Indians of the last fifty years would result in the discovery of the immense place that Christian thought, life and even phraseology have in modern Indian expression. From whence have these been obtained? It is clear that the two main sources have been, firstly, Schools and Colleges, and, secondly, the circulation of literature."[1] If Christianity were to be judged by the influence that it exerts upon the minds of India's most honoured leaders, no one could doubt that it is now an Indian possession, no longer an intruder but actually grafted upon the ancient Indian tradition.

But apart from this leavening process which is held by some leading missionary educators to be the primary aim of the Christian College, the actual accessions that it has brought to the Christian Church have been notable in quality. Though the number of converts from among the higher classes has always been comparatively limited, their influence in the Church and in its extension has been very great. The Brāhman converts that were the fruit of Duff's educational work in not a few instances became apostles bearing the message of their faith to the people of the United Provinces and the Punjab, while converts of a similar type from John Wilson's College in Bombay laboured with marked success among the out-castes of the Nizam's Dominions. Thus the influence of the few who became Christians from among the privileged

[1] *The Christian Task in India*, pp. 3 f.

classes extended throughout the whole Church and played a part in the moulding of Indian Christianity that is not less significant than the part played by the unprivileged who have come into it in such multitudes. How and where these multitudes came into the Church we must now consider. We can do little more than indicate the various provinces in which "mass movements" have taken place, some of the circumstances that produced them, and some of the general characteristics that they bear.

We have seen that movements of this kind accompanied the preaching of St. Francis Xavier. In the case both of that older movement and these modern ones the causes that were at work were in the main spiritual. A message of deliverance and hope and a messenger who won trust and admiration—these two elements have been present, we may claim, in all these tidal movements, creating them. And as such they were of God. The effect of this spiritual gravitation that drew so many to God would inevitably be most marked amongst those least bound by tradition and social prejudice and most obviously in distress and need. That there was a relationship between famines and these awakenings need not surprise us. Hunger is an experience that reaches deep and the compassion that relieves it may be truly a divine revelation. Accordingly we find that it was everywhere the oppressed and the despised that flocked into the Church in such numbers and that these events date from the great famine of 1876–79, when, we are told, in the Tamil and Telugu areas of the South hundreds of thousands died.

Up till that time the converts that had been obtained by Protestant Missions in the South were from the Sudra classes, that is to say, the classes at the lower extremity of the caste spectrum, but not outside of it. According to the census of 1851 there were 74,176 "native Christians" in the Madras Presidency, the great majority of them being Sudras.[1] When in 1881 this number had

[1] Richter, *op. cit.*, p. 232.

grown to 299,742 the situation was entirely different. The increase had come about by accessions almost entirely from among the Panchamas or outcastes. On the other hand the Church in the Tinnevelly area, which contained a strong body of Christians converted in early days from the Sudras, after obtaining a large increase during the famine period, has actually in recent decades diminished in numbers. This stagnation is due, we are told, in some degree at least, to caste disputes between Sudra and outcaste.[1] There are problems to be solved ere the ancient yokes are broken and the new liberty achieved, but the coming together of these classes under the common influence of the discovery of a new spiritual world and of the experience of a new source of spiritual strength is undoubtedly making possible, as could never have been the case before, the solution of these problems and the achievement of that liberation.

In another great area of the South, that of the Telugu-speaking people, over two hundred thousand entered the Church between 1851 and 1900. These came from two outcaste communities each of which is as jealous of its social separateness as ever against the other, as in the case of the castes that despise them. The Mālas were the first to become Christian and when the Mādigas—scavengers and leather workers—followed, the battle of prejudice began. A new reconciling power was, however, at work. "Within the course of a few years," the Wesleyan historian of this movement tells us, "there were Mādiga Christians in every village, and presently 'Mādiga' and 'Māla' as terms of distinction were quietly dropped. They were brothers."[2]

In this case at least those caste conflicts that have caused so much trouble in the history of Christianity in South India have been overcome. And later within this

[1] Sharrock, *South Indian Missions*, p. 307.

[2] F. C. Sackett, *Vision and Venture, a Record of Fifty Years in Hyderabad*, p. 131.

same area the power within Christianity that is able to exorcise these ancient enmities even at their worst was fully demonstrated when the constraint of Christ laid its grasp upon the classes that had proved hitherto the most stubborn in their resistance. The caste people, Brāhmans and Sudras—those among whom caste prejudice had been so stubborn—have now begun, drawn by the lives of the outcaste Christians, to seek in steadily increasing numbers the fellowship within the Christian Church of those whom they had formerly despised. The Sudras, whom we may describe as the lower middle classes of the Hindus, are the slowest of all to be moved by any new idea, the most conservative in clinging to the traditions of the past. Where elsewhere in the South they had become Christians they had often clung tenaciously to their caste arrogance and in consequence, it would seem, had frustrated the divine purpose. But here no such denial of the spirit of Christ by those who desired to follow Him was for a moment tolerated. It may well prove that we have in this movement the opening of a new era in the history of the Christian Church in India.

These great quickenings of the South have had through the last hundred years their parallels among similar communities in the North of India. There also, great communities from among the unprivileged and neglected classes—the outcastes and the hill-tribes—have cast themselves upon the compassion of the Christian Church, claiming admission within it. Thus in the United Provinces the number of Christians increased in the latter half of last century from one thousand to one hundred thousand—almost wholly from the outcaste classes. In the Punjab there have been similar accessions, so that there is at the present time, we are told, a Christian community of 85,000 in connection with one Presbyterian Mission and of 40,000 in connection with one Anglican Mission. So also from among the hill peoples of Bihar there has emerged, under the guidance mainly of the

Gossner Mission a strong Christian community able now in large measure to shape their own course as a self-governing Church. Another example of the swift but genuine transformation that the coming of the Christian message has accomplished can be seen in the case of the aboriginal tribes in the Lushai Hills in Assam. From head-hunting savages large numbers of them have been transformed into earnest Christians, active in evangelising others. The Lushai Christian community is now reported as numbering over 55,000 persons. The increase in the figures at the census of 1921 was so great that the census officer doubted the accuracy of the enumeration. Further enquiry, however, showed that there was no mistake but that, as he says, " a sort of revivalist wave " had passed over the whole Lushai population."[1]

These must suffice as examples of the rapid growth of the Christian community throughout North India during the last two generations. It has, of course, to be fully recognised at the same time that a complete transformation of such multitudes in so brief a time from the degradation to which as outcastes and aborigines they had for so long been subjected to all that Christianity signifies could not, even in the most favourable conditions, be achieved. It has been seen that in South India one difficulty that hindered the progress of converts and caused division was the survival of the old caste spirit among them. This has proved less of an obstacle in the North than in the South, where the tyranny of caste is seen at its worst. It is said that the two evils that proved so deadly in the case of the early converts in Tanjore and Trichinopoly were " caste and the eleemosynary spirit." [2] If the former was not so powerful a hindrance to spiritual progress in the North, the latter, among classes that were

[1] The census officer " quotes an instance of the rigorous standard adopted by the new converts : the five-year-old son of Christian parents being entered as an Animist because the young scoundrel was so greedy that he failed to say grace before meals." *Indian Census Report, Assam*, 1921, p. 54.

[2] Sharrock, *South Indian Missions*, p. 46.

almost all in the lowest depths of poverty, was an evil less easy to be on one's guard against and not less fatal in its consequences. This can be seen specially in the United Provinces where the classes affected were the degraded Chamars (leather workers) and Sweepers, and where, according to the census officer, the Mission that was chiefly concerned was "satisfied with a lower standard of appreciation of the tenets of Christianity than many other Missions require from their converts."

Whether this charge is just or not, it is one that has been widely brought against the Missions that have had —with very inadequate staffs of workers—to face the overwhelming demands that those mass movements make upon them. It is well, accordingly, that we should have before us, as representative of many criticisms that the mass movements have provoked, the views set forth in the Census Report of 1901 of the character of this particular movement in the United Provinces. "In the early days of Christian Missions," Mr. Burn writes, "it was almost a necessity that the Missions should provide the means of subsistence for their converts, and the result of this is still felt as a hindrance in Mission work, and the charge is freely made that converts change their religion for material gain. Such a charge cannot be maintained now when numbers have increased so enormously, while the expenditure of this Mission shows a lower rate per head than of any Mission in these provinces. . . . The number of converts was increasing so rapidly that instructions had to be issued to the native pastors to use more discretion in baptising people, and the difference between the number of members at the close of any year and the sum of the baptisms in that year and the number of members at the close of the preceding year shows that a considerable number disappear or are struck off. . . . From enquiries made it appears that the customs hardest to change amongst these low-class converts are their old ceremonies at birth, marriage and death, the belief in spirits and the loathing at contact with sweepers who still practise their old occupation. From one district it was reported that images and shrines of the *Lalguru* are still resorted to in secret. It would therefore seem that these numerous conversions somewhat resemble those of Hindus in Eastern Bengal and Assam, with the exception that greater care is taken to instruct and look after the spiritual welfare of the Converts. These results constitute a serious problem for the future."[1]

That this problem is a very serious one is certain, but it is not new in the experience of the Christian Church, though seldom, perhaps, has it had to be faced on such a scale as in these movements in India, The task of deepening what must in multitudes of instances be a very superficial experience and a very unstable resolve is being undertaken to the limit of the resources that are available. It is not our purpose here, however, to estimate the quality of Indian Christianity, but to note its extent and the outward conditions of its establishment in the country. A rapid survey has been made of its spread in various provinces and among various classes of the people. How deeply it has rooted itself and what spiritual values it is creating in those who have submitted themselves to its influence we have yet to consider. It is enough at this point to note what has already been indicated, that in one great area the witness of the changed lives of the out-castes is exercising its power in subduing the stubborn hearts of those who had so long scorned them. We may adapt to a different situation the old phrase about captive Greece and captor Rome, and say that the oppressed out-caste is bringing under his mild yoke his once cruel oppressor. There could be no more convincing evidence than this of the reality of the transformation that is coming about in the lives of those who not only were formerly despised but—though the blame was not theirs—who were despicable.

[1] *Census of India*, 1901, Vol. I, Part I, pp. 390 f.

CHAPTER XVIII

ITS CHARACTERISTICS AND ITS SPIRITUAL VALUE

WHEN we turn from the history of the establishment of Christianity in India through the centuries and endeavour to consider it as it is today in its wholeness and its significance, we are inevitably hindered by facts which our historical survey will have made plain. It is difficult to unify what has come into being by such varied agencies, at such widely separated periods, throughout so vast a country and so diverse a population. It is true that along with so much that divides there is a profound element which is common to all the sections and strata of the Christian people; it is true also that that harmonising element is being greatly reinforced by the circumstances of today. At the same time it seems best, with a view to clearness of comprehension, that we should consider each of the three great Christian types separately before we endeavour to obtain a single view of Indian Christianity as a whole.

A. *The ancient Syrian Church* should be the easiest of the three to sum up and describe, for it is formed of a compact group that have lived continuously together as Christians for at least fifteen centuries. The mere passage of time must have made them one in nature if not in name. We have seen, however, what elements of strife have entered among them from without, dividing and distracting them and making this Church with its brave record of endurance appear today a lamentable thing of shreds and patches. This victim of ecclesiastical jealousies and ambitions deserves, indeed, far more our admiration than our censure. When one remembers what it has had to endure, surrounded by the debasing influences of Hinduism and Islam, isolated from Christendom or, worse still, harassed and deceived by its unworthy emissaries, one cannot doubt that it has carried all the time within it an unquenchable flame of divine life that will yet burn with a clear and steadfast light. A shrewd observer, Mr. Howard, who had both personally acquainted himself with the condition of the Syrian Christians and made as well a careful study of their history, gave in 1864 a considered estimate of their Christian character which deserves to be stated in full. He quotes the testimony of Dr. Kerr, who sixty years earlier had been like himself an Anglican Chaplain in the Madras Presidency, to the effect that their character was "marked by striking superiority over the heathens in every moral excellence" and that they were "remarkable for their veracity and plain dealing."[1] His own account of them confirms this earlier estimate in language of warm appreciation. He testifies to "the character that they still retain as a simple, honest people, remarkable for modesty and truth" and to "the respect with which they are consequently regarded by the heathen." "Their Churches," he goes on, "are numerous and in different parts of the country, and are served by an abundant staff of native clergy, thoroughly acquainted with the language and manners of the people. Even in the present depressed condition of the Church its influence must be widely felt among the heathen. What would that influence be if the Church were restored to the purity and zeal of early times?"[2]

Again in a concluding passage of his interesting study of the Church he summarises his impressions. "The Church has had a full share of those vicissitudes which have been the lot of so many others. . . . We trace

[1] G. B. Howard, *The Christians of St. Thomas and their Liturgies*, pp. 58 f.

[2] Howard, *op. cit.*, p. 111.

with pain the worldly ambition, the intrigues and struggles for power, which, even to the present day, disfigure the pages of its history; but there are, I trust, not a few who, remembering that features such as these must of necessity be the most prominent in any history, will love to cherish the belief that, from the day when it was first planted in Malabar, the Gospel has ever done its work in pious souls; that in many a village . . . remote from the scenes of strife, men and women have lived quiet and peaceable lives in all godliness and honesty and in faithful dependence on their Redeemer; that in the Church of Travancore, as elsewhere, beneath the troubled surface there has ever been and still is a deep underflow of piety which, from its gentle aud unobstusive character, is not chronicled in human records but whose fruit will be found at the great day to the praise and glory of God."[1]

At the time when this witness to their character and influence was borne the Romo-Syrians in the two States of Travancore and Cochin are said to have numbered 119,000, while the rest of the community, known generally as Syrian-Jacobites numbered 116,483. If these figures can be relied upon as accurate, the increase in their numbers during the fifty years that followed is remarkable. The census of 1911 gives the number of Romo-Syrians in the two States as 394,573; of Jacobites and Chaldeans as 234,241; and of Reformed or Mar Thoma Syrians as 75,462. The increase in the number of Romo-Syrians is specially notable. These figures would seem to indicate that Syrian Christianity is not the stagnant thing that it is often supposed to be. The Abbé Dubois, the famous Roman Catholic missionary and savant, estimated their numbers when in 1823 he published his *Letters on the State of Christianity in India*, as seventy or eighty thousand in all, both Roman and non-Roman. "They are all designated," he adds,

[1] Howard, *op. cit.*, p. 167.

"under the contemptuous name of Nazarany, and held by the pagans in still greater contempt than the Christians of this part of the country."[1]

It seems probable that the figure he gives for the Syrian population is too low and his account of the estimation in which they were held too depreciatory. The census of the State of Cochin was conducted in 1901 by a Hindu State officer, but he gives a very different account of the Syrian community. He notes that in certain respects they were influenced by their Hindu environment, some of them even joining on occasion in Hindu worship. More widespread in its effect upon them is the caste prejudice that is so marked a feature of the Hindus in that area of South India. This is seen in their attitude to the outcaste people whom, he says, "they do not admit within their premises . . . even after their conversion to Christianity." He pays a tribute, however, to their high standard of education and goes on, "in enterprises of all kinds they are considerably ahead of their Hindu and Muslim brethren. In every walk of life they are making their mark by their industry and enterprise."[2]

This testimony to the position of honour held by the Syrians in 1901 could be borne in still stronger terms a generation later. In that period, in spite of the contentions that still, as through the centuries, enfeeble them, there has been steady progress towards a fuller realisation of the duty and responsibility of a Christian Church. The Jacobite and Mar Thoma sections of Syrian community have, through little groups of men and women, deeply concerned for the spiritual good of the ancient Church to which they belong, come together in common tasks of Christian service. One such group have established the Alwaye College in which they have united in a spirit of fellowship and of self-sacrifice in order that they may together serve their

[1] That is, Mysore.

[2] *Cochin Census Report*, 1901, p. 60.

fellow-countrymen and seek to fulfil the Church's long neglected missionary duty. A new hope for the future is dawning through the flame that these ardent spirits are kindling. One of them, a leading personality in the Mar Thoma section of the Church, Mr. K. K. Kuruvilla, may be quoted to indicate how, even in the midst of the conflicts that seem as far from reconciliation as ever, there are some who can look beyond them and foresee the coming of a happier time. He refers to a recent secession to Rome as a serious set back, but, he goes on, "more than that, the Church's organic connection with the backward diocese of Antioch and her involvement in law suits have sapped the life and enthusiasm of the Church and dwarfed her growth. But here and there have arisen men who see visions for their Church, and the most hopeful thing about the Jacobite Church today is the presence of such men who, in spite of great odds, still hope for a happy future for their Church and look to the day when her differences will be healed and her life renewed."

Another distinguished son of this ancient Church, Mr. P. O. Philip, also a member of the Mar Thoma section, has furnished the writer with a valuable estimate of some of the influences that through the centuries have been at work within the Syrian community, preserving its vitality when on every side there was so much to deaden and corrupt. In spite of the pressure of evil about them, "the Syrian Christians," he writes, "have always maintained a high level of morality in accordance with Christian standards." Referring to social and civil disabilities that they had to suffer in former days, he says, "they were able to hold their own with Hindus only by demonstrating to their rulers that they were loyal and hard-working people, bringing peace and prosperity to the country by their toil as agriculturists and by their enterprise as traders."

This able Syrian Christian goes on to give an account

of the forces that are at work at the present time in his community which may be accepted as just and discerning. "Is there anything," he asks, "that is distinctive in the religious life of the Syrian Churches? Probably very little. The Syrian Christians of today found in the Indian States of Travancore and Cochin will strike an outside observer as a self-centred community concerned about their own welfare and progress like the Hindu communities of that area. They seem to thrive as peasant proprietors, traders, planters, bankers and government servants. Their religion may not be much in evidence, except perhaps through the interminable litigations over ecclesiastical property in which the Bishops and other dignitaries of the Church seem always to be deeply involved. This is religion breaking down under the stress of dissension. But fortunately this is not the whole of the picture. About eighty years ago a group of men who were influenced by the evangelical purpose of Christianity had the faith and courage to stand alone against opposition from those in power and influence in the Church. The stand they took was the beginning of a liberalising evangelical movement in the Church which is represented today by the Mar Thoma Syrian Church. Evangelistic work among outcastes done by this Church has brought in hundreds of these people to Christianity. With its limited resources of men and money this Church is engaged in various forms of Christian service both within the Malayalam country and without.

"The Orthodox section of the Church has also been roused in recent years to its missionary responsibility. But for the unfortunate dissensions going on in this Church for the last twenty years between the Patriarch of Antioch and the Indian Metropolitan in regard to temporal powers, this Church would have made great advance in evangelistic and missionary work."

Mr. Philip concludes his survey of the outlook of his Church today as follows: "The above facts are hopeful for the future of the Syrian Church. Worldliness, self-seeking, indifference to the high Christian calling and questionings about Christian values—all these are to be found among the Syrian Christians in South India as among any other large group of Christians in any part of the world. But there are also many to whom prayer is real and faith in Christ is a power that is sufficient to meet and overcome the perils and temptations of life. Such men and women, scattered through the congregations and often found in humble walks of life, are eager to share their spiritual experience with others."

B. *The Roman Church* must bear a share of the blame for the sorrows of the Syrian Christians and for the divisions that have rent them. When we turn to consider the fruit of their own missionary efforts throughout India we cannot fail to be impressed by the fact that their comparative failure in the earlier period of their missionary activity, in spite of much heroism on the part of individuals, was due in large measure to two hostile factors. These were the mistaken policy of the Jesuits and the unfortunate alliance formed by the Church with Portugal. To these matters we need not refer further except to quote the considered opinion of Abbé Dubois addressed by him in 1823 to the Directors of the East India Company maintaining " the desperateness of the attempt to convert India to the Christian faith." He bases this conclusion largely on the Jesuit failure and on the fact that for the Indians—when they discovered that the Jesuit missionaries were not, as they claimed, " men coming from another world,"—the ultimate and unanswerable argument was, " your religion is the religion of the *Fringy* "[1] and so radically bad. To the Abbé it appeared that " if any form of Christianity were to make an impression and gain ground in the country, it is undoubtedly the Catholic mode of worship, whose external pomp and show appear so well suited to the genius and

[1] That is, of the Portuguese.

dispositions of the natives; and that when the Catholic religion has failed to produce its effects and its interests are become quite desperate, no other sect can flatter itself even with the remotest hope of establishing its system."[1]

The despair of the Abbé was the result of the collapse of Roman Catholic Missions at the close of the eighteenth century. This collapse, we may claim, was due not to the failure of the Christian religion, but to the failure of propaganda in behalf of such a Catholicism as the Abbé describes, of methods of compromise and accommodation such as the Jesuits followed, and of a policy which made the words "Portuguese" and "Christian" synonymous.[2] If the position of Roman Catholicism in India is different today it is because a more spiritual religion is preached and more spiritual methods employed. The weaknesses that still mark this section of the Christian community may be said to be largely due to the evil inheritance that has come down from those earlier days.

This evil inheritance is present wherever the Christians trace their descent from converts of the days of Portuguese aggression. Thus the province of Goa is to all outward appearance a Roman Catholic country and has been so since the latter part of the sixteenth century, but it is only gradually that the effects of the unspiritual methods of early evangelisation have given place to a conformity that is more truly Christian. The belief that their Christianity was often purely nominal has made the Christians in this area objects of attention from the emissaries of the "Suddhi" movement which in recent years has been seeking to win back to the Hindu fold those who had left it. "In spite of rumours that have occasionally been heard within the last half century," the

[1] *Letters on the State of Christianity*, pp. 23 f.

[2] "The question in the Catechism, 'Dost thou desire to become a Christian?' was then worded: 'Wilt thou enter the caste of the Prangui?'" Footnote to p. 56 in Richter's *History of Missions in India*. The "Prangui" or "Fringy" (above) were the Europeans, and primarily the Portuguese, as in this particular case.

Census Report of 1901 informs us, "those who have lived amongst these classes give evidence of the reality of their adherence to the faith of their adoption."[1] In spite of the survival among them of Hindu practice alongside of Christian profession not much success seems to have attended the efforts to persuade them to abandon the Christian name. Thus the Census Report of 1921 gives an interesting account of the failure of efforts to win back to Hinduism the Christian Kolis of Bombay, a fishing caste that seemed to have little real hold of Christianity. "These Kolis," the Report tells us, "combine the worship of idols with the worship of the Christian Trinity, figures of Hindu godlings being kept behind the altar and covered with a cloth when a priest comes to celebrate Mass." Dr. Goodier, the Roman Catholic Archbishop of Bombay, wrote to the census officer in regard to them, "Though we call them Christians, one has to give a very broad definition in order to include them." All the same they were unwilling to give up this nominal connection. In 1920, according to Dr. Goodier, an effort by a Hindu Society was made to win them. "It gave indications at first of being far-reaching but ended with the reception of twenty persons only."[2]

It is not necessary to dwell further upon characteristics of Roman Catholic Missions which result from methods adopted by them in other parts of the world as well as India. Some of these methods, such as the recognition of caste, have been adopted also, as we have seen, by some Protestant Missions, but not for more than a brief period and never as an accepted policy. Even in the Roman Missions the old evil tradition of such recognition is not always maintained. In the Bombay Presidency, we are told in the 1921 Census Report, the distinction between castes was abolished in one village with the

[1] *Bombay Census Report*, Vol. I, p. 51.

[2] *Census Report*, 1921, Vol. VIII, Part I, p. 73 (Bombay Presidency).

result that a considerable number of the Christians who claimed to be of higher castes "seceded and were readmitted as Hindus by the local members of their original castes."[1] Some Protestant Missions in South India have had experiences of a not dissimilar kind.[2]

When, a century ago, Gregory XVI decided to ignore the claim of Portugal to spiritual lordship over India and opened the land to all Roman Catholic missionaries a new era for Roman Catholicism began. The establishment in France in 1822 of the Society called *La Propagation de la Foi* and twenty years later of its juvenile branch, *La Sainte Enfance*, would seem to mark a definite change to a more spiritual plane in missionary effort. During the century that followed there has been a continuous increase in activity in this direction. This has culminated in the notable efforts, in which India has largely shared, that have been made during the last decade under the impulse of the missionary passion of Pope Pius XI.[3]

One direction of great significance in which a determined advance is being made is the training of native clergy. In an encyclical Pius XI declared this to be the first duty of missionary leaders and called for the establishment of seminaries for this purpose. Such a policy was indeed demanded by the urgent need for more training in the Christian faith of the large numbers of nominal Catholics that there were in India as in other lands. Accordingly a large part of the activity of the missionaries has been directed to education and in this department of work the Jesuits have been no less prominent than they were in earlier times.

This change in the character of their missionary effort —which is no less evident in Protestant than in Roman Catholic Missions—is indicated by the fact that there are

[1] *Census Report*, 1921, Vol. VIII, Part I, p. 73 (Bombay Presidency).
[2] See Sharrock, *South Indian Missions*, pp. 183 ff.
[3] See *The World-Wide Christian Mission*, 1922–32, pp. 258 ff. (*The International Review of Missions*.)

now throughout India fourteen Catholic Arts Colleges preparing students for degrees in Arts. "Catholic Colleges," we are told, "were established primarily for the education of Catholic students, the remote preparation of a Catholic priesthood and the formation of a Catholic *élite*. The *praeparatio evangelica* for conversions came in only gradually with the admission of non-Christian students."[1] In this department of work they claim to have had remarkable success. "St. Joseph's College, Trichinopoly," the Rector of St. Xavier's College, Calcutta, writes, "has alone produced more converts these last ten years than the thirty-eight Protestant Colleges put together."[2] This writer is able to speak of "the enormous contribution (of the Colleges) to the progress of the Missions."

In these ways both the Colleges and the Seminaries for the training of priests are being used to establish the Christian faith more securely in the minds of the Catholic youth and to extend its conquests. The policy that Robert de Nobili initiated has not been wholly abandoned, though it has been purged of the objectionable features that are usually associated with his name. While some of the Jesuit Colleges have obtained honourable distinction for their researches in various departments of science, other missionaries of the same Order have been giving much study to the points of contact between the Hindu and the Christian philosophical constructions. These scholars maintain and seek to prove that the Vedānta systems of Śankara and Rāmānuja "move in the same direction as the Catholic philosophy" of St. Thomas Aquinas. Referring to the work which these Jesuit Fathers have done through their magazine, *The Light of the East*, published in Calcutta, M. de la Vallée Poussin, the Belgian Sanskritist, writes, "Without

[1] Rev. M. Vermeire, S.J., in *The Catholic Educational Review*, Christmas, 1931.
[2] *Ibid.*

adopting, like Robert de Nobili in former days the Brāhman dress, these very modern apologists have made for themselves a very modern psychology, thoroughly Thomist and yet Bengali. While their brothers are civilising the totems of Chota Nagpur they win over this intellectual aristocracy that found Buddhism irrational and Allah too simple." They are seeking to lead India "vers le Christ par le Vedānta."[1]

It is interesting to find the old Vedic road being explored by this group of members of the same Society to which belonged the reputed author of the Fifth Veda. They were, indeed, anticipated by a Bengali Catholic, Brahmabandhav Upadhyaya. This remarkable Bengali convert to Catholicism, who died in Calcutta in 1905, sought in his own person to explore this road of compromise. When he died he was under the censure of his Church, his religious and political nationalism having brought him under suspicion. The tragedy of his death, in the opinion of a Catholic historian of the Indian nationalist awakening, is "the fact that the impression was thereby created as if there were a necessary antithesis between Swaraj[2] and Catholicism."[3] It would appear that in the quarter of a century that has elapsed since then the attitude of the Roman Church has become more favourable to attempts to "convert India through Hinduism,"[4] for the adventures of the Jesuits of Calcutta in the region of a Hindu-Christian syncretism bear the papal *imprimatur*.

These are indications of the desire to plant Catholic Christianity deeper and more securely in the Indian spirit, the resolve to be no longer content with a mere acceptance by the convert of the outward symbols of the

[1] *Vers le Christ par le Vedanta*, by Pierre Johanns, S.J. I. Śankara et Rāmānuja, p. vii.

[2] That is, the Indian nationalist demand for political independence.

[3] *Renascent India*, by H. C. E. Zacharias, p. 28. For an account of this Bengali Catholic and another kindred spirit belonging to the same Church, see pp. 25 ff. of this book.

[4] *Op. cit.*, p. 29.

faith. This is seen not only in the case of those who sought to win converts from Brāhmanism but in the case also of " their brothers " who, in the words of M. de la Vallée Poussin already quoted, " are civilising the totems of Chota Nagpur." When, at the beginning of this century, a " Mass-movement," almost as remarkable in its results as those of the days of St. Francis Xavier, brought into the Church in that region more than 100,000 converts from animism, their instruction, and especially the instruction of the children, was organised on a scale that, at the earlier date, much as the saint desired it, was not possible. We learn from the Census Report of 1921 that 354 schools are maintained for the education of the children of this community while their general supervision and care is undertaken by a staff of over a hundred European and Indian missionaries. Such facts as these give evidence of the great advance that has been made in the last century in all parts of India where the Roman Church has responsibilities. By such means as these reality is being given to the profession of the Christian faith and the reproach that so often attached to it is being removed. The level of Christian intelligence in the masses of the people is being steadily raised, while, in the words of Father Vermeire quoted above, " a Catholic *élite* " is being created who are taking an increasing share in the public life of their country and playing their part in the remaking of the nation.

C. *The Churches of the Protestant Missions*. When now we turn to estimate in terms of character and life the value of Indian Christianity as represented by the products of the missionary effort of the non-Roman Churches of the West we find the same problems demanding solution as in the case of the Roman Missions and the same mistakes being made. Deep-rooted social ills have to be faced by both sections alike, ills that require for their overthrow nothing less than the faith that can remove mountains. This much of difference may, however, be claimed on a just and impartial survey of the whole situation, that while both types of missions have fallen at times into the error of recognising caste or of being content with a superficial and unreal religion, these were always viewed by the Missions of the Protestant Churches as dangerous errors of which the young Churches that were arising in India must be warned and against which they must be guarded. Protestantism has always had two marks which individuals might forget but which every Missionary Church remembers—its recognition of the inward and spiritual character of religion and its belief in the equality before God of all His children. For that reason, while sometimes "Mass movements" have been mishandled by Protestant Missions also, the unworthy admitted to the Church and the ignorant left in their ignorance, and while sometimes the evil of caste has been condoned, these things have been done by individuals in the face of the condemnation of the Missions they served. In 1833 Bishop Wilson laid down in the clearest terms the Christian attitude to the evil social order of Hindu tradition. By it, he declared, "all the intercommunity of the body of Christ is violated and destroyed." "His strong and decisive campaign against all caste distinctions," writes Mr. Mayhew, "determined for the future the policy of Protestant Missions."[1] That was in South India where this evil was most powerfully entrenched and where the danger was greatest lest the Church should succumb to it. At a still earlier date William Carey and the Baptist Mission in Bengal had taken up a position that was equally uncompromising. From that day until the present there has been no division of view on this subject among the Missions of Protestantism; the only question that has concerned them has been the methods by which the young Christian Church may be most effectually purged and protected from a spirit that is so manifestly not of Christ. That the methods used have been wholly

[1] *Christianity and the Government of India*, p. 155.

successful in achieving their purpose cannot indeed be claimed.

As a typical example of what is being done in every Province of India to exorcise this evil from the Church we may cite the experience of the Church Missionary Society in Nadia in Bengal. There the Christian community includes a considerable number from a despised and outcaste company who work in leather, eat half putrid flesh and live in squalor. The conditions they have come forth from are the normal consequences of the oppression and contempt that they and so many like them have had for centuries to endure. A Mission Report of a generation ago writes in regard to them as follows: " The Church, even at the present time " (that is, after these people had been for many years Christians) " finds it hard to receive them in a whole-hearted way, sometimes even refusing to eat or smoke with them. The problem how to get the Bengali Church to receive them . . . has vexed all right-thinking Christians for many years. In former years feasts were given and all were invited and were more or less forced to eat together, but such harsh methods were not entirely crowned with success. The more successful way has been by education to try to raise their social status." This is the method that has been everywhere resorted to, with the result that the despised outcaste is now compelling recognition and respect.

The danger that arises here, as is widely recognised, is " that Christianity should be identified with civilisation and schools thought more of than Churches."[1] That this danger, however, has been kept constantly before the wisest among those who have the difficult task of leading the outcastes up from slavery, two testimonies must suffice to prove. Dr. Sidney Cave writes from personal experience of a " Mass-movement area " in the extreme south of the peninsula among those people who were as stubble before the flame that glowed in the heart of

[1] Dr. Sidney Cave in *International Review of Missions*, Vol. VII, p. 479.

Francis Xavier, but whose evil ways brought him to despair. There Ringeltaube at the beginning of the nineteenth century had a success almost as remarkable as his had been and shared, as well, in his predecessor's disappointment. "They are great rogues," he wrote of his converts. "The poorest of them count to be made proselytes for money and good words, and after they cleave to you like leeches. I have about 600 of them and therefore I am quite poor." Writing a hundred years later Dr. Cave can say that "of the people whom in his bitterness Ringeltaube so described has come a great Christian Church in which the notes of the Holy Spirit are today unmistakable."[1]

The Church can indeed be delivered from this evil spirit only when in all classes alike within it Christ dwells and is manifest. It is because this has come about in the Telugu area, as we have already noted, that the sight of the transformed and purified lives of the outcastes has drawn the Hindus of higher caste into new relations with them of respect and honour and made them even wish to become such Christians as they are. This "attractive power," as the Bishop of Dornakal tells us, has taken the place of the old repulsion. "It takes various forms," the Bishop goes on. "In one case it is the advance in education and civilisation that has been made by the outcastes; in another their honesty and truthfulness; in another their growth in soberness and in sexual morality; in yet another their clean speech."[2] Here again we have evidence that the power that beyond all others can avail to expel the old heritage of caste intolerance from the hearts of those in whom it is so deeply implanted is just the power that can remake them all—high caste and low caste alike—in the image of Him that created them. There is no place for despair in the hearts of those who can look back and compare what once was in these people

[1] *International Review of Missions*, Vol. VII, p. 473.
[2] *Ibid.*, Vol. XXI, pp. 460 f.

with what now is and is coming to be. "'Are we not different?' they themselves ask. 'We men and women go to prayers together every night; we do not now commit burglary; we do not now drink; we enjoy heaven here and now; we were in hell before.'"[1]

These two examples of the most effective way of escape from the caste evil may be taken at the same time as examples of the way of escape from the danger lest the Church should remain content, especially when multitudes are coming into it, with a religion without depth or reality. To see these people beginning to grow in the grace and knowledge of the Lord Jesus Christ is to have the assurance that the plant of the Christian faith is striking its roots downwards and, in consequence, bearing fruit upwards. This religion is not ritual alone but life and faith. Even the simple evidence that the Bishop of Dornakal adduces proves this. "Christians," he says of the field labourers in the Andhra country, "have been given extra wages, and can in many villages command higher wages because they are known to be honest and need no supervision." "Honesty," he adds, "is the proof of real religion."[2] If it is asked what that culture of the soil is by means of which it has been so transformed from barrenness to fertility, the question may be answered by such an enumeration as the Bishop of Dornakal has given us from his own experience. "Participation in daily prayer and worship, regular instruction in the Christian faith, constant recital of religious song and ritual, education of the young, the practical exemplification of the doctrine in the lives of the teacher and his wife, monthly visits from the pastor for inspiration and advice, and most of all the cleansing waters of baptism and the receiving of the laying on of hands in confirmation—these so do their work in the hearts and upon the minds and even the physical features of the converts, that higher

[1] *International Review of Missions*, Vol. XVIII, p. 511.
[2] *Ibid.*, Vol. XVIII, p. 515.

motives, nobler thoughts and fresh achievements in character manifest themselves and call public attention to the new creation that has been wrought in them through the acceptance of the new religion."[1] In every part of India where men and women are entering the Church, these methods, with differences of emphasis and differences of effectiveness, are being followed. As a consequence the Churches which are composed largely of men and women who have been lifted up from the slough of untouchableness are beginning to clothe themselves in raiment befitting the Church of Christ. They are learning as Christians to put on Him in whom they have been called.

That consummation seems often remote enough still in the case of the majority. "From among the sons of Hindu India," writes a Syrian Christian, looking out upon his fellow-Christians, "have arisen men and women who have attained nearer the Christ ideal than the Christians around them. Daily, hourly, the Church in India is confronted with this challenge."[2] But it is responding to that challenge as Hindu India has never responded to the challenge of the untouchables. Mr. Gandhi is not willing, it would seem, to admit that Christianity is raising these submerged multitudes, but the facts cannot be disputed. It is not Hinduism but Christianity that is actually able to remake these "tattered outlaws of the earth" into "people of God,"[3] as Mr. Gandhi now calls them. Even the Syrian Church, which was so far subdued to its evil surroundings in the past as to become "a silent sanctioner and approver of untouchability,"[4] has awakened to its duty, and one group at least of educated young men are giving themselves in Travancore with much devotion to the task of making reparation.

At the same time it has to be recognised that a spirit

[1] *International Review of Missions*, Vol. XVIII, p. 510.
[2] K. K. Kuruvilla in *An Indian Approach to India*, p. 141.
[3] "Harijan," which may be so translated.
[4] *Mahatma Gandhi's Ideas*, by C. F. Andrews, p. 175.

is abroad in India today that in the case of all classes—Hindu, Muslim, Christian—is creating a new sense of that brotherhood which the caste spirit denies. This is the spirit of nationalism which is opening the eyes of high-caste Hindus to the crime against national unity and self-respect of which they have been guilty in placing these fellow-Indians beyond the pale. This same spirit is at work among the Christians also, breaking down the wall of separation that often isolates them from those who follow other faiths. A charge, constantly brought against the work of Christian Missions—and with justice—is that it has tended to denationalise those who enter the Christian Church. The awakening of the national spirit has done much in recent years to cure this evil and to draw the Christians into the life of the nation. That nationalism has its perils for the Christian as for the non-Christian is obvious. It often becomes a frenzy, breaking down higher obligations and arrogating to itself an authority that supersedes the claims alike of religion and of morality. But these are its extravagances. Its value lies in the power it possesses to shake the torpor from men's minds, driving them to recognise their duties to each other within the State. In this way nationalism is arousing not a few in India at the present time to an appreciation of their solidarity as those who inherit common traditions and travel by a common road. We have already noted an instance of this in the case of the Bengali Roman Catholic, Brahmabandhav Upadhyaya. He has his parallels among non-Roman Christians. The political movement has compelled many men and women of ability from among the Christians to abandon their attitude of aloofness and to respond to the national call and devote themselves to national service. Under this influence they have become fused with their fellow-Indians of other faiths in a way that was not formerly the case and have thus proved in their persons that Christianity is no longer an alien, but is truly Indian.

But a political unification, even if it is a unification so real as to make men one in suffering for its achievement, is not the only or the chief means by which it may be demonstrated that the Christians are not aliens in the life of their land. There are filaments of sentiment and aspiration and thought that unite the Indian soul and the Christian soul, and these, sometimes too hastily broken, when an Indian accepted the Christian faith, are now being reknit. It is in many cases, though they may be little aware of it, an ancient heritage of longing for God that draws the Indian seekers to the feet of Christ. Sir Denzil Ibbetson in his Punjab Census Report many years ago pointed out that the religion of the outcaste Churahs of the Punjab is nearer to Christianity than any other religion in India, and most of the members of that community are now within the Christian Church. Similarly at the other extreme of Hindu Society, the Brāhman, N. V. Tilak journeyed to Christ, he tells us, over the bridge of the Bhakti of the Marāthā poet-saint, Tukārām, who was—if ever there was one—a *mens naturaliter Christiana.* Bhakti indeed, in many of its expressions, as we have seen, is a prophecy and a forecast of the Christian revelation.

These facts—and many others that could be advanced—point to a parallelism and an affinity between some of the deepest probings of the Hindu spirit and the discovery that the Gospel makes to men. The Christian need, therefore, be no alien in India, nor need we find any incongruity in the term Indian Christianity. Indian Christian scholars are exploring more and more these affinities, exhibiting " Christianity as Bhakti Mārga " and " Jesus as the Avatār."[1] Thus it is being demonstrated that Christianity is at home in its Indian environment and is establishing itself securely in the context of Indian thought. There are, of course, perils that will beset all

[1] These are the names of two books by Indian Christians, published by the Christian Literature Society, Madras.

such adventures of discovery as these scholars are embarking upon. The Christian who sets out across the "unplumbed, salt, estranging sea" of Hinduism on such a quest must have before him always the chart which will secure him against shipwreck.

Not only are there Christians who are seeking thus to acclimatise Christianity in the thought-worlds of the Indian people. In other ways also this religion is proving that to it India is no strange land. The traditional *sannyāsi*[1] of Hinduism has been reinterpreted in Christian terms by Sadhu Sundar Singh, while he remains still essentially Indian; Pandita Ramābai was acclaimed at the close of her life of Christian devotion as one whose name still had its place in the calendar of Hindu saints; and B. C. Sircar in his shrine at Puri practised a yoga that was always Christian. There are many others besides these who in humbler places all over the land have borne a true Indian witness to Christ Jesus. The Indian Christians have their own songs by means of which, with the music and in the devout spirit of the old saints of Hinduism, they lift their hearts to God. "They are made one with Brahma with a song," said Tukārām of the old saints among whom he himself had so great a place, and Narayan Vaman Tilak and H. A. Krishna Pillai have rendered the same service to the Marāthā and the Tamil Christians, bringing them into the far richer fellowship with God that is by Christ Jesus. When a religion sings it has laid hold of the heart, and the Christian religion is demonstrating in these ways that it is indeed laying hold of the heart of India.

Syrian, Roman and Protestant—whatever the channel by which the message of Christ has come to them—all alike have in some measure received it and are following it, however far off. Few, indeed, and feeble they appear—six millions though they may be—dispersed among multitudes of Hindus and of Muslims who are dominated

[1] The Hindu ascetic.

by ancient and arrogant beliefs. Yet this little company may yet fully realise—indeed there are indications that they are beginning to realise—their great mission and great opportunity. Mr. Mayhew in his recent book on *Christianity and the Government of India* quotes as "wise words that might well be adopted as a guiding principle of the whole Christian community in India" a passage from a memorial presented to the Simon Commission by an association of Christians of low-caste origin. "Christianity," they say, "represents a religious spirit. . . . It is a life dominated by the love of Christ; it is a life of continual sacrifice of one's dignity, wealth and health for the sake of others. It never made an Englishman a Scotchman or vice versa. It does not in India confer a new skin or a new bone nor does it make its adherents into a separate caste."[1]

These humble Christians have realised that their vocation is not just to add one more religion to the many already established in the land, but, as Mr. Mayhew says, to become "a spiritual power house" for the remaking of India. For that end what matters most is the quality of their religion and not the number of those who profess it. The religious spirit which Christ creates in men, the "life of continual sacrifice for the sake of others" which he exhibits, dwells in many who are not enumerated in the census as Christians and we may say that "winds and waves and waters as they roll work with it silently." Mr. Mayhew takes as its symbol the fertilisation of millions of acres of Punjab desert by the Government engineers. That is a symbol of the effect that Christianity has produced "on the soil of Indian thought and feeling and social life." Through its agency "have come the ideas that are fertilising that soil, and the power, like that of the sun and the rain, which swells the seed."[2] It is a bold claim to make and many in India today would reject it, but there are many facts in

[1] Mayhew, *op. cit.*, p. 248. [2] *Op. cit.*, p. 250.

the history of the rebirth of the land during the last century to confirm its truth. Ram Mohan Roy, who died in 1833, was the pioneer of the new age and we may say that he declared what throughout the whole of the succeeding century has been its inward spring of energy and inspiration when in 1820 this Hindu reformer published a collection of the words of Christ bearing the title *The Precepts of Jesus, the Guide to Peace and Happiness.* A hundred years later, in 1922, when the latest and greatest in the prophetic line that followed Ram Mohan Roy, Mahatma Gandhi, was sent to prison, "all India," Mr. K. T. Paul tells us, "seemed to have become suddenly aware of the Cross." "The parallel," Dr. H. C. Zacharias comments, "may seem to many far-fetched; that it was so spontaneously and universally made is at all events a very significant fact and one which shows the great role that the Mahatma is playing, unwittingly, in India's *praeparatio evangelica*."[1]

In many directions this leaven has been at work throughout this whole period of rejuvenation. At an earlier date the Brahmo movement had no hesitation in acknowledging its debt to Christ, and indeed by the lips of Keshab Chunder Sen proclaimed it boldly. The Brahmo movement has been followed in later times by the Rāmakrishna Mission which, as we have seen, seeks to identify its worship in certain respects with that of Christianity. Its attitude is similar to that of the Mithraic priest who said to St. Augustine, "Et ipse Pileatus Christianus est." We may translate and adapt these words as: "The man who wears a turban is also a Christian." A similar approach from another direction is made by an outstanding contemporary figure in Indian philosophic study, Sir S. Radhakrishnan. His aim has been, as the editor of the *Indian Social Reformer*, Mr. K. Natarajan, points out with approval, "to form a synthesis of the teachings of Jesus with the teachings of the

[1] Zacharias, *op. cit.*, p. 216.

Upanishads and the Gītā." These influences which are, and have been for a hundred years, at work among the educated Hindus, have been similarly influential among Parsis and, to a certain extent, among Muslims as well. The standard by which life's values are measured is openly accepted by the most thoughtful as that of Christ. India may learn to ignore Him but it will only be if India abandons her great tradition as a God-intoxicated people. God still holds India by the roots of her being, and therefore Christ speaks to her and His Church has a witness to bear to her.

BIBLIOGRAPHY

The following brief list of books is meant to guide the student in following up the studies to which this book is an introduction. The sacred books of each religion should, of course, be the centre around which such study must always move and to which it must have reference. No books about the religions can take the place of the books themselves, which are their starting-point and from which they derive their authority. It is not necessary nor possible to give a list of these here, but most of them may be found among the *Sacred Books of the East*.

Hinduism

For Hinduism I would name three books by J. N. Farquhar—his *Primer of Hinduism*, which is provided with an excellent Bibliography, his *Outline of the Religious Literature of India*, an indispensable work, and his *Modern Religious Movements in India*, which, however, is being rapidly left behind by the changing conditions of the land. The volumes on Hinduism in the Religious Quest of India Series may also be commended, as well as the briefer studies of many aspects of Hindu life and thought which will be found in the volumes of the Heritage of India Series and the Religious Life of India Series (all published by the Oxford Press). The standard books by scholars who base their studies upon the ancient literature need not be named. Of books that have recently appeared two that treat of aspects of Bhakti may be mentioned. These are Professor Rudolf Otto's *India's Religion of Grace* (Student Christian Movement Press) and Professor R. D. Ranade's *Mysticism of Maharashtra* (Aryabhushan Press, Poona).

Indian Islam

Indian Islam, by M. T. Titus (Religious Quest of India Series), and *The People of the Mosque*; an Introduction to the Study of Islam, with special reference to India, by L. Bevan Jones, Student Christian Movement Press. Also the account of the Ahmadiya Movement, by H. A. Walter in the Religious Life of India Series.

BIBLIOGRAPHY

The Religion of the Jainas

The Heart of Jainism, by Mrs Sinclair Stevenson (Religious Quest of India Series); *La Religion Djaina*, by A. Guérinot, and Glasenapp's *Der Jainismus*.

The Religion of the Sikhs

The Adi Granth, translated by Dr E. Trumpp; and *The Sikh Religion*, a translation of the Granth with lives of the Gurus, by M. A. Macauliffe (6 vols.).

The Religion of the Parsis (Zoroastrianism)

Early Zoroastrianism and *The Treasures of the Magi* (both by J. H. Moulton) cover the whole subject of the beginning of Zoroastrianism and its Parsi period. In addition, *Zoroastrian Studies*, by the leading student of this subject, A. V. Williams Jackson, and *Zoroastrian Theology*, by a learned Parsi priest, M. N. Dhalla, should be studied. There are valuable articles on all these religions in the *Encyclopædia of Religion and Ethics*, but the articles on Zoroastrianism are perhaps specially useful and important.

Indian Christianity

Of the Syrian Churches, *The Lesser Eastern Churches*, by Adrian Fortescue, gives an account from the point of view of Rome, while G. M. Rae's, *The Syrian Church in India*, approaches the subject from another angle. The history of the other Churches must be obtained from a large variety of sources, histories of Missions, biographies, etc. No account of the whole development from the point of view of the indigenous Church has as yet appeared, but such a study is now in preparation by Mr Stephen Neill and should appear within a short time.

INDEX

INDEX

INDEX